About This Book

Why is this topic important?

Organizational consulting generally has a broader focus than training. Whereas a trainer might develop people's understanding of team roles, a consultant might help a dysfunctional team function. Similarly, a trainer might deliver a workshop on developing good time management and productivity skills, whereas a consultant might be contracted to analyze and reorganize workflow through a team or through an entire division or operating unit. There are clearly similarities between training and consulting—and the terms are often used interchangeably—but each has a unique focus and requires divergent approaches, tools, and techniques.

What can you achieve with this book?

Offering entirely new content each year, the consulting edition of *The Pfeiffer Annual* showcases the latest thinking and cutting-edge approaches to organization development and performance improvement contributed by practicing consultants, organizational systems experts, and academics. Designed for both the dedicated consultant and the training professional who straddles both roles, the *Annual* presents a unique source of new knowledge and ideas, as well as practical and proven applications for facilitating better work processes, implementing and sustaining change, and improving organizational effectiveness.

How is this book organized?

The book is divided into four sections: Experiential Learning Activities (ELAs); Editor's Choice; Inventories, Questionnaires, and Surveys; and Articles and Discussion Resources. The materials can be freely reproduced for use in the normal course of an assignment. ELAs are the mainstay of the *Annual* and cover a broad range of consulting topics. The activities are presented as complete and ready-to-use designs for working with groups; facilitator instructions and all necessary handouts and participant materials are included. Editor's Choice pieces allow us to select material that doesn't fit the other categories and take advantage of "hot topics." The instrument section introduces proven survey and assessment tools for gathering and sharing data on some aspect of performance. The articles section presents the best current thinking about workplace performance and organization development. Use these for your own professional development or as resources for working with others.

About Pfeiffer

Pfeiffer serves the professional development and hands-on resource needs of training and human resource practitioners and gives them products to do their jobs better. We deliver proven ideas and solutions from experts in HR development and HR management, and we offer effective and customizable tools to improve workplace performance. From novice to seasoned professional, Pfeiffer is the source you can trust to make yourself and your organization more successful.

Essential Knowledge Pfeiffer produces insightful, practical, and comprehensive materials on topics that matter the most to training and HR professionals. Our Essential Knowledge resources translate the expertise of seasoned professionals into practical, how-to guidance on critical workplace issues and problems. These resources are supported by case studies, worksheets, and job aids and are frequently supplemented with CD-ROMs, websites, and other means of making the content easier to read, understand, and use.

Essential Tools Pfeiffer's Essential Tools resources save time and expense by offering proven, ready-to-use materials—including exercises, activities, games, instruments, and assessments—for use during a training or team-learning event. These resources are frequently offered in looseleaf or CD-ROM format to facilitate copying and customization of the material.

Pfeiffer also recognizes the remarkable power of new technologies in expanding the reach and effectiveness of training. While e-hype has often created whizbang solutions in search of a problem, we are dedicated to bringing convenience and enhancements to proven training solutions. All our e-tools comply with rigorous functionality standards. The most appropriate technology wrapped around essential content yields the perfect solution for today's on-the-go trainers and human resource professionals.

www.pfeiffer.com

Essential resources for training and HR professionals

The Pfeiffer Annual Series

The Pfeiffer Annuals present each year never-before-published materials contributed by learning professionals and academics and written for trainers, consultants, and human resource and performance-improvement practitioners. As a forum for the sharing of ideas, theories, models, instruments, experiential learning activities, and best and innovative practices, the *Annuals* are unique. Not least because only in the *Pfeiffer Annuals* will you find solutions from professionals like you who work in the field as trainers, consultants, facilitators, educators, and human resource and performance-improvement practitioners and whose contributions have been tried and perfected in real-life settings with actual participants and clients to meet real-world needs.

The Pfeiffer Annual: Consulting
Edited by Elaine Biech

The Pfeiffer Annual: Human Resource Management
Edited by Robert C. Preziosi

The Pfeiffer Annual: Training
Edited by Elaine Biech

Call for Papers

How would you like to be published in the *Pfeiffer Training* or *Consulting Annual?* Possible topics for submissions include group and team building, organization development, leadership, problem solving, presentation and communication skills, consulting and facilitation, and training-the-trainer. Contributions may be in one of the following three formats:

- Experiential Learning Activities

- Inventories, Questionnaires, and Surveys

- Articles and Discussion Resources

To receive a copy of the submission packet, which explains the requirements and will help you determine format, language, and style to use, contact editor Elaine Biech at Pfeifferannual@aol.com or by calling 757-588-3939.

Elaine Biech, EDITOR

The *2005*
Pfeiffer
ANNUAL

CONSULTING

Pfeiffer
A Wiley Imprint
www.pfeiffer.com

ISBN: 0-7879-6933-8
ISSN: 1046-333-X

Acquiring Editor: Martin Delahoussaye
Director of Development: Kathleen Dolan Davies
Developmental Editor: Susan Rachmeler
Editor: Rebecca Taff
Senior Production Editor: Dawn Kilgore
Manufacturing Supervisor: Bill Matherly
Interior Design: Chris Wallace
Illustrations: Leigh McLellan Design

Printed in the United States of America

Printing 10 9 8 7 6 5 4 3 2

Contents

Experiential Learning Activities

Editor's Choice

Inventories, Questionnaires, and Surveys

Articles and Discussion Resources

Preface

Fast, Fresh, and Functional

"How do I stay on top of all the information coming my way?" "How will I find time to create new ideas?" "Where can I find a resource that will provide me with tools that are practical and guaranteed to work?" "How can I live up to my boss's expectations to get my tasks done faster than ever?" and "How do I take care of me: learning new things and networking with others?"

If you've been asking yourself more questions lately than you have answers for, join the crowd! I call it the fast, fresh, and functional dilemma! Everyone in your life wants everything faster than ever. As a trainer or consultant, you are most likely turning projects around at a pace you never dreamed possible. But in addition to fast, your projects must be fresh. Your clients, customers, bosses, and participants want new ideas, new activities, new tools. Yes, and in addition to fast and fresh, all of your projects must be successful—they must be functional!

If this is true for you, you have come to the right place. The content of the *2005 Pfeiffer Annual: Consulting* is fast, fresh, and functional! Let me share some of the highlights with you.

Kristin Arnold's experiential learning activity (ELA), "The Hats We Wear," takes about one-half hour to introduce a fresh way to discuss problem roles on a team. Have you been challenged to find a fresh way to discuss organizational values? Check out Cher Holton's ELA. It takes one to two hours, but that's better than some of the full-day sessions I've been through! And it works! Really fresh is Lorraine Ukens' fable-based activity that allows participants to examine the influence of various factors on performance issues. Very creative!

Also in the Consulting *Annual*, Ira Morrow shares two instruments to provide teams with constructive quantitative feedback regarding their performance in presentations. This should be useful to many of you. Jeffrey and Linda Russell share their successful model for leading change in organizations. They present a model for understanding the emotional impact of change on individuals, especially as it relates to our current fast-paced world. Ever wish the teams you work with were more functional? Warner Burke presents his thoughts about that topic in his article, "What If We Took Teamwork Seriously?"

So if your job is asking you to do the impossible, the *Pfeiffer Annual* has resources to help you produce fast, fresh, and functional. What else is happening that you should know about?

What's New to Take Care of You?

What about you? What are you doing to refresh yourself? After being in the middle of the fast, fresh, and functional milieu, you need to be sure that you are finding ways to continue to learn and to network with other professionals. Whether you are a trainer or a consultant, you will be happy to know that there is something new out there for you.

Trainers

The American Society for Training and Development (ASTD) released its 2004 competency study, Mapping the Future. It is the icon for the profession, and its impact on the workplace learning and performance community is expected to be huge. The model provides content required to develop competencies that ensure trainers think more strategically and link learning and performance to results. Even more significantly, however, is that ASTD will launch a certification program for learning and performance professionals in 2005. This provides the credibility to the training field that has been sorely lacking for a long time.

The best news of all for trainers everywhere is that the certification effort will spawn well-thought-out, practical training for you to do your jobs better, or shall we say, fast, fresh, and functional? More information about the competency study and certification is available on ASTD's website, www.ASTD.org.

Consultants

A new association, Independent Consultants Association (ICA), has formed recently to help consultants be more successful. ICA will offer free listings to consultants in its directory, which will be published online and in a hard-cover library edition. In addition, the Association will feature a newsletter, seminars, interactive web events, a national conference, daily tips, and consultant news on its website. Tom Peters will chair the Advisory Council.

This is great news for all consultants. Finally a fresh new association exists that understands the independent consultant and your needs. Get involved on the ground floor, become a member, attend the first national conference, or at least list yourself in the directory. Looking for networking opportunities? This looks like a big one to me! Visit ICA's website at www.ica-assn.org.

What Is the *Annual?*

The 2005 Pfeiffer Annual: Consulting presents a collection of practical materials written for trainers, consultants, and performance-improvement technologists. This source for experiential learning activities, resource for instruments, and reference for cutting-edge articles has inspired human resource development (HRD) professionals for thirty-three years.

The Pfeiffer Annual: Consulting focuses on skill building and knowledge enhancement and also includes cutting-edge articles that enhance the skills and professional development of consultants.

Whether you are a trainer, a consultant, a facilitator, or a bit of each, you will find tools and resources that provide you with the basics and challenge (and we hope inspire) you to use new techniques and models.

Annual Loyalty

The *Pfeiffer Annual* series has many loyal subscribers. There are several reasons for this loyalty. In addition to the wide variety of topics and implementation levels, the *Annuals* provide materials that are applicable to varying circumstances. You will find instruments for individuals, teams, and organizations; experiential learning activities to round out workshops, team building, or consulting assignments; ideas and contemporary solutions for managing human capital; and articles that increase your own knowledge base, to use as reference materials in your writing, or as a source of ideas for your training or consulting assignments.

Many of our readers have been loyal customers for a dozen or more years. If you are one of them, we thank you. And we thank each of you who provided input about the new features and the improvements we initiated last year. The cover design, the binding style, and the CD-ROM all received rave reviews. The *Annuals* owe most of their success, though, to the fact that they are immediately ready to use. All of the materials may be duplicated for educational and training purposes. If you need to adapt or modify the materials to tailor them for your audience's needs, go right ahead. We only request that the credit statement found on the copyright page (and on each reproducible page) be retained on all copies. Our liberal copyright policy makes it easy and fast for you to use the materials to do your job. However, if you intend to reproduce the materials in publications for sale or if you wish to reproduce more than one hundred copies of any one item, please contact us for prior written permission.

If you are a new *Annual* user, welcome! If you like what you see in the 2005 edition, you may want to consider taking out a standing order. By doing so, you are guaranteed to receive your copy each year straight off the press and receive a discount off the cover price. And if you want go back and have the entire series for your use, then the *Pfeiffer Library*—which contains content from the very first edition to the present day—is available on CD-ROM. You can find information on the *Pfeiffer Library* at www.pfeiffer.com. I often refer to many of my *Annuals* from the 1980s. They include several classic activities that have become a mainstay in my team-building designs. But most of all, the *Annuals* have been a valuable resource for over thirty years because the materials come from professionals like you who work in the field as trainers, consultants, facilitators, educators, and performance-improvement technologists whose contributions have been tried and perfected in real-life settings with actual participants and clients to meet real-world needs.

To this end, we encourage you to submit materials to be considered for publication. We are interested in receiving experiential learning activities; inventories, questionnaires, and surveys; and articles and discussion resources. Contact the Pfeiffer Editorial Department at the address listed on the copyright page for copies of our guidelines for contributors or contact me directly at Box 8249, Norfolk, VA 23503, or by email at pfeifferannual@aol.com. We welcome your comments, ideas, and contributions.

Acknowledgments

Thank you to the dedicated, friendly, thoughtful people at Pfeiffer who produced the *2005 Pfeiffer Annual: Consulting:* Kathleen Dolan Davies, Martin Delahoussaye, Dawn Kilgore, Susan Rachmeler, Laura Reizman, and Rebecca Taff. Thank you to Lorraine Kohart of ebb associates inc, who assisted our authors with all the details of submission and who ensured that we met all the deadlines. Most important, thank you to our contributors, who have once again shared their ideas, techniques, and materials so that trainers and consultants everywhere may benefit.

Elaine Biech
Editor
September 2004

The Difference Between Training and Consulting:
Which *Annual* to Use?

The two volumes of the *Pfeiffer Annuals*—training and consulting—are resources for two different but closely related professions. Each *Annual* serves as a collection of tools and support materials used by the professionals in their respective arenas. The volumes include activities, articles, and instruments used by individuals in the training and consulting fields. The training volume is written with the trainer in mind, and the consulting volume is written with the consultant in mind.

How can you differentiate between the two volumes? Let's begin by defining each profession. A trainer can be defined as anyone who is responsible for designing and delivering knowledge to adult learners and may include an internal HRD professional employed by an organization or an external practitioner who contracts with an organization to design and conduct training programs. Generally, the trainer is a subject-matter expert who is expected to transfer knowledge so that the trainee can know or do something new. A consultant is someone who provides unique assistance or advice (based on what the consultant knows or has experienced) to someone else, usually known as "the client." The consultant may not necessarily be a subject-matter expert in all situations. Often the consultant is an expert at using specific tools to extract, coordinate, resolve, organize, expedite, or implement an organizational situation.

The lines between the consulting and training professions have blurred in the past few years. First, the names and titles have blurred. For example, some external trainers call themselves "training consultants" as a way of distinguishing themselves from internal trainers. Some organizations now have internal consultants who usually reside in the training department.

Second, the roles have blurred. While a consultant has always been expected to deliver measurable results, now trainers are expected to do so as well. Both are expected to improve performance; both are expected to contribute to the bottom line.

Facilitation was at one time thought to be a consultant skill; today trainers are expected to use facilitation skills to train. Training one-on-one was a trainer skill; today consultants train executives one-on-one and call it "coaching."

The introduction of the "performance technologist," whose role is one of combined trainer and consultant, is a perfect example of a new profession that has evolved due to the need for trainers to use more "consulting" techniques in their work. The "performance consultant" is a new role supported by the American Society for Training and Development (ASTD). ASTD has shifted its focus from training to performance improvement.

As you can see, the roles and goals of training and consulting are not nearly as specific as they once may have been. However, when you step back and examine the two professions from a big-picture perspective, you can more easily differentiate between the two. Maintaining a big-picture focus will also help you determine which *Pfeiffer Annual* to turn to as your first resource.

Both volumes cover the same general topics: communication, teamwork, problem solving, and leadership. However, depending on your requirement and purpose—a training or consulting need—you will use each in different situations. You will select the *Annual* based on how you will interact with the topic, not on what the topic might be. Let's take a topic such as teamwork, for example. If you are searching for a lecturette that teaches the advantages of teamwork, a workshop activity that demonstrates the skill of making decisions in a team, or a handout that discusses team stages, look to the Training *Annual*. On the other hand, if you are conducting a team-building session for a dysfunctional team, helping to form a new team, or trying to understand the dynamics of an executive team, you will look to the Consulting *Annual*.

The Training *Annual*

The materials in the Training volume focus on skill building and knowledge enhancement as well as on the professional development of trainers. They generally focus on controlled events: a training program, a conference presentation, a classroom setting.

Look to the Training *Annual* to find ways to improve a training session for 10 to 1000 people and anything else that falls in the human resource development category:

- Specific experiential learning activities that can be built into a training program;

- Techniques to improve training: debriefing exercises, conducting role plays, managing time;

- Topical lecturettes;

- Ideas to improve a boring training program;

- Icebreakers and energizers for a training session;

- Surveys that can be used in a classroom;

- Ideas for moving an organization from training to performance; and

- And ways to improve your skills as a trainer.

The Consulting *Annual*

The materials in the Consulting volume focus on intervention techniques and organizational systems as well as the professional development of consultants. They generally focus on "tools" that you can have available just in case: concepts about organizations and their development (or demise) and about more global situations.

Look to the Consulting *Annual* to find ways to improve consulting activities from team building and executive coaching to organization development and strategic planning:

- Skills for working with executives;

- Techniques for solving problems, effecting change, and gathering data;

- Team-building tools, techniques, and tactics;

- Facilitation ideas and methods;

- Processes to examine for improving an organization's effectiveness;

- Surveys that can be used organizationally; and

- Ways to improve your effectiveness as a consultant.

Summary

Even though the professions and the work are closely related and at times interchangeable, there is a difference. Use the following table to help you determine which *Annual* you should scan first for help. Remember, however, there is some blending of the two and either *Annual* may have your answer. It depends . . .

Element	Training	Consulting
Topics	Teams, Communication, Problem Solving	Teams, Communication, Problem Solving
Topic Focus	Individual, Department	Corporate, Global
Purpose	Skill Building, Knowledge Transfer	Coaching, Strategic Planning, Building Teams
Recipient	Individuals, Departments	Usually More Organizational
Organizational Level	All Workforce Members	Usually Closer to the Top
Delivery Profile	Workshops, Presentations	Intervention, Implementation
Atmosphere	Structured	Unstructured
Time Frame	Defined	Undefined
Organizational Cost	Moderate	High
Change Effort	Low to Moderate	Moderate to High
Setting	Usually a Classroom	Anywhere
Professional Experience	Entry Level, Novice	Proficient, Master Level
Risk Level	Low	High
Professional Needs	Activities, Resources	Tools, Theory
Application	Individual Skills	Usually Organizational System

When you get right down to it, we are all trainers and consultants. The skills may cross over. A great trainer is also a skilled consultant. And a great consultant is also a skilled trainer. The topics may be the same, but how you implement them may be vastly different. Which *Annual* to use? Remember to think about your purpose in terms of the big picture: consulting or training.

As you can see, we have both covered.

Introduction

to *The 2005 Pfeiffer Annual: Consulting*

Getting the Most from This Resource

The 2005 Pfeiffer Annual: Consulting is the forty-fifth volume in the *Annual* series, a collection of practical and useful materials for professionals in the broad area described as human resource development (HRD). The materials are written by and for professionals, including trainers, organization-development and organization-effectiveness consultants, performance-improvement technologists, facilitators, educators, instructional designers, and others.

This *Annual* has three main sections: experiential learning activities; inventories, questionnaires, and surveys; and articles and discussion resources. A fourth section, editor's choice, has been reserved for those unique contributions that do not fit neatly into one of the three main sections, but are valuable as identified by the editorial staff. Each published submission is classified in one of the following categories: Individual Development, Communication, Problem Solving, Groups, Teams, Consulting, Facilitating, Leadership, and Organizations. Within each category, pieces are further classified into logical subcategories, which are identified in the introductions to the three sections.

"Cutting edge" topics are identified in each *Annual*. This designation highlights topics that present information, concepts, tools, or perspectives that may be recent additions to the profession or that have not previously appeared in the Annual or are currently "hot topics."

The series continues to provide an opportunity for HRD professionals who wish to share their experiences, their viewpoints, and their processes with their colleagues.

To that end, Pfeiffer publishes guidelines for potential authors. These guidelines are available from the Pfeiffer Editorial Department at Jossey-Bass, Inc., in San Francisco, California. Materials are selected for the *Annuals* based on the quality of the ideas, applicability to real-world concerns, relevance to current HRD issues, clarity of presentation, and ability to enhance our readers' professional development. In addition, we choose experiential learning activities that will create a high degree of enthusiasm among the participants and add enjoyment to the learning process. As in the past several years, the contents of each *Annual* span a wide range of subject matter, reflecting the range of interests of our readers.

Our contributor list includes a wide selection of experts in the field: in-house practitioners, consultants, and academically based professionals. A list of contributors to the *Annual* can be found at the end of the volume, including their names, affiliations, addresses, telephone numbers, facsimile numbers, and email addresses. Readers will find this list useful if they wish to locate the authors of specific pieces for feedback, comments, or questions. Further information is presented in a brief biographical sketch of each contributor that appears at the conclusion of each article. We publish this information to encourage "networking," which continues to be a valuable mainstay in the field of human resource development.

We are pleased with the high quality of material that is submitted for publication each year and often regret that we have page limitations. In addition, just as we cannot publish every manuscript we receive, you may find that not all published works are equally useful to you. Therefore, we encourage and invite ideas, materials, and suggestions that will help us to make subsequent *Annuals* as useful as possible to all of our readers.

Introduction
to the Experiential Learning Activities Section

Experiential learning activities ensure that lasting learning occurs. They should be selected with a specific learning objective in mind. These objectives are based on the participants' needs and the facilitator's skills. Although the experiential learning activities presented here vary in goals, group size, time required, and process, they all incorporate one important element: questions that ensure learning has occurred. This discussion, led by the facilitator, assists participants to process the activity, to internalize the learning, and to relate it to their day-to-day situations. It is this element that creates the unique experience and learning opportunity that only an experiential learning activity can bring to the group process.

Readers have used the *Annuals'* experiential learning activities for years to enhance their training and consulting events. Each learning experience is complete and includes all lecturettes, handout content, and other written material necessary to facilitate the activity. In addition, many include variations of the design that the facilitator might find useful. If the activity does not fit perfectly with your objectives, within your time frame, or to your group size, we encourage you to adapt the activity by adding your own variations. You will find additional experiential learning activities listed in the "Experiential Learning Activities Categories" chart that immediately follows this introduction.

The 2005 Pfeiffer Annual: Consulting includes fourteen activities, in the following categories:

Individual Development: Sensory Awareness

Picture Yourself: Gaining Self-Awareness, by Deborah Spring Laurel

Individual Development: Self-Disclosure

Take a Risk: Practicing Self-Disclosure, by Ira J. Morrow

Individual Development: Diversity

At the Movies: Building Cross-Cultural Sensitivity, by Teresa Torres-Coronas

Communication: Awareness

All Power Is Relative: Checking Ourselves Against Others, by Robert Shaver

Communication: Listening

The Association for Community Improvement: Dealing with Hidden Agendas, by Donna L. Goldstein and Luis R. Morales

Problem Solving: Generating Alternatives

Give Brands a Hand: Generating Ideas, by Arthur B. VanGundy

Problem Solving: Consensus/Synergy

Pass It On: Using an Alternate Brainstorming Technique, by Brenda Hubbard and Susan Crosson

Groups: Competition/Collaboration

Altair the Ant: Influencing Performance, by Lorraine L. Ukens

Teams: Roles

The Hats We Wear: Understanding Team Roles, by Kristin J. Arnold

Teams: Feedback

The Last Team Member: Building a Team, by Connie Phillips

Consulting and Facilitating: Facilitating: Opening

Plunge In: Using Openers to Connect Groups and Their Work, by M.K. Key

Want/Give Walkabout: Sharing Expectations, by Gail Hahn

Leadership: Motivation

Three Roles of Leaders: Understanding Leadership, by Parth Sarathi

Organizations: Vision, Mission, Values, Strategy

To Be the Best: Determining Aspirational Values, by Cher Holton

To further assist you in selecting appropriate ELAs, we provide the following grid that summarizes category, time required, group size, and risk factor for each ELA.

Category	ELA Title	Page	Time Required	Group Size	Risk Factor
Individual Development: Sensory Awareness	Picture Yourself: Gaining Self-Awareness	11	50 to 60 minutes	10 to 20	Moderate
Individual Development: Self-Disclosure	Take a Risk: Practicing Self-Disclosure	17	90 minutes	Any number of work teams of 3 to 5	Low to Moderate
Individual Development: Diversity	At the Movies: Building Cross-Cultural Sensitivity	25	Approximately 2 hours	Any size	Low to Moderate
Communication: Awareness	All Power Is Relative: Checking Ourselves Against Others	35	45 to 60 minutes	10 to 20	Moderate to High
Communication: Listening	The Association for Community Improvement: Dealing with Hidden Agendas	43	Approximately 2 hours	16 to 24	Moderate to High
Problem Solving: Generating Alternatives	Give Brands a Hand: Generating Ideas	55	Approximately 60 minutes	5 to 7 per group	Low
Problem Solving: Consensus/Synergy	Pass It On: Using an Alternate Brainstorming Technique	59	30 to 45 minutes	6 to 25	Low
Groups: Competition/Collaboration	Altair the Ant: Influencing Performance	63	90 minutes	15 to 25	Moderate
Teams: Roles	The Hats We Wear: Understanding Team Roles	69	Approximately 50 minutes	6 or more	Moderate
Teams: Feedback	The Last Team Member: Building a Team	73	Approximately 60 minutes	20 or fewer	Low to Moderate
Consulting, Training, and Facilitating: Facilitating: Opening	Plunge In: Using Openers to Connect Groups and Their Work	77	Approximately 25 minutes	6 to 30	Low
Consulting, Training, and Facilitating: Facilitating: Opening	Want/Give Walkabout: Sharing Expectations	81	15 to 20 minutes	8 to 100	Low
Leadership: Motivation	Three Roles of Leaders: Understanding Leadership	85	Approximately 90 minutes	15 to 30	Low to Moderate
Organizations: Vision, Mission, Values, Strategy	To Be the Best: Determining Aspirational Values	91	90 to 120 minutes	5 to 25	Moderate

Experiential Learning Activities Categories

Picture Yourself:
Gaining Self-Awareness

Activity Summary

This mildly physical activity allows participants to gain a different perspective of themselves and their lives.

Goals

- To demonstrate the usefulness of metaphor in increasing self-awareness.

- To develop participants' awareness of their feelings about themselves and their lives.

Group Size

10 to 20 participants in groups of 5.

Time Required

50 to 60 minutes.

Materials

- One Picture Yourself Instruction Sheet for each participant.

- One Picture Yourself Worksheet for each participant.

- Colored markers or pencils for participants.

- Blank sheets of paper for participants.

Physical Setting

Writing space for the participants. Ideally, they should be seated 5 to a table.

Facilitating Risk Rating

Moderate.

Process

1. Give everyone copies of the Picture Yourself Instruction Sheet and read the directions aloud to the participants.

2. Emphasize the fact that during this activity they are not to be concerned with their artistic ability or accuracy. Rather, the focus should be on selecting a metaphor that best describes the "climate" or "feel" of their roles and relationships.

3. Offer the participants colored markers or pencils and blank paper on which to draw if they would prefer a larger surface than exists on the Instruction Sheet.

4. Give the participants 10 minutes to create their drawings.

5. Check their progress and assist those who are hesitant to draw or who are having difficulty selecting a metaphor.

6. When the 10 minutes is almost up, or most participants have completed their drawings, remind them to write some words that describe the details in their drawings or better explain the reasons for their choices. *(10 minutes.)*

7. Indicate that it is time for the participants to show their drawings and explain to the other people at their tables what they chose to draw and the underlying reasons for their choices. Explain that the small groups should decide which of the drawings should be described to the group at large. *(15 minutes.)*

8. Ask for participants to volunteer to show and explain their drawings. Allow 8 to 10 minutes for this show-and-tell activity.

9. Give the participants copies of the Picture Yourself Worksheet and ask them to fill it out, indicating what they learned from this exercise. Provide 5 to 10 minutes for completion of the individual worksheets.

10. Lead a directed group discussion regarding the degree to which this activity gave the participants additional information regarding themselves, their roles, and their relationships. Ask what they might do differently if they were to make a new drawing.
(15 minutes.)

Variations

- Instead of asking for volunteers, ask for the individual(s) with the most interesting drawings at each table to show their drawings to the group at large and explain what they chose to draw and the underlying reasons for their choices.

- Provide an opportunity for participants to draw or picture the "new you" at the end of the activity.

Submitted by Deborah Spring Laurel.

Deborah Spring Laurel, *president of Laurel and Associates, Ltd., is an international management training consultant who specializes in the design and presentation of skill building, participant-centered workshops in personnel management, interpersonal relations, leadership, organization development, and train-the-trainer. She is also a Certified Professional Consultant to Management, with expertise in human resource management, organization development, and performance consulting. She has her master's degree from the University of Wisconsin-Madison.*

Picture Yourself Instruction Sheet

Instructions: In this exercise, you will have an opportunity to look at yourself from a new perspective. Imagine that you are a vehicle, an animal, or a food, and draw yourself as well as you can. Don't worry about your artistic accuracy. Instead, concentrate on adding details that you feel capture the "climate" of your role and your relationships. For example, if you choose to describe yourself as a car, consider whether it has air conditioning or electric windows. Remember, any type of vehicle, air, land, or sea, can be chosen. If you choose to describe yourself as a horse, consider whether it is wild or tame, a racehorse or a plow horse. If you choose to describe yourself as a loaf of bread, consider whether it is fresh or stale, whole wheat or Wonder bread. After you have drawn your vehicle or animal or food, write down a few words or phrases that describe it. For example, if it is a car, is it expensive, old, conservative, or flashy? If it is an animal, is it soft and cuddly or withdrawn and snappish. If it is a food, is it sweet, dry, bitter, or spicy?

Picture Yourself Worksheet

- What metaphor did you choose?

- Why did you choose this metaphor?

- What does your drawing tell you about how you feel about yourself?

- What does your drawing tell you about how you feel about your role(s)?

- What does your drawing tell you about how you feel about your relationships?

- How content are you with the status quo as described in your drawing?

- What, if anything, do you want to change about what you drew?

- If you made the changes you desire, what would the drawing of the "new you" look like?

Take a Risk:
Practicing Self-Disclosure

Activity Summary

Team members learn about the importance of and practice self-disclosure.

Goals

- To demonstrate and practice self-disclosure.

- To provide an opportunity to discuss the relationship between self-disclosure, risk taking, developing trust between individuals, and team development.

Group Size

Any number of intact work teams of 3 to 5 participants. Break larger teams into smaller groups.

Time Required

90 minutes.

Materials

- One Take a Risk Lecturette for the facilitator.

- One copy of the Take a Risk Questionnaire for each participant.

- One copy of the Take a Risk Post-Activity Rating Form for each participant.

- A flip chart and felt-tipped markers.

- Pens or pencils for participants.

Facilitating Risk Rating

Low to moderate.

Process

1. Present the Take a Risk Lecturette.
   (10 minutes.)

2. Give participants copies of the Take a Risk Questionnaire and pens or pencils and have them complete the questionnaire individually.
   (30 minutes.)

3. Have participants form into their work teams, 3 to 5 members per group. Larger work teams should form several smaller groups. Instruct participants to share their answers to the questions on the Take a Risk Questionnaire with the other members of their teams in a round-robin manner, with each participant in turn disclosing his or her answer to question 1, and then moving on to question 2, and so on. Encourage participants to elaborate on their answers, to provide examples, or to ask each other for further explanation, clarification, or elaboration.
   (30 minutes.)

4. Ask team members to reflect on and to discuss with each other the following questions:

   • What observations did you make about this activity and its impact on people?

   • What did you notice about yourself and about others during this activity?
   (10 minutes.)

5. Give team members copies and ask them to complete the Take a Risk Post-Activity Rating Form. After they have all completed the form, tell teams to calculate an average team score for each of the four questions. Post the four average scores for each team on a flip chart.

6. Lead a discussion about the scores and what they suggest about the impact of the activity. For example, high scores (in the 4 to 5 range) for questions 1 and 2 suggest that the activity had considerable impact on the team(s), whereas low scores (in the 1 to 2 range) suggest that the activity for one reason or another had little impact. These reasons might be that the team members already knew each well beforehand; the activity was of too short a duration to have much impact; despite instructions, members were not willing to engage in adequate

self-disclosure; or the questions did not lend themselves to adequate self-disclosure. With regard to questions 3 and 4, point out that it is reasonable to predict that scores for question 3 should be higher than for question 4. The reason for this is that people generally feel that they themselves are being honest, but one can never know for certain whether someone else is being completely honest. You may wish to determine whether this predicted pattern is borne out by the data.

7. Ask what additional thoughts they have based on the Post-Activity Rating Form. Ask what they might do differently back on the job as a result of this activity.

    (10 minutes.)

Submitted by Ira J. Morrow.

Ira J. Morrow *is an associate professor of management at Pace University's Lubin School of Business in New York City. He has a Ph.D. in industrial-organizational psychology from New York University and has consulted extensively in the private and public sectors, primarily in the areas of selection and assessment.*

Take a Risk Lecturette

Most people in our society are not in the habit of disclosing personal information to strangers or casual acquaintances. People may reasonably feel that self-disclosure entails a certain degree of risk taking since the information provided to others may reveal potentially embarrassing flaws, weaknesses, or shortcomings, and that such information may be used to the person's detriment at some point in the future.

As people gradually come to know one another better, they may open up and be more willing to share information about themselves with others. This process generally takes place in a gradual manner, which suggests that people are willing to share such information as they develop trust in one another. Conversely, people are also more willing to trust one another as they share information. This relationship between self-disclosure and the development of trust can be said to be cyclical and mutually reinforcing so that we can say that the more people trust one another, the more willing they are to self-disclose, and the more willing people are to self-disclose, the more they will trust one another. Just as we cannot definitely answer the classic problem of which came first, the chicken or the egg, so too is it difficult to say which comes first, trust or self-disclosure.

We are commenting here on a general expected pattern and, of course, exceptions are possible. For example, the disclosure-trust cycle may be disrupted and broken if one self-disclosing party has seen that previously provided information has indeed been misused.

The requirements of contemporary life, particularly in organizational work and educational settings, are such that people, including strangers, near strangers, or casual acquaintances, are often thrust together into groups or teams for the purpose of working together to accomplish certain goals. Often the ability to work together effectively in order to attain important outcomes is dependent on a team's ability to be cohesive. Cohesiveness may in turn be dependent on developing trust in one another, and this in turn is related to the team's ability and willingness to engage in self-disclosure.

Because of organizational pressures and of the need to do things quickly, team members often do not have the luxury of implementing the trust-disclosure cycle in the gradual manner that is generally the case in our personal lives. The process, in other words, often has to be short-circuited and sped up. This experiential learning activity is designed to help team members speed up the development of the trust-disclosure cycle so that teams can enhance their cohesiveness in order to improve team member satisfaction and performance.

Take a Risk Questionnaire

Instructions: As frankly and honestly as possible, please respond to the following questions.

1. What are five adjectives that best describe you?

2. Describe the skills that have helped you the most in your career, education, or life.

3. Describe the limitations that have hindered you the most in your career, education, or life.

4. What actions do you need to take to overcome these limitations?

5. What actions do you think that you realistically will take to overcome these limitations?

6. What kind of help or support from others do you need to overcome these limitations?

7. What steps can you take to obtain this help from others?

8. What is the most important thing that has happened to you in the past year?

9. What is the most important change that you would like to see in your life in the next two years?

10. What concerns do you have about this team's ability to perform effectively?

11. How do you feel about answering questions of this type? Why do you feel this way?

Take a Risk Post–Activity Rating Form

Instructions: Using a 1 to 5 rating scale, where 1 = not at all, 3 = to some extent, and 5 = to a great extent, please respond to the following questions. Give a number value and insert any comments about why your answer is true for you.

_____ 1. To what extent do you know the other members of your team better now?

_____ 2. To what extent do you trust the other members of your team better now?

_____ 3. To what extent were you honest with the other members of your team?

_____ 4. To what extent were the other members of the team honest with you?

At the Movies:
Building Cross-Cultural Sensitivity

Activity Summary

Participants assess their own cultural values by viewing films and taking an inventory.

Goals

- To build understanding and awareness of cultural differences.

- To discovery one's own cross-cultural attitudes as part of a critical reflective-learning approach.

- To build participants' competencies required for operating in a cross-cultural milieu.

Group Size

Any size group.

Time Required

Approximately 2 hours.

Materials

- "Film as a Learning Resource" article offered by Professor Joe Champoux from New Mexico University, downloaded from www.swlearning.com/management/champoux.

- One At the Movies Cross-Cultural Sensitivity Inventory for each participant.

- One At the Movies Guide for Understanding the Cross-Cultural Sensitivity Inventory for each participant.

- Three different films rented on video, set ahead of time to the indicated scenes. (Your player may be slightly different from these numbers, so be sure to double-check.):

  > *L'auberge Espagnole,* directed by Cedric Klaspisch in 2003 and distributed by Fox Searchlight. 185 minutes. [You will show 1:07:16 to 1:16:02.] (Synopsis: Xavier, a young French economics student getting his first taste of the rest of Europe, moves into an apartment in Barcelona with a group of other European students, including guys from Italy, Denmark, and Germany and girls from England, Belgium, and Andalusia. Together, the septet share a series of adventures.)

  > *My Big Fat Greek Wedding,* directed by Joel Zwick in 2002 and distributed by IFC Films. 95 minutes. [You will show 1'40 to 6'17 and 1:02:48 to 1:09:20] (Synopsis: Everyone in the Portokalos family worries about Toula. Still unmarried at 30, she works at Dancing Zorba's, the Greek restaurant owned by her parents. Vowing that she'd rather stab herself in the eye with a red-hot poker than work in the restaurant for the rest of her life, Toula is ready for a change.)

  > *The Mexican,* directed by Gore Verbinski in 2001 and distributed by DreamWorks Pictures. 123 minutes. [You will show 11:37 to 12:38.] (Synopsis: A bungling gangster has promised his girlfriend that he'll go straight, but first he has to do one last job for his boss: secure a "cursed" antique pistol known as The Mexican.)

- A monitor and a video player.

- A flip chart and felt-tipped markers.

- Pencils for participants.

Physical Setting

No special requirements are needed except that everyone must have a view of the video screen.

Facilitating Risk Rating

Low to moderate.

Preparation

1. Use the instructors' free resource "Film as a Learning Resource" offered by Professor Joe Champoux from New Mexico University to familiarize yourself with using film in teaching. (Go to http://champous.swcollege.com to download the article.)

Process

1. Administer the At the Movies Cross-Cultural Sensitivity Inventory at the beginning of the session, giving everyone copies of the inventory and a pencil. Allow time for participants to properly score their own inventories. It is important to ensure confidentiality of responses given that some participants may be sensitive about their results.
   (15 minutes.)

2. When everyone has finished the scoring process, give participants copies of the At the Movies Guide for Understanding the Cross-Cultural Sensitivity Inventory to determine their own levels of cross-cultural sensitivity.
   (5 minutes.)

3. Engage the group in a discussion of cross-cultural issues using the following questions:

   - Were you surprised by your results on the inventory? In what way?

   - Why do people usually lack cultural sensitivity?

   - It is difficult to become more cross-culturally sensitive? What are the main drawbacks we face?

   - Which kinds of behaviors would be useful to help us develop our cross-cultural sensitivity?

   - What kind of behaviors would you like to start practicing to increase your own cross-cultural sensitivity?

   - Why is it important to do so?
   (20 minutes.)

4. Summarize the learning from the session at this point. Use a flip chart to write down participants' observations.
   (10 minutes.)

5. Show the clip from L'auberge Espagnole (Min. 1:07:16 to 1:16:02). This scene takes place in the international students' dinning room. The English student's brother, who has just arrived in Barcelona, is talking about an encounter he has had with a Spanish man on the train. Stereotypes and misunderstandings quickly arise.
   (10 minutes.)

6. Engage the group in a discussion of the following questions and issues:

   - How has the sensibility of the Spanish girl been damaged?

   - In which cross-cultural sensitivity subscales from the inventory would the English boy score the lowest?

   - Can this kind of behavior be avoided? If so, how?
   (10 minutes.)

7. Show the two clips from My Big Fat Greek Wedding:

   - First show scene number 1 (Min. 1'40 to 6'17). Toula is reflecting about what being a Greek girl means.

   - Next show scene number 2 (Min. 1:02:48 to 1:09:20). In this scene Toula's Greek family meets the Anglo-Saxon family of Toula's boyfriend.
   (15 minutes.)

8. Engage the group in a discussion of the following questions and issues:

   - What are the main characteristics of the Greek culture from Toula's point of view? Is she proud of her cultural background?

   - What kind of cultural stereotypes can be observed in scene 2? Which could be the origins of these stereotypes? What are the consequences?
   (10 minutes.)

9. Show the clip from the film The Mexican (Min. 11:37 to 12:38). In this scene Brat Pitt is trying to rent a car after his arrival at a Mexican airport. Stereotypes about expected cultural behaviors easily arise.
   (5 minutes.)

10. Engage the group in a discussion of the following questions and issues:

    - What does this scene show us about cultural archetypes?

    - How are these four movies scenes related?

- What can we learn from these scenes about our understanding of other cultures?

- What can we learn about our own cultural perceptions?
  (10 minutes.)

11. Summarize the learning of the session at this point. Use a flip chart to write down participants' points.
    (10 minutes.)

12. Thank the participants for sharing their knowledge and encourage them to continuously work on developing cross-cultural awareness.

Variation

- Carry the theme further by having participants make plans for more culturally sensitive behavior back on the job.

References

Cushner, K.(1986). *The inventory of cross-cultural sensitivity.* Kent, OH: School of Education, Kent State University.

Submitted by Teresa Torres-Coronas.

Teresa Torres-Coronas *has a bachelor's degree in economics and a Ph.D. in management. She is the author of* Valuing Brands, *co-author of* Retrieve Your Creativity, *and co-editor of the forthcoming* Changing the Way You Teach: Creative Tools for Management Educators. *She is a professor in the Universitat Rovira i Virgili and is one of the Spanish associates of the Center for Research in Applied Creativity, Canada.*

At the Movies Cross-Cultural Sensitivity Inventory*

Instructions: Circle the number that best corresponds to your level of agreement with each statement below.

1 = Strongly Disagree   7 = Strongly Agree

1. I speak only one language.   1 2 3 4 5 6 7

2. The way other people express themselves is very interesting to me.   1 2 3 4 5 6 7

3. I enjoy being with people from other cultures.   1 2 3 4 5 6 7

4. Foreign influence in our country threatens our national identity.   1 2 3 4 5 6 7

5. Others' feelings rarely influence decisions I make.   1 2 3 4 5 6 7

6. I cannot eat with chopsticks.   1 2 3 4 5 6 7

7. I avoid people who are different from me.   1 2 3 4 5 6 7

8. It is better that people from other cultures avoid one another.   1 2 3 4 5 6 7

9. Culturally mixed marriages are wrong.   1 2 3 4 5 6 7

10. I think people are basically alike.   1 2 3 4 5 6 7

11. I have never lived outside my own culture for any great length of time.   1 2 3 4 5 6 7

12. I have foreigners over to my home on a regular basis.   1 2 3 4 5 6 7

13. It makes me nervous to talk about people who are different from me.   1 2 3 4 5 6 7

14. I enjoy studying about people from other cultures.   1 2 3 4 5 6 7

15. People from other cultures do things differently because they do not know any other way.   1 2 3 4 5 6 7

*The Cross-Cultural Sensitivity Inventory is reprinted with permission of the copyright holder, Kenneth Cushner, College of Education, Kent State University.

16. There is usually more than one good
    way to get things done.   1 2 3 4 5 6 7

17. I listen to music from another culture
    on a regular basis.   1 2 3 4 5 6 7

18. I decorate my home or room with
    artifacts from other countries. 1 2 3 4 5 6 7

19. I feel uncomfortable when in a
    crowd of people.   1 2 3 4 5 6 7

20. The very existence of humanity depends
    on our knowledge about other people. 1 2 3 4 5 6 7

21. Residential neighborhoods should be
    culturally separated.   1 2 3 4 5 6 7

22. I have many friends.   1 2 3 4 5 6 7

23. I dislike eating foods from other cultures. 1 2 3 4 5 6 7

24. I think about living within another
    culture in the future.   1 2 3 4 5 6 7

25. Moving into another culture would
    be easy.   1 2 3 4 5 6 7

26. I like to discuss issues with people from
    other cultures.   1 2 3 4 5 6 7

27. There should be tighter controls on the
    number of immigrants allowed into
    my country.   1 2 3 4 5 6 7

28. The more I know about people, the
    more I dislike them.   1 2 3 4 5 6 7

29. I read more national news than interna-
    tional news in the daily newspaper. 1 2 3 4 5 6 7

30. Crowds of foreigners frighten me. 1 2 3 4 5 6 7

31. When something newsworthy happens,
    I seek out someone from that part of
    the world to discuss the issue with. 1 2 3 4 5 6 7

32. I eat ethnic foods at least twice a week. 1 2 3 4 5 6 7

Scoring the Cross-Cultural Sensitivity Inventory

The Cross-Cultural Sensitivity Inventory can be scored by subscales. Simply enter the number you gave for each question you answered in the space provided under each subscale heading. Reverse the values for the items marked with an asterisk (*). For example, reverse scoring results in 7 = 1, 6 = 2, 5 = 3, 4 = 4, 3 = 5, 2 = 6, 1 = 7

Your total score is obtained by adding the various subscale scores together.

Scale C		Scale B		Scale I		Scale A		Scale E	
Item	Score	Item	Score	Item	Score	Item	Score	Item	Score
1*		2		3		4*		5*	
6*		7*		8*		9*		10	
11*		13*		14		15*		16	
12		19*		20		21*		22	
17		25*		26		27*		28	
18		30		31		Total		Total	
23*		Total		Total					
24									
29*									
32									
Total									

Subscale	Score
Cultural Integration (C Scale)	
Behavioral Scale (B Scale)	
Intellectual Interaction (I Scale)	
Attitude Toward Others (A Scale)	
Empathy Scale (E Scale)	
TOTAL SCORE	

Determining Sensitivity to Cross-Cultural Diversity

Subscales	Low Sensitivity	Average Sensitivity	High Sensitivity
Cultural integration	10–30	31–50	51–70
Behavioral response	6–15	16–30	31–42
Intellectual integration	6–15	16–30	34–42
Attitudes toward others	5–14	15–24	25–35
Empathy	5–14	15–24	25–35
Total score	32–95	96–160	161–224

My Overall Sensitivity: _____

At the Movies Guide for Understanding the Cross-Cultural Sensitivity Inventory

The Inventory of Cross-Cultural Sensitivity (ICCS) (Cushner, 1986) is a thirty-two-item self-report inventory to tap five major aspects of one's cross-cultural sensitivity.

1. Cultural integration reflects one's willingness to integrate with other cultures.

2. Behavioral response taps into perception of one's behavior toward others.

3. Intellectual interaction reflects one's intellectual orientation toward interactions with other cultures.

4. Attitudes toward others taps one's attitudes toward people from other cultures.

5. Empathy reflects one's ability to empathize with people from other cultures.

As proposed by Loo (1999) the ICCS can be used to stimulate the self-examination and self-discovery of cross-cultural attitudes as part of a critical reflective-learning approach to learning and to encourage group discussions about cross-cultural attitudes among participants. It is hoped that participants will identify aspects of their attitudes and behaviors that could be changed.

References

Cushner, K.(1986). *The inventory of cross-cultural sensitivity.* Kent, OH: School of Education, Kent State University.

Loo, R. (1999). A structured exercise for stimulating cross-cultural sensitivity. *Career Development International, 4*(6), 321-324.

All Power Is Relative:
Checking Ourselves Against Others

Activity Summary

The exercise helps new supervisors understand alternative sources of power.

Goals

- To show how easily power stereotypes surface.

- To help people become aware of the various sources of power and influence.

Group Size

10 to 20 participants in a supervisory training group or who have been recently promoted.

Time Required

45 to 60 minutes.

Materials

- One copy of the All Power Is Relative Survey for each participant.

- Pens or pencils for participants.

- Two flip charts.

- Felt-tipped markers.

Physical Setting

A room with tables and chairs, as well as enough open space for two large groups to assemble.

Facilitating Risk Rating

Moderate to high.

Process

1. Briefly explain the goals of the activity. Then give each person a copy of the All Power Is Relative Survey and a pen or pencil and ask everyone to complete the survey. (See the Consultant's Note below.)
   (10 minutes.)

2. After participants complete and score the survey, ask them to gather in an open space at the front or back of the room. Have them arrange themselves in a line by their scores, low to high.

3. Divide the participants, who are standing in line by score, into two subgroups based on a natural break in their scores on the survey. Try to have the one-third of those with the highest scores form the first subgroup and the remaining participants (lowest scores) form the second subgroup. Seat the groups as far apart as possible. Assign each group to a flip chart that cannot be read by the other group and provide markers.

4. When everyone has been seated, ask the group: "What influenced your scores the most?" After waiting for answers and writing them on the flip chart, say:

   "Self-perceptions are important, but who you chose to compare yourself with is also critical. For example, I may note that I am older than a former President and think that I have not accomplished much in my life compared to him. Or I might think of myself as much more successful than someone who is still struggling up the ladder or works in a different part of the organization. It is easy to feel powerless if I choose the wrong person to compare myself to or powerful if I choose someone who is perceived as lower on the organizational hierarchy."

5. Ask that people share the information from their surveys within their groups, including something about the people they used for comparison.
   (10 minutes.)

6. For the next part of the exercise, you must be a provocateur, willing to seed the discussion. For example, privately start the high-power group with the following:

    "I know that none of you would ever say or believe such things, but I'll bet that you have heard others speak about those people who have little or no power. You know, like those people over there, the low scorers, the sheep, the followers. What are some of the stereotypes you have heard others share?"

    As soon as the group shares a few, turn them loose to fill up the flip chart with other stereotypes, reminding them not to let the other group see what they write.

7. Move to the low-power group and say something like:

    "I know that none of you would ever say or believe such things, but I'll bet that you have heard others speak about those people who have a lot of power. You know, like those people over there, the high scorers, the power hungry ego-maniacs. What are some of the stereotypes you have heard others share?"

    Again, after they begin leave them alone to write their list.

8. It will take each of the groups about 5 minutes to fill up one sheet of flip-chart paper. Some of the typical examples include:

Stereotypes of High Power	Stereotypes of Low Power
Abrasive	Insincere, Average, Ordinary
Aloof, Know-It-Alls	Bottlenecks, Parasites
Arrogant, Manipulative	Clock Watchers, Sheep, Climbers
Overachievers	Complacent, Slackers
Condescending, Power Hungry	Lemmings, Unmotivated
Conceited, Self-Centered	Mediocre, "Warm Bodies"
Dominating Snobs	Meek Whiners

    (10 minutes.)

9. Ask each subgroup to elect a leader to present its list of stereotypes to the other subgroup. Say that they are to take turns sharing one item at a time from their lists with the other group (which requires that the total list remain hidden from view in some fashion). When both groups have finished sharing their lists, step in for the debriefing. Make the following points and ask these questions:

    *   Did you notice how easy it was to come up with stereotypes based on power? All of these stereotypes exist in the workplace. If you are in a position of power, someone is just waiting to see whether you will use, misuse, or abuse that power. I am certain that none of you wants

to be labeled with any of these stereotypes, yet it is easy to have them hung on us.

- What sources of power have you developed? Which should you be developing?

- What steps are you taking to avoid the negative perceptions that exist about those who have power and misuse it?

(15 minutes.)

Consultant's Note

For the ensuing discussion, it is important to direct the participants in their selection of people for comparison when completing the survey. For example, if they compare themselves to their managers, their subsequent scores will usually be very low. In contrast, if they compare themselves to their direct reports, their scores will usually be very high. In addition, some may not have direct reports, so ask the participants to compare themselves with their peers. Peers should be people inside the organization, people over whom they have no direct authority, but people they rely on to be successful in the performance of their jobs. Peers would also include those they would be competing with for their next promotion.

Variations

- After listing stereotypes, ask the participants to return to their groups and to identify the five to seven sources of power that are least likely to intimidate others (for example, 3, 4, 13, 17, 21, 33, 36, 37). It doesn't matter what the groups select. What is important is their expanded awareness of the significant number of sources of power beyond formal authority. Very few things will create more ill will than a supervisor's reliance on formal authority (e.g., "Because I said so!").

- Use the results as a transition to other exercises in communication, conflict resolution, management of change, and emotional intelligence. For example, How does a person's level of power influence his or her behaviors—the content of communications (e.g., withhold bad news), the level of disclosure and feedback (e.g., fear of retaliation), trust in the workplace, and so forth?

- Use the following quotes to introduce or summarize the activity:

  o "Even a nod from a person who is esteemed is of more force than a thousand arguments or studied sentences from others." (Plutarch)

  o "Power is never absolute; it is always relative." (Anonymous)

Submitted by Robert Shaver.

Robert Shaver *is a faculty associate with Executive Education, a continuing education unit of the University of Wisconsin-Madison, School of Business. As the director of the Basic Management Certificate Series Program, he is responsible for the development, marketing, staffing, and management of an adult education program serving about seven hundred first-line supervisors each year. He works with companies throughout the Midwest, designing and delivering custom, in-house training programs. Shaver received his bachelor's degree in communication, economics, and business administration from the University of Wisconsin-Stevens Point and his M.B.A. from the University of Wisconsin-Madison.*

All Power Is Relative Survey

Instructions: For each of the following dimensions, compare yourself with a peer in your organization you routinely interact with, using the following scale:

> +1 = Much Greater Than This Person
> 0 = About the Same as This Person
> −1 = Much Less Than This Person

For example, if you feel you are more adaptable than the person with whom you are comparing yourself, you would give yourself a +1 on the first item. Keep the same person in mind as you complete the survey.

1.	Adaptability (flexibility; openness to change; ability and readiness to learn)	+1	0	−1
2.	Ambition (competitive spirit; desire to be successful; results oriented)	+1	0	−1
3.	Amusing\Performing Skills (sense of humor; fun; flair for showmanship)	+1	0	−1
4.	Attitude (work habits; work ethic; commitment to excellence; attention to detail)	+1	0	−1
5.	Balance in Life (multiple interests; sources of nourishment and support)	+1	0	−1
6.	Coaching\Training (mentoring; counseling; reinforcement; instruction; lecturing; tutoring)	+1	0	−1
7.	Coercive Power (ability and willingness to instill a fear of retaliation)	+1	0	−1
8.	Common Sense (sound and prudent judgment, often unsophisticated; street smart)	+1	0	−1
9.	Communication Skills (oral; written; nonverbal; listening)	+1	0	−1
10.	Decision-Making Skills (ability and willingness to make difficult decisions in a timely fashion)	+1	0	−1
11.	Delegation Skills (ability and willingness to let go of tasks)	+1	0	−1

+1 = Much Greater Than This Person

0 = About the Same as This Person

−1 = Much Less Than This Person

12. Discipline Skills (timely and constructive feedback; confronting skills) +1   0   −1

13. Emotional Maturity (healthy self-esteem without arrogance; self-confidence) +1   0   −1

14. Energy (sense of urgency; passion; infectious to others; resiliency; stamina) +1   0   −1

15. Ethics (personal and professional integrity) +1   0   −1

16. Expert Power (technical competency or specialized skills that are respected and desired by others) +1   0   −1

17. Feeling, Sensing, Empathy Skills (tact; compassion; sensitive and responsive to feelings of others) +1   0   −1

18. Formal Authority (title or office; ownership) +1   0   −1

19. Image\First Impression (demeanor; grooming; confidence; naturalness) +1   0   −1

20. Information Power (not same as expert power; access to information as a result of experience or connections) +1   0   −1

21. Interpersonal Skills (ability to work with, get along with, and relate to others with diverse backgrounds, opinions, and values) +1   0   −1

22. Intellectual Power (creativity; memory; formal education) +1   0   −1

23. Leadership Skills (enlisting and synergizing others toward course of action) +1   0   −1

24. Luck\Karma (ability to capitalize on circumstances) +1   0   −1

25. Meeting Management Skills (facilitating; controlling) +1   0   −1

26. Management\Supervision Skills (monitoring individual and group behavior) +1   0   −1

27. Negotiation Skills (mediating; arbitrating; compromising; reconciling) +1   0   −1

+1 = Much Greater Than This Person

0 = About the Same as This Person

−1 = Much Less Than This Person

28. Perseverance Skills (ability to remain steady and focused in face of adversity)   +1   0   −1

29. Persuading Skills (inspiring; convincing; motivating; ability to sell intangibles)   +1   0   −1

30. Physical Power (fitness; strength; resiliency)   +1   0   −1

31. Public Speaking Skills (for large groups; media relations)   +1   0   −1

32. Referent Power\Charisma (extent to which others desire to be identified with you)   +1   0   −1

33. Reputation\Track Record\Stature (ability; commitment; share rewards; trust; how you will treat others who make mistakes; accept responsibility)   +1   0   −1

34. Reward Power (ability and willingness to provide valued resources and outcomes)   +1   0   −1

35. Risk Orientation (risk seeking or risk aversion)   +1   0   −1

36. Service Skills (followership; collaboration)   +1   0   −1

37. Social Power (interpersonal alliances; affiliations; networking; external connections)   +1   0   −1

38. Skill at Coping with Stress (healthy or dysfunctional)   +1   0   −1

39. Tolerance for Ambiguity (versus need for certainty)   +1   0   −1

40. Vision (ability to see the forest for the trees; clarity of purpose and direction)   +1   0   −1

Total your numbers for the forty items
and wait for instructions from the facilitator.   _____ _____ _____

The Association for Community Improvement:
Dealing with Hidden Agendas

Activity Summary

This role play/simulation activity pits three grassroots organizations against each other, with the goal of securing a large community improvement grant from the County Commission. One group has an ethnocentric hidden agenda, which may or may not be recognized during the process.

Goals

- To develop collaboration skills through the experience of developing an effective group presentation/proposal.

- To improve communication, listening, and persuasion skills.

- To develop the skill to identify hidden motives, which may be racist or ethnocentric in nature. (Do not share this goal until the end of the activity.)

Group Size

16 to 24 participants who are members of the same organization in four roughly even subgroups.

Time Required

Approximately 2 hours.

Materials

- Copies of The Association for Community Improvement Form A for all members of Subgroup 2.

- Copies of The Association for Community Improvement Form B for all members of the Commission.

- Copies of The Association for Community Improvement Form C for all members of Subgroups 1 and 3.

- Copies of The Association for Community Improvement Form D for all participants.

- Copies of The Association for Community Improvement Form E for members of Subgroups 1 and 3.

- Copies of The Association for Community Improvement Form F for members of Subgroup 2.

- Paper and writing utensils for all participants.

- (Optional) A stack of play money (at least $150,000 worth) in large denominations to be delivered to the winning team, or small prizes as desired.

Physical Setting

One large room, with a table at the front, where the "Commissioners" will sit and later preside. The three subgroups should be seated at tables (round if possible), some distance from each other, to plan their presentations. It is especially important that the groups work privately. If necessary, one or more of the subgroups can go to another room or work in a hallway.

Facilitating Risk Rating

Moderate to high.

Process

1. Break the large group into four teams of 4 to 6 members each.

2. Designate one group as the County Commission and each of the other three groups as three different "Associations for Community Improvement." One group, 2, has a divisive hidden agenda, which is outlined in Form A. None of the other groups must know about this, including the County Commis-

sion, so when you hand out the forms, do not give away the fact that the groups are receiving different instructions.

3. Give an overview of the role play/simulation and the first two goals:

   "In this activity, three groups, all calling themselves 'The Association for Community Improvement,' will each be vying for a major grant. These funds, to the tune of $150,000, will be presented at the end of the simulation to only one group chosen by the County Commission. You will receive full instructions and a time frame. Once you read your instructions as a group, I will circulate to answer any questions. Good luck to you all."

4. Give Form A to Group 2, Form B to the County Commission, and Form C to the other two groups, both also "Associations for Community Improvement." *(10 minutes.)*

5. After 4 or 5 minutes ensure that both Groups 1 and 3 have determined what their mission is. Also check to assess, as needed, that the Commission is preparing a useful checklist to evaluate the presentations. Additionally, ensure confidentially that Group 2 understands its ulterior motive and its role in the simulation.

6. Observe all four groups and periodically give updates on how much time is left. Also remind them that at least two members from each group will make the presentations to the Commission. If they should ask, groups may use any "props" that they find in the room or vicinity for their presentations. *(20 minutes.)*

7. After approximately 20 minutes, check with each group to ensure that they have completed their tasks. Give an additional 5 to 10 minutes if necessary, as time is available.

8. Hand out Form D to all participants and tell them to pay close attention and to take notes on Form D regarding the effectiveness of each presentation. Ask Group 1 to come to the front and, facing the Commissioners' table, make their "pitch." The Commission has 5 to 10 minutes to probe and ask questions while the first group is presenting. *(15 minutes.)*

9. Repeat the process for the additional two groups. Since you (the consultant) recognize the ulterior motive of Group 2, be careful not to let on or impact the presentation or evaluation process. Again, the other groups will assess the presentations when they are not presenting. It is imperative that participants

stay focused on the proceedings, since one group may pick up something that the Commission may miss!

(30 minutes.)

10. Once all three groups have finished, tell the Commission to reconvene privately for about 10 minutes to evaluate each group and determine their selection. Remind them that the grant stipulates only one winner. Concurrent to this, ask the other three groups to reconvene. Hand out Form E to all members of Groups 1 and 3 and Form F to members of Group 2 and ask them to complete the forms and discuss their group process.

(10 minutes.)

11. When the Commission is ready and the groups have finished filling out their forms, reassemble the large group and ask the Commissioners to speak to each group, one group at a time, sharing the criteria that were used to evaluate their proposal and the strengths and weaknesses that were noted. Also ask for any additional feedback from the other participants on the presentations they heard, based on what they wrote on Form D.

(15 minutes.)

12. When all three groups have received feedback, ask the Commission to announce the winner. Lead the whole group in a discussion of the choice that was made. The following are options for how the discussion might proceed:

a. If Group 2, with the hidden agenda, is NOT chosen, ask one of their members of that group to read their instruction sheet (Form A) aloud. Ask the larger group (if necessary), "Did anyone pick up any indication of the hidden agenda of this group?" and discuss why this was so.

b. If Group 2 is awarded the grant, ask them to "share" their motivation and what they really intend to do with the money. Then discuss this with the larger group.

(10 minutes.)

13. Debrief with questions appropriate to what the group experienced. A few samples might include:

- What are some of the ways "improvement" has been defined?

- Was there anything the Commission missed?

- Has anyone ever experienced a similar situation?

- Have you ever observed racist or ethnocentric behavior in a group? How did you confront it? With what results?

- What can or should we do if we become aware of covert hidden agendas? *(10 minutes.)*

14. Wrap up the activity by thanking everyone for their time and attention and cite any person or group whose role seemed especially difficult. Ask participants, "What learning experience was most significant for you?"

Consultant's Note

Be sure to debrief this activity carefully, so that every person who participated understands that it was a simulation and not the real view or intent of any of the participants or of the organization.

This activity is based on a true-life incident. An organization with a very nebulous name like "The Association for Community Improvement" and a divisive hidden agenda secured a fairly large community improvement grant from a local government agency. Unbeknownst to the funding agency, this group began to use these funds to attempt to block the development of affordable housing and the influx of immigrants into their community.

After learning about this fiasco, it occurred to us that the funding board needed to "dig deeper" to discover possible hidden motives. We also recognized that a phrase like "community improvement" could mean many different things to different people. For someone who is ethnocentric, thinking "my people" (same race, ethnic background, religion, or income level) are better than everyone else, the goal of keeping the "others" out could seem like a commendable mission.

The activity also demonstrates that even though, in many cases, overt racism or ethnocentrism has lessened, it is still very much alive in our world. The process will assist you and your participants to become more aware of these challenges. It can also help you begin a dialogue on ways to combat these divisive forces in your own community and organization.

Variation

- The activity can be used as a way to review an organization's diversity, EEO compliance, or other related policies.

Submitted by Donna L. Goldstein and Luis R. Morales.

Donna L. Goldstein, Ed.D, *is the managing director of Development Associates International, a human resource consulting and training group that helps organizations excel. An executive coach and team-building expert, she has contributed to nineteen books and has written dozens of articles on contemporary HR issues. Over the past twenty-five years, she has trained over 100,000 individuals and has provided training and consulting services to more than three hundred organizations worldwide, including Barclays Bank, IBM, and MTV Networks.*

Luis R. Morales *receive his MA in psychology from Boston University with additional graduate studies in adult education and interpersonal dynamics. He became a member/trainer of NTL Institute for Applied Behavioral Science in 1969 and an associate of Development Associates International in 1997. He has worked in most of Hispanic America and the United States. Some of his clients include: Searle and Co., Venezuelan Executives Association, U.S. Department of Agriculture, Central American Episcopal Bishops, Digital Equipment, Inter American and Development Bank.*

The Association for Community Improvement Form A

Instructions: In this activity, which is based on a true incident, you are being asked to participate in a role play that may go against some of your beliefs. Nevertheless, we ask that you comply with these instructions as faithfully as possible. Your cooperation is essential to achieving the goals of this program. Your "forced task" will be revealed to the entire group at the end of the activity.

You are a loosely knit group of twenty-five citizens made up of long-time residents of your community who call yourselves "The Association for Community Improvement." As a group, you are quite concerned with maintaining the original ethnic integrity and character of your community. You now see an excellent opportunity for this in the form of a new $150,000 grant, which will be awarded by the County Commission. You are quite proud that your group has performed some important services to the community in the past, such as organizing a successful "crime watch" program.

Your group is now concerned with the large influx of new immigrants into your community. You would like to develop strategies to prevent what you feel is further erosion of the original ethnic makeup of your neighborhood.

You are aware that your mission may be perceived as "politically incorrect," and you must work to hide or disguise this fact, within the contents of your proposal. You will have 20 to 25 minutes to prepare a 3-minute presentation to the County Commission. At least two members of your group will deliver the presentation.

The Association for Community Improvement Form B

Instructions: You are a local governing body whose task is to ensure that your county thrives in what are challenging economic times. You are particularly concerned with ensuring both the safety and attractiveness of your community and preserving the dollars brought in by tourism.

Your local community has been awarded a $150,000 grant from a regional community development agency with the stipulation that it be given in one lump sum to the community-based, grassroots organization you believe will have the greatest positive impact in your increasingly diverse community.

Curiously, three grassroots groups, all calling themselves the "The Association for Community Improvement," have registered to present their proposals to you. Each group will have 3 minutes to make a presentation, and you will have several minutes to ask them questions about their organizations and their requests. Be sure that you are extremely clear about the mission and goals of each group and how that group would propose to spend the monies, if awarded.

Your first task is to develop a list of criteria and guiding questions, which you will use to evaluate each group's proposal. In order to expedite the evaluation process, it is suggested that you create a checklist with criteria you will use to evaluate each of the presentations. You will have 20 to 25 minutes to do this, while the three groups are preparing the proposals they will present to you.

The Association for Community Improvement Form C

Instructions: Imagine that you are a grass-roots lobbying group of citizens and developers in an imaginary community. The name of your organization is "The Association for Community Improvement." Your task is two-fold. First, you must determine, as a group, the mission of your organization. Given the ambiguous name of your group, you can choose one of any number of community improvement goals, such as reducing litter, improving roads, landscaping of public places, better street lighting, improving after-school or daycare programs, etc.

Take no more than 5 minutes to determine your group's mission. Once this has been determined, you will have 20 to 25 minutes to prepare a 3-minute presentation to give to the County Commission requesting grant funding. The Commission will award only one $150,000 grant to the most worthy proposal they receive from a community group. At least two members of your group will be responsible for making the presentation. It may be necessary to make up some facts, but have them mirror at least part of your community as closely as possible.

The Association for Community Improvement Form D

Instructions: Use this form to evaluate how well the other groups did in their presentations to the Commission.

1. How clear were they about their goals and mission?

2. How specific were they about how the funds would be spent to achieve their goals?

3. How persuasive were the presenters?

4. How convincing were they in justifying why they should receive the funds?

    Rate each group on the scale below and give one reason for your rating.

    0 = Unconvincing   5 = Strong Justification

5. How strong was their delivery? Rate delivery on a 0 to 5 scale with rationale for why you rated it the way you did.

    0 = Weak delivery   5 = Powerful Delivery

The Association for Community Improvement Form E

Instructions: Complete this form as a group while the Commission is deliberating.

1. To what degree were the goals of your proposed project clearly defined?

2. Compared to the other groups, how persuasive were you?

3. Were the skills, talents, and experiences of your group members adequately used?

4. If you had the opportunity to do your presentation again, would you do anything differently?

The Association for Community Improvement Form F

Instructions: Complete this form as a group while the Commission is deliberating.

1. How did you feel when you read your role-play task?

2. To what degree were you able to disguise your hidden motives?

3. How well did your group collaborate, even on an unpleasant or difficult task?

4. Compared to the other groups, how persuasive were you?

Give Brands a Hand:
Generating Ideas

Activity Summary

This is a provocative thinking activity designed to revitalize a brand or generate ideas, very loosely based on the Hegelian dialectic involving thesis, antithesis, and synthesis.

Goals

- To help an organization (profit or nonprofit) revitalize a brand.

- To provide a different way for small groups to generate new ideas.

- To demonstrate how two opposing points of view can be reconciled and merged to achieve something new.

Group Size

Subgroups of 5 to 7 participants from the same organization.

Time Required

Approximately 60 minutes.

Materials

- One flip chart and markers for each small group.

- (Optional) One overhead projector.

- A prepared flip-chart sheet or transparency listing the three ingredients of a Hegelian dialectic: (1) Thesis, (2) Antithesis, (3) Synthesis.

Physical Setting

A room large enough to accommodate all subgroups and their flip charts with sufficient space between groups.

Facilitating Risk Taking

Low.

Process

1. Organize the participants (members of the same organization) into small groups of three to six people each.

2. Use the prepared flip chart or an overhead transparency to show all the participants a management challenge or current vision statement for the organization, for example, "To become the premier soft drink brand in the United States."

3. Inform the groups that they are going to use a modified Hegelian dialectic involving: (1) thesis, (2) antithesis, and (3) synthesis.

4. Tell the groups to defer judgment and generate at least ten ideas to achieve the vision or resolve the challenge.

5. Have the groups assign a recorder, use a flip chart to record the ideas, and then select one idea they can agree on. As an example, "Have a modern beauty contest." (This is the "thesis.")
    (10 minutes.)

6. Tell them to discuss some opposite, contradiction, or variation of the idea they have chosen that might make it less appealing or effective. For instance, make it an "old-fashioned" contest from the 1960s and have "Miss Fizzo" with carefully coifed hair walking down a runway in a bathing suit. This is the "antithesis" and implies that the brand is dying or has died. (Note that the antithesis does not have to be a direct reversal of the thesis.)
    (10 minutes.)

7. Ask the groups to create a new campaign, but to incorporate or combine elements of both the original "thesis" and the "antithesis." Thus, they might create a branding campaign that involves a satirical, updated beauty contest using a "Mizz Fizz" (instead of "Miss Fizz") from Chicago who exudes "attitude" and strength of character. (This is the "synthesis.")
    (15 minutes.)

8. Have the groups use the result of the synthesis as the thesis for another round of the dialectic. So the antithesis of "Mizz Fizz" might be a "Mister Siss," which might lead to the idea of a campaign using men dressed in drag. Tell the groups to use the two concepts they have come up with to create a synthesis such as a quirky married couple with a "soda-drinking problem."
   (15 minutes.)

9. After all of the groups have gone through at least two rounds, bring everyone back together and tell small groups to share their ideas, in turn, with the larger group. Record any new ideas that might be stimulated by the sharing.

10. Summarize with a discussion of the following questions.

    • What worked?

    • What happened to your thinking during the process?

    • How could you use this process in other areas back on the job?
    (10 minutes.)

Submitted by Arthur B. VanGundy.

Arthur B. VanGundy, Ph.D., *is considered a pioneer in his work on idea generation techniques and has written twelve books, including* Brain Boosters for Business Advantage, 101 Great Games & Activities, *and* Orchestrating Collaboration at Work: Using Music, Improv, Storytelling, and Other Arts to Improve Teamwork. *He founded All Star Minds, a global Internet "e-storming" business and specializes in facilitating brainstorming retreats for new products and processes as well as providing training in creative problem solving. He has received leadership service awards from the Creative Education Foundation and the Singapore government.*

Pass It On:
Using an Alternate Brainstorming Technique

Activity Summary

This is an alternative brainstorming and consensus-building technique that involves everyone in narrowing down the choices.

Goals

- To create a climate where the ideas generated have equal weight by removing individual bias, persuasion, and groupthink.

- To reach consensus quickly using a process perceived as fair and objective.

Group Size

6 to 25 participants.

Time Required

60 to 90 minutes.

Materials

- A flip chart and markers.

- Masking tape.

- Pads of 3 x 5 Post-it® Notes (at least one pad per every two people).

- A black ink or fine-point felt-tip pen for each participant.

Physical Setting

An area large enough to allow participants to be seated at a table(s), wall space for hanging flip-chart sheets, and room for a flip chart and for participants to walk to the flip-chart area.

Facilitating Risk Rating

Low.

Process

1. Introduce the issue or topic and the intended outcome of the activity, for example, "When we're finished today, we'll have a list of items that we agree are the most important for us to work on over the next six months."

2. Introduce the brainstorming process. Review the key points of a brainstorming session:

   - Every idea is a good idea.

   - Contribute your idea even if you don't think it's possible to achieve since it may give someone else an idea that is achievable.

   - Be objective, don't advocate your cause.

   - Don't judge the merits of others' ideas.

   Let them know that today's brainstorming exercise will help them learn to follow these rules.

3. Give everyone Post-it Notes and pens or markers. Ask participants to think of three ideas (or any quantity you wish) within a set time limit (generally 3 to 5 minutes). Ask them to neatly write their ideas on the Post-it Notes, listing one idea per sheet. If they are sharing pads, ask them to remove several sheets so that each person has some to use. It's okay if an individual generates fewer or more ideas, just not a "runaway" list. Ask participants to be as descriptive as possible so that their ideas can be understood easily.
   (5 minutes.)

4. Have them remove their sheets of ideas from the pads and exchange these ideas with a neighbor for verbal feedback. After a few minutes of exchange, ask participants to add any required clarifications to their own ideas. (The purpose of this exchange is to allow for idea validation and refinement.)
   (5 minutes.)

5. Ask participants to randomly pass their idea sheets around so no one knows which are whose. (If necessary, provide assistance as to what direction the sheets should be passed.)

6. After a few minutes, ask participants to review the idea sheets they have in front of them and to vote on whether each idea is important (as defined by you, for example, "to work on over the next six months") or not by making a plus mark on the ideas they deem viable and no marks on the other sheets. After this process is finished, ask participants to pass the idea sheets to the left and for those people to record their "votes" on the ideas they believe to be feasible. Continue until all participants have voted on all the ideas. *(10 minutes.)*

7. Ask each participant one at a time to come to the flip chart and present and post the ideas he or she ended up with. Tell participants to read each idea aloud, describe it, and explain why the idea is a good one or not. Since the idea is not one of their own, they may not understand the intent behind it or may even disagree with its viability. (Only ask the originator of the idea to volunteer information if absolutely necessary.)

8. Post the ideas on the flip chart, still on their Post-it sheets. Continue until all ideas have been posted. Use additional flip-chart sheets as necessary. *(10 minutes.)*

9. Begin to look for themes and similar or repetitive ideas at the onset of the exercise. Starting with a new flip-chart sheet and the markers, begin to identify categories and rearrange the ideas under those categories using the assistance of the group.

10. Let the group discuss the ideas presented. With their permission, remove duplicate items. Also post new ideas when any emerge that may be totally different or a combination of one or more ideas. The result should be a list of ideas that falls under themes or categories. *(10 to 15 minutes.)*

11. Number the ideas or identify them in some fashion. Ask each participant to select three ideas that satisfy the intended outcome of the activity and to vote for them by putting their numbers on a blank Post-it Note. Collect the Post-it votes and display them on the flip chart. Take a 10-minute break so participants can informally review the voting. *(10 to 15 minutes.)*

12. After the break, tabulate the ideas with the most votes. "Most" is an arbitrary number; look for a natural breaking point. If necessary, take the ideas with the most votes and vote again until the list is narrowed down to a number that is appropriate for the intended outcome.
    (10 minutes.)

13. Bring closure to the exercise. Ask what they thought of the process. Ask how they might be able to use the process in other situations. Review the outcome and confirm agreement with participants. Thank them for their time and willingness to participate, and congratulate them on success in achieving the goal!
    (5 to 10 minutes.)

Submitted by Brenda Hubbard and Susan Crosson.

Brenda Hubbard, *an accounting education program manager, works in the area of continuing education and career development for a statewide association of certified public accountants. A key part of her job is developing instructional materials, managing volunteers, and speaking to educator groups. She is currently writing a dissertation toward her doctorate in instructional systems at Florida State University.*

Susan Crosson, *professor and faculty coordinator of accounting, has more than twenty years of college and university teaching experience. She is known for her innovative application of pedagogical strategies online and in the classroom. She is a recipient of an Institute of Management Accountants' Faculty Development Grant to blend technology into the classroom; the Florida Association of Community Colleges Professor of the Year Award for Instructional Excellence; and the University of Oklahoma's Halliburton Education Award for Excellence.*

Altair the Ant:
Influencing Performance

Activity Summary

This fable-based activity allows participants to examine the influence of individual and organizational factors on performance issues.

Goals

- To discover individual and group views of performance.

- To examine how personal perspectives influence performance.

- To discuss how organizational culture affects performance.

Group Size

15 to 25 from the same organization in subgroups of 3 to 5.

Time Required

90 minutes.

Materials

- One copy of The Adventures of Altair the Ant for each participant.

- A pen or pencil for each participant.

- Blank paper for participants.

- A flip chart and a felt-tipped marker for recording.

- Masking tape for posting flip-chart sheets.

Physical Setting

A room large enough for the groups to work without disturbing one another. Writing surfaces should be provided. Wall space is required for posting flip-chart sheets.

Facilitating Risk Rating

Moderate.

Process

1. Introduce the session by explaining that the participants will be using the fable-like story of an ant's explorations to examine performance issues.

2. Distribute a copy of The Adventures of Altair the Ant and a pen or pencil to each participant. Read the story aloud while they follow along, taking notes if they wish.

3. Tell the participants that each individual is to develop a creative ending for the story that conveys some message to the reader. Provide each participant with additional paper.

4. Allow approximately 7 minutes for the task, giving the participants a 2-minute warning before calling time.
   (7 minutes.)

5. Direct the participants to form groups of three to five persons each. Ask the group members to share their story endings with one another and then to discuss similarities and differences among the various stories. Allow approximately 15 minutes for the task, giving the participants a 2-minute warning before calling time.
   (15 minutes.)

6. Explain that the members of each group will write an ending to the original story that represents the combined views of all members. Announce that groups will have approximately 20 minutes for this task. Provide additional paper, if necessary. Give the participants a 2-minute warning before calling time.
   (20 minutes.)

7. Ask a representative from each group to read aloud the story ending that was created. When all groups have finished reading their story endings, ask

the following questions, using flip-chart sheets to record significant issues and posting the sheets as necessary:

- What message did you find in the beginning of the story? How did the various endings affect the beginning of the tale?

- Did all members of your group share similar ideas in terms of their individual story endings? What were some differences, if any?

- Was it difficult to incorporate the individual endings into one cohesive ending? Why or why not? How do individual viewpoints affect group performance?

- How did the original part of the story relate to the concept of task accomplishment? To goal setting? To individual performance? To group performance?

- In what way(s) did the story ending that your group created support these concepts?

- How do you think it would feel to be the ant in your group's final story? Would you have felt any differently in the tale using your personal ending? Why or why not?

- What three adjectives would you use to describe Altair the ant? Why? How does this image affect your personal view of individual performance?

- Altair is a unisex name of Greek and Arabic origins that means "star" (Baby Name World, 2003). In what ways did Altair support or refute the idea of a "star" performer?

(30 minutes.)

8. Explain to the participants that each organization has a unique set of values, norms, beliefs, and practices that govern how it functions. This is referred to as "organizational culture" or "organizational climate." Ask the following questions:

- What are some organizational culture factors in your own workplace?

- In what ways can organizational culture have an impact on individual viewpoint and performance?

- How might organizational culture affect the ability of a group to perform effectively?

(10 minutes.)

9. Referring to the posted flip-chart sheets, tell the participants that there are a variety of factors, both individual and organizational, that influence performance issues.

10. Lead a concluding discussion based on the following questions:

   - How can you relate the story of Altair the Ant to performance issues in your own workplace?

   - Why is it important for organizational members to become aware of the "the bigger picture" represented by the organization as a whole? How does this awareness influence overall performance?

   - In what ways can you apply what you have learned to your own organizational environment?

   (10 minutes.)

Variation

   - Have the groups develop a list of actionable items that can be undertaken to gain greater insight into the strategic goals and/or organizational culture of their organization.

References

Baby Name World. (2003). Retrieved February 16, 2004, from www.babynameworld.com/a.asp

---

Submitted by Lorraine L. Ukens.

Lorraine L. Ukens, *owner of Team-ing With Success, is a performance improvement consultant who specializes in team building and experiential learning. She is the author of several training activity books, games, and consensus simulations, including* Energize Your Audience, Working Together, The New Encyclopedia of Group Activities, *and* Adventure in the Amazon. *She also teaches a graduate course in training and development at Towson University in Maryland and is a past president of the Maryland Chapter of ASTD.*

The Adventures of Altair the Ant

One day, Altair was assigned a task that took the ant outside the anthill for the very first time. The task was to bring back a dead grasshopper killed by the elders in a raid the previous day.

The young champion set out, and upon exiting the anthill was profoundly impressed and even shocked at the size of the outside world. Altair had heard tales that the world was vast, but never had the ant experienced such massive dimensions.

As the search continued, the ant carefully followed detailed directions, but a barrier was soon encountered that seemed insurmountable. Altair decided to crawl under this obstacle. Upon so doing, the ant was confronted with another shock! The outside world was immensely larger than ever could have been dreamed. It seemed that the anthill was located under a bushel basket and what was thought to be the outside world was only the area covered by the basket. Altair realized there was no way to have fully understood this environment until the larger world had been approached. Only now did Altair realize that the anthill had been covered by a bushel basket.

Because the grasshopper had not yet been found, Altair continued on until encountering another barrier that could not be burrowed under. The ant was forced to retrace some steps, then zig and zag in several directions until an opening appeared. Once on the other side of the barrier, Altair was once again shocked with the realization that the bushel basket was located within a greenhouse and that what was thought to be the big wide world was actually only the small greenhouse.

Now that Altair was outside this greenhouse,

WRITE A CREATIVE ENDING FOR THIS TALE THAT CONVEYS A MESSAGE TO THE READER.

The Hats We Wear:
Understanding Team Roles

Activity Summary

This non-threatening activity provides a way to discuss problem roles on a team.

Goal

- To demonstrate the concept of informal roles and how they affect team dynamics and the decision-making process.

Group Size

6 or more participants from the same team or organization.

Time Required

Approximately 50 minutes.

Materials

- Six baseball caps (hidden in a bag until used) with the following labels on five of the caps and a sixth cap with nothing written on it.
  - Obey me.
  - Ask my opinion.
  - Ask my opinion, but ignore it.
  - Ignore me.
  - Laugh at me.

  You can print these instructions on index cards and tape the cards to the front of the hats or print the caps with liquid paint.

- One copy of a list of ten items that must be prioritized (of pertinence to the group) for each participant.

- Pens or pencils for participants.

Physical Setting

A room that can be arranged with six chairs in a circle in the center with space for observers around the perimeter.

Facilitating Risk Rating

Moderate.

Process

1. Begin with a list of ten (or so) items that the group needs to prioritize. (*Note:* you may have to put together a list based on previous team discussions, but make sure that the list is meaningful and relevant to the group.) Hand out copies of the list and pens or pencils to all participants. Ask the participants to individually rank the importance of each item from 1 to 10 (or so) with 1 being the most important.
    (10 minutes.)

2. When the participants have completed their individual rankings, ask for six volunteers. Ask them to bring their chairs and sit in the middle of the group in a circle. Ask those who remain to be process observers and watch how this team of six individuals accomplishes the task.
    (5 minutes.)

3. Tell the team of six:

    > "Your task will be to reach consensus on the priority of items on the list within 10 minutes. However, before you start, you must follow a few ground rules. I have several hats, which I will place on your heads. Please do not take them off until I tell you that you may. For those of you who are looking at these hats, follow the instructions on them to whatever extent you choose. Process Observers, please watch how the team achieves its objective. You have 10 minutes."

    The team may be uncomfortable and will probably ask you for clarification. Simply repeat the ground rules. After 10 minutes, if the team has not finished, allow them 30 additional seconds.
    (10 minutes.)

4. Then debrief the team: (*Note:* Do not let them look at their hats yet.) Ask the team these questions:

   - Who has the final list that the team agrees to?

   - Do you like the result? What do you like/not like about it?

   - What did you like about the activity? What did you not like about it?

5. Begin to debrief each of the six participants in turn. Ask: "Can you guess what is written on your hat?"

6. Have each participant look at his or her hat. Ask, "Are you surprised?"

   (*Note:* Save the participant wearing the hat with nothing printed on it for last. This participant will think that there is something on it—reemphasizing the point that we all come together with "hats" on.)

6. Facilitate the debriefing of the entire team:

   - What did you think about this activity?

   - How do the roles we play affect our teams' goals?

   - What do you think about the hats we wear when we come together on a team?

   - How do our hats affect our decision-making process?

   - What can we incorporate from this activity into our future work as a team?

   (15 minutes.)

Variation

   - Print other roles on the caps that are more pertinent to your team.

Submitted by Kristin J. Arnold.

Kristin J. Arnold, CPF, CMC, CSP, *helps corporations, government, and nonprofit organizations build high performance teams. She specializes in facilitating executives and their teams, as well as training others to facilitate teams to higher levels of performance. An accomplished author as well as a featured columnist in the* Daily Press, *she is regarded as an expert in process and team development. She graduated with high honors from the U.S. Coast Guard Academy and earned her MBA with an emphasis on marketing strategy from St. Mary's College in California.*

The Last Team Member:
Building a Team

Activity Summary

Team members assess their strengths and weaknesses; provide feedback to each other; and develop objective criteria for the knowledge, skills, and abilities (KSAs) desired in a new team member.

Goals

- To facilitate an honest assessment of team members' strengths and weaknesses in relation to others' and perceived team needs.

- To encourage feedback among group members.

- To develop a description of desirable traits in a new member of an intact team.

Group Size

Any intact team with 20 or fewer members, broken into subgroups of 3 to 4 members.

Time Required

Approximately 60 minutes.

Materials

- Enough flip charts for each subgroup to have one.

- Enough easels for each flip chart.

- Markers.

- A chair for each participant.

Physical Setting

A room large enough for subgroups to have open discussion without interfering with other subgroups.

Facilitating Risk Rating

Low to moderate.

Process

1. Form subgroups of 3 to 4 participants (either randomly or by assignment) and give each a flip chart and markers. Each subgroup should appoint a recorder.

2. Explain the objectives of the activity.

3. Read the following to participants:

    "James Collins, in his book *Good to Great,* talks about the organizational journey and the importance of deciding who is going on the journey before deciding where, or the destination of the journey. Collins believes that the organizational 'destination' may change as companies change vision, products, and/or services. The right people in the right places can adjust to changing priorities. Great people will decide on and complete great journeys. Leadership must decide on who first, and then where."

4. Next read the following aloud to the group.

    "Imagine that your organization is going to put your group on a special task force for six months to a year. There will be several projects that need special attention. You don't know what the tasks are yet; however, they will be significant projects with impact on the whole organization.

    "You have all been appointed to this task force and have the ability to appoint one more member. Your task now is to review the current strengths and resources within this group and decide what traits (knowledge, skills, and abilities [KSAs]) you would like your last team member to possess. You do not need to select the person you would like to be the last member of your group. Your task is simply to develop a checklist of KSAs this person will need and that are not readily available in other group members."

5. Have groups work independently for 20 to 25 minutes and prepare their checklists of desired knowledge, skills, and abilities.
   (20 to 25 minutes.)

6. Bring the total group together and have each subgroup share its checklist of desired traits for a new team member.
   (10 minutes.)

7. Debrief the exercise using the following questions as a guideline.

   Sharing (What Happened?)

   - What was your process for deciding on the traits?

   - What traits did you consider?

   - How comfortable was the exercise for you? Who felt the same? Or differently?

   - What did you observe?

   - What KSAs were common across all groups?

   - What areas did particular groups focus on that others did not?

   Interpreting (So What?)

   - Were there particular areas that each group missed or avoided?

   - Why do you think that happened?

   - What did you learn about your ability to talk about your own strengths and weaknesses?

   - What did you observe about giving and receiving feedback?

   - What behaviors demonstrated by group members assisted with this task?

   - What behaviors were not helpful to the process?

   Application (Now What?)

   - How do we usually form teams? How was this different?

   - Under what circumstances could you use this exercise in the workplace?

   - Can you make any generalizations about giving and receiving feedback?

   - What factors must be in place among group members for this exercise to be successful?

   (20 minutes.)

Variations

- If the group seems to be having trouble starting or if limited time is available, you may want to provide them with the following framework of skills for a successful team from Katzenbach and Smith (1993):

  - Technical or functional skills

  - Problem-solving and decision-making skills

  - Interpersonal skills

- You may want to have all-female and all-male groups and compare answers.

- If you have a team that actually does need a new member, they can use this exercise, knowing what the task will be.

References

Collins, J. (2001a). First who . . . then what. In *Good to great.* New York: HarperCollins. Chapter 3, p. 41.

Collins, J. (2001b). From good to great. *Fast Company, 51,* p. 90+.

Katzenbach, J.R., & Smith, D.K. (1993). *The wisdom of teams.* Boston, MA: Harvard Business School Press.

Submitted by Connie Phillips.

Connie Phillips *manages training and organization development programs for the City of Anaheim, California. She also consults with other public sector organizations. She has master's degrees in library science and in organizational leadership and had fifteen years' experience as a line manager before moving to HR. She has taught at local colleges and for the Orange County Sheriff's Academy. Additionally, she is a certified trainer for the International Personnel Management Association's (IPMA) Core Competency Program.*

Plunge In:
Using Openers to Connect Groups and Their Work

Activity Summary

This opener for meetings allows the team to immediately begin to work on its task.

Goals

- To connect the team to the work at hand, addressing task and group process at the same time.

- To enable the learning of a new tool that will help the team at a later time.

Group Size

6 to 30 participants from any team formed for a specific purpose.

Time Required

Approximately 25 minutes.

Materials

- One Plunge In Modified Affinity Diagram Process Sheet for each participant.

- Flip chart and markers.

- Masking tape.

- 3 x 5 inch Post-it® Notes for participants.

Physical Setting

Room for all participants first to sit and then to stand and move about easily. Sufficient wall space for hanging flip-chart sheets.

Facilitating Risk Rating

Low.

Process

1. Introduce the aim/purpose of the meeting and name the problem they are there to work on.

2. Explain the object of the opener (avoid words like "icebreaker" and "warm-up"). Say something like, "We will be using an opener to get our thoughts connected to the work at hand, allow us to begin to work together as a team, and teach us the use of a new tool."

3. Distribute Post-its to everyone and ask them to silently brainstorm (sometimes called Nominal Group Technique) the root causes of the problem they are there to solve. Tell them to list only one idea per Post-it.

4. While they are recording ideas, tape two blank flip-chart sheets to the wall. Write whatever the problem statement is at the top.
    (5 minutes.)

5. When the writing appears to be slowing down, ask all participants to meet you at the flip-chart sheets and begin to silently group the Post-its into clusters of ideas that seem to go together. (Often this will produce laughter and moving each other's ideas around.)
    (10 minutes.)

6. When the grouping stops, help participants refine their clusters and name them. Write the cluster names on the charts next to each.

7. Tell the group they have just learned a modified affinity diagramming process. Ask for their reflections on the process.

    *   What worked best?

    *   Why do you think it worked?

    *   What did not work?

- Can you think of ways to improve the process?

- When might you use this technique in the workplace?
  (5 minutes.)

8. Provide everyone with a copy of the Plunge In Modified Affinity Diagram Process Sheet for later use.

Variations

- If wall space is not available, use a tabletop.

- Use a cause-and-effect diagram, but leave the bones bare to receive the Post-its.

- Post the final chart in a public area where others who have knowledge about the problem can add their ideas.

Submitted by M. K. Key.

M.K. Key, Ph.D., *is a clinical-community psychologist and the founder and principal of Key Associates in Nashville, Tennessee. She is a nationally recognized speaker on leadership, releasing the creative spirit, mediation of conflict, and team development. She has authored over thirty publications on such topics as change management, continuous quality improvement, strategic business issues, and leadership during turbulent times. She has served as adjunct professor of organization and human development at Vanderbilt University.*

Plunge In Modified Affinity Diagram Process Sheet

The purpose of an affinity diagram is to distill ideas into groups in order to analyze a problem. The steps are listed below.

Steps

1. Write ideas on Post-it Notes® with markers, one idea per Post-it, each idea in fewer than six words.

2. Randomly place the Post-its on a tabletop or wall chart.

3. Organize the ideas in meaningful clusters, grouping things that seem to go together.

4. If ideas go in more than one category, encourage the creation of duplicates.

5. Discourage the evaluation of the ideas; only allow clarification.

6. When the grouping is finished, name the clusters, writing their titles in another color.

7. Only then vote on or prioritize ideas for use with the group.

Want/Give Walkabout:
Sharing Expectations

Activity Summary

This icebreaker is used to identify participants' expectations and to encourage networking.

Goals

- To introduce participants to each other at the beginning of a consulting experience.

- To expose expectations, wants, and needs of participants and share what they can contribute from this time together.

- To create connections among participants.

Group Size

8 to 100 participants.

Time Required

15 to 20 minutes.

Materials

- Two different colored Post-it® Note pads 2 by 3 inches or 3 by 3 inches.

- Pens or pencils for participants.

- A prepared piece of flip-chart paper with two columns labeled "Wants" and "Gives."

- Masking tape.

Physical Setting

Conference room or any space large enough for participants to mingle.

Facilitating Risk Rating

Low.

Process

1. Hand out one each of the two different colored Post-it Notes and a pen or pencil to each person. Tell them that one color will be for "wants" and the other will be for "gives." Have them write "Want" at the top of the colored note you designate and "Give" on the top of the other colored note. Tell them to write something they want out of this experience and something they can give to the process or to the other people in the room on the appropriate notes.

2. Tell them to put their names on their notes and then to stick the notes on their clothing and walk around the room for 5 to 10 minutes speaking to at least three other people to share their Wants and Gives.
    (10 minutes.)

3. Once the time has ended, have the group members post their notes on the prepared flip-chart page. Have them take their seats. Lead them in matching the Wants and Gives. If there is a natural match, stick those together onto a different sheet of flip-chart paper. Help them to match any of the Wants and Gives to create natural clusters on the flip-chart sheet and help them to see what types of categories are represented.

4. Bring closure with the following actions:

    *   Read examples of the matches so everyone hears both the consistency and the differences across participant desires.

    *   Encourage participants to connect with others who match their Wants or Gives to help create a learner-centered environment and to ensure they have their needs met.

    *   If appropriate, include some of the things that are wanted from the group into the program or process with the group.

5. Keep the flip charts on the wall for the duration of the day, session, or experience so people can see who may have what they are looking for. If de-

sired, check at the end of the session to see who took advantage of the opportunity and in what ways.

Variation

- Names can be omitted from the sticky notes—if it is deemed to be too high-risk, but teaming people up would then be done in the large group or after the workshop on a volunteer basis only.

Submitted by Gail Hahn.

Gail Hahn, MA, CSP, CPRP, CLL, *is the chief energizing officer of Fun*cilitators and author of* Hit Any Key to Energize Your Life *as well as contributing author to over sixteen other books. She is an international keynote speaker, corporate trainer, and an award-winning team-building facilitator who holds certifications as a Speaking Professional, Parks and Recreation Professional, Laugh Leader, and Strength Deployment Inventory Facilitator.*

Three Roles of Leaders:
Understanding Leadership

Activity Summary

This combination of physical and imaginative activities in dyads and small groups allows participants to experience the process of leadership.

Goal

- To experience and conceptualize three important leadership processes: envisioning; aligning others toward the vision; and ensuring execution or implementation.

Group Size

15 to 30 participants.

Time Required

Approximately 90 minutes.

Materials

- One copy of Three Roles of Leaders for each participant.

- A flip chart and markers.

Physical Setting

A room large enough for grouping participants in dyads and small groups comfortably. Chairs may be placed along the walls, keeping the central space open.

Facilitating Risk Rating

Low to moderate.

Process

1. Ask participants to form pairs, preferably with others they do not know well.

2. State that they are going to participate in an activity in which one person plays the role of a sculptor and the other the raw material. The raw material, however, is living and can think and decide whether to respond or not to the instruction of the sculptor. Provide a few minutes' time to the participants and answer their questions.

3. Ask the "sculptors" to visualize a pose or an object or an act that appears artistically impressive and that can be made by using the given "raw material," that is, the other participant in the dyad. Tell them not to disclose any information verbally about what they want. If the sculptors want to use pencil and paper, they can do so without showing their envisioned object to their partners or to others.
    (5 minutes.)

4. Announce that the sculptors will make or construct the object or pose that they have visualized using the raw material. Also announce that, during the creation process, neither the sculptor nor the raw material may speak. The sculptor should give his or her instructions nonverbally. Remind them that the material is free to respond or not respond; act or react; or do whatever is preferred. Tell them they have 5 minutes. Observe the action.
    (5 minutes.)

5. Ask those who finish early to remain near their objects and ask the objects to remain in the same poses if possible.

6. Ask all sculptors to observe each other's creations in the room. After they have seen each other's creations, ask them to sit down in their seats and allow the objects to sit down also. Ask them about their feelings, and summarize on a flip chart. Urge them to share their experiences through answering the following questions.

    *   How did you feel when visualizing the pose or object?

    *   How did the raw material feel when he or she was instructed by the sculptor? Did the raw material obey?

    *   What did the sculptor do when the material did not respond positively?

- How did the sculptors persuade or influence the material to do what was wanted? How did the sculptors make the raw material understand the images that were visualized?

(10 minutes.)

7. Add any observations or highlights you experienced during the activity.

8. Ask the group to divide into groups of 5 or 6 people each. Ask each group to choose a sculptor again. This time, in every group there will be one sculptor and the remaining members will be the raw materials.

9. After they have formed groups and chosen their sculptors, ask the sculptors to raise their hands so that they are identified. Announce, "This time every member of the group, not just the sculptor, will visualize a pose, object, or scenery that can be executed by all the members of the group together, again nonverbally. Please close your eyes and visualize a pose, object, or scenery that appeals to you."

(5 minutes.)

10. After 5 minutes, ask them to open their eyes and verbally share their images/ visions with their group members and try to select any one vision to enact by discussion and convincing, not by voting. As modifications are suggested, the members must agree or not. The agreed-on images/poses/vision may be explained to all members in the group. Allow 15 minutes for them to share, discuss, and decide on one image, pose, scenery, or vision for presentation. (Groups may go to different rooms for discussion if they desire.)

(15 minutes.)

11. After 15 minutes, have all participants reconvene. Ask each group to make a 5-minute presentation of its vision to the large group by enacting/executing it nonverbally, as before, but with all members in the group as raw material and thus taking part in the presentation. Remind everyone that it is to be nonverbal.

12. After each presentation, have others guess what they were trying to depict.

13. After the presentations are over, have all members of the large group, including the sculptors, share their experiences.

- What was different the second time around? Why do you think this was true?

- What is the message you take from this activity? How will you act differently in the future as a result of your experience?

(10 minutes.)

14. Provide the Three Roles of Leaders handout to each person and ask them to read it silently. After a few minutes, conclude by giving a brief presentation based on the handout. Ask participants how this activity was related to each of the three leadership roles described. Ask how each type of relationship transfers to the real world. Again ask participants what they might do differently in the future if they were creating another vision.
(15 minutes.)

15. Summarize with a reminder of the three leadership roles.

Variation

- In the first round, instead of only one raw material (model), the sculptor may use two or three at a time and visualize accordingly.

Submitted by Parth Sarathi.

Parth Sarathi *is a practicing manager with a diverse background. He started his career after obtaining a degree in metallurgical engineering and subsequently obtained PG qualifications in industrial engineering and management (H.R.). He is an accredited Behavior Process Facilitator, Thomas Profile Licensee, and Competency Assessor. An accomplished trainer and consultant, he has authored a number of books and articles and is currently working as a general manager (HRD) at Human Resource Development Institute (BHEL).*

Three Roles of Leaders

Leaders have to do different things depending on their areas of activity, roles, and responsibilities, as well as on their own desires and goals.

The three tasks are common: envisioning, aligning followers to their vision, and ensuring execution. In all three roles, influencing remains the core skill.

Envisioning

The leader envisions the organization in the future, i.e., what will the organization be five years or ten years from now? This is the dream for the future organization: "the vision." The vision may be made more specific by formulating a mission. Envisioning essentially is dreaming, and dreaming requires imagination. A leader who is highly imaginative, intuitive, and creative envisions spontaneously. But many are strong analytical thinkers, and for them dreaming may be difficult. They have to depend on others—insiders or outsiders—to translate their dreams.

Aligning People Toward the Vision

For implementation, the leader's vision has to become the vision of followers—a shared vision. For this, the leader has to involve others and also involve them in the mission. The leader influences top management and key people of the organization through his or her skills and charisma. These key people, after internalizing the vision and mission, start converting others and aligning them toward the vision and mission.

When influencing people, four types of strategies are frequently used:

- *Rewards:* This strategy uses some rewards, tangible or intangible, for making people agree or do what the leader wants them to agree to or do.

- *Reason:* The leader tries to convince others or accomplish tasks by using rationale, logic, facts, and figures. Leaders explain the reasons for accomplishing the task or reaching an agreement.

- *Relationships:* A leader using this strategy focuses on the interpersonal needs, specifically the emotional needs of followers. The leader remains in the position of follower and tries to feel or experience the same feelings, reactions, and responses. Using the interpersonal needs (inclusion, control, and affection) (Schutz, 1967), the leader wants to gain the acceptance of the followers. These leaders use emotional intelligence and empathy extensively.

- *Group Appeal:* This is a very powerful strategy used by visionary leaders. They identify a powerful super-ordinate goal and try to convince and invite followers to accept and align themselves with it. The charisma of the leader, as well as his or her visibility and credibility, help a lot.

Ensuring Execution

This leadership task is essential for actualizing the dreams. The leaders specifies tasks, activities, and targets that must be carried out for achieving the vision and mission at different levels and by different groups. Agencies that will carry out the tasks are defined and spelled out clearly, as is a time frame.

Once the activities are assigned to the appropriate people by the leader, he or she uses various strategies and styles to be sure the tasks are completed. Two types of leader behavior are important here: task behavior and relationship behavior. Hersey and Blanchard (1976) list four styles of leadership against four maturity levels in their Situational Leadership® model.

References

Hersey, P., & Blanchard, K.H. (1976). Leadership effectiveness and adaptability descriptions (LEAD). In J.W. Pfeiffer & J.E. Jones (Eds.), *The 1976 annual handbook for group facilitators.* San Francisco, CA: Pfeiffer.

Schutz, W.C. (1967). FIRO B. Palo Alto, CA: Consulting Psychologists Press.

To Be the Best:
Determining Aspirational Values

Activity Summary

This is a safe activity to address desired organizational values.

Goals

- To create buy-in for an organization's aspirational value(s).

- To generate discussion around organizational goals and behaviors.

Group Size

5 to 25 participants from the same organization in subgroups of 5 or 6.

Time Required

90 to 120 minutes.

Materials

- One set of 5 to 8 behavior statements on index cards for each participant (chosen from the To Be the Best Sample Statements).

- A flip chart with plenty of paper.

- Felt-tipped markers.

- Masking tape.

- A timer.

Physical Setting

A room large enough for participants to mill around, with tables set up to accommodate small groups. (Round tables are the best, set for 5 or 6 per table.)

Facilitating Risk Rating

Moderate.

Preparation

1. Prior to the group sessions, create two lists of statements reflecting (1) attitudes and behaviors exhibited in the company now and (2) attitudes and behaviors that one might wish to see exhibited or that management could be looking for in the company, in other words, aspirational values—those values not currently exhibited, but that a company must have to achieve success.

2. Create a deck of cards on index stock, with one statement per card. Write out enough sets of cards so there are at least 5 cards per person. You may duplicate statements if you wish, which would shorten the time required. (See the To Be the Best Sample Statements for some possible cards.)

Process

1. Remind participants of their company's defined core values. Review them with the group and display them on a piece of flip-chart paper. Then introduce the concept of aspirational values, saying:

   "Aspirational values are those values that we are not exhibiting as part of our culture right now, but they reflect something we believe we need to develop in order to achieve the success we desire. In this session we will sort out our aspirational values from the values we are living now and find ways for the company to live the new values too."

2. Explain that you have created a deck of cards that contains some values to which they may aspire and some they live now, with each card containing a statement about one such value, expressed as an attitude or behavior they incorporate now OR may wish to incorporate in the future. Share a few sample statements.

3. Continue by telling the group:

   "We will be completing this activity in several phases, and I will give directions as we go along. During Phase 1, I will be distributing cards to everyone. Take time to read the cards you receive. Your goal will be similar to a hand of Rummy or Poker in which you want to create a set of cards in your hand where each statement is one you feel strongly about and also believe to be representative of a value the company SHOULD be practicing right now, but is not.

"When I give the signal, we will begin moving around the room doing a blind trade. Select any number of cards you want to trade (those you feel represent values that are NOT important to our success or that we already practice well). Hold them separately from the other cards you receive, and then walk around the room communicating the number of cards you want to trade. Find someone willing to trade the same number of cards and, without reading the cards first, make the trade. Review what you received; add them to your card set if they represent your aspirational values for the company. Then decide which cards you still want to trade. Keep trading as often as you want until I call time. You cannot discard any cards during this phase of the activity."

Respond to any questions from participants.

4. Distribute five to eight cards to each person and tell them to begin the trading phase.
   (10 minutes.)

5. After 10 minutes, call time and ask everyone to stand where they are while you give directions for the next phase. Assure any unhappy people who don't like the cards they ended up with that relief is on the way!

6. Say, "In preparation for Phase 2, we will need to divide into smaller groups. When I say go, line up in descending order by the length of time you have worked at this company." Indicate where the line should begin. "Ready? GO!"

7. Once everyone has lined up, have them count off in the number of teams you want to create. For example, if you want four small groups, have them count off 1, 2, 3, 4, 1, 2, 3, 4 . . . with their number representing the group number. (By doing this, you quickly create small groups made up of people with varying levels of seniority in each group.)

8. Tell the participants with the same numbers to convene at the tables, taking their final card hands with them. Continue with directions for this phase after they are settled:

   "Your small group will now prioritize the statements you all have on your cards and select aspirational statements that your group believes are the most important for the company's future success—that is, those values that, if practiced, would make the most difference. You may begin by discarding any cards that the group as a whole agrees are not contenders for the final selection. These could be cards showing values you all believe are already practiced well or those values you all believe are not important for the company's future. Your discards will go into our 'open bank.' [Identify the location where all groups will put their discards.] You may send team members to the 'open bank' any time throughout this phase of the activity to review the cards that are there and take any of them back to your group for consideration."

(20 minutes.)

9. Allow 20 minutes for this phase and then call attention and give further instructions:

> "Once you have a set of eight to ten cards that everyone in your group agrees represent the most important aspirational values for your organization, discuss them until you determine the three to five most important as far as impact on the success of your company. Be prepared to explain your results to the entire group in 20 minutes."

Respond to questions, and then have everyone begin. During this phase, it is important to visit each group as an observer to be sure they are on-track and working toward the desired goal.

(20 minutes.)

10. After 20 minutes, call time. Begin Phase 4, during which they will make a case for their group's choices. Explain to everyone that, during this phase, each small group will share its results with everyone. Ask each group in turn to post the statements that they selected on the wall on flip-chart paper and explain briefly why the value that each represents is important to the future success of the organization.

(30 minutes.)

11. When all groups have finished, facilitate a discussion reviewing all the feedback, using the following questions:

- What themes or trends do you see as you look at the results posted by the groups?

- What critical areas are reflected in these trends?

- What do these high-priority statements tell us about what we need to focus on to be more successful?

- What was not on any of the cards that you wish had been there? (or) If you could have prepared these cards, what additional statements would you have written?

- If we focused on [pick any statement selected by the team], what impact would it have on you personally? On the organization as a whole?

- Describe a world where [pick a trend/topic area the group identified] was a core value.

- How do these statements correlate to (or dilute) our core values?

- If we could only focus on one thing, where would you suggest we put our emphasis?

- How can we begin to practice some of these aspirational values?
(20 to 30 minutes.)

Variations

- Prior to the session, determine up to five potential contenders for the most critical aspirational value, such as effective and caring communication; teamwork; continuous development; trust; risk taking; creativity and innovation; and so on. Assign a color to each value you select. Develop your statements around these specific values, and color code each card to match the value it reflects.

  Conduct Phase 1 of the activity. Then allow individuals to prioritize their cards and select their personal "Top 3" statements.

  Post a pie chart on the wall, divided into the same number of segments as you have potential values, each segment in the appropriate color. Have individuals post their selections by matching the colors of their cards to the colored segments.

  Once everything is posted, identify the value that corresponds to each color. Then announce: "Now that you understand what value each color represents, does anyone want to move their statements to back a different value?"

  This variation provides a visual depiction of where the majority of preferences lie. Then you can move to the next phase, allowing small groups to discuss the results.

- Allow the team members to write their own statements. Simply provide blank cards and have everyone write five to ten statements, one per card, that identify specific things they would like to see more of in the company. Collect all the cards, and proceed with the activity.

- Ask groups to create action plans for their chosen aspirational values.

Submitted by Cher Holton.

Cher Holton, Ph.D., *president of The Holton Consulting Group, Inc., is an impact consultant focusing on rekindling the human spirit. She is a Certified Speaking Professional and Certified Management Consultant and is author of* The Manager's Short Course to a Long Career; Living at the Speed of Life: Staying in Control in a World Gone Bonkers!; Suppose . . . Questions to TurboCharge Your Business and Your Life; *and* From Ballroom to Bottom Line . . . in Business and in Life.

To Be the Best Sample Statements

I know what performance is expected of me.

Communication is very important to the success of our company.

People do not know what is expected of them.

We satisfy our customers, no matter what the cost.

This is a fun place to work.

Everyone is on the same page in terms of our mission goals.

Employee personal growth is a priority.

The rumor mill runs wild around here.

It is important for everyone to understand each other's roles.

We function as a unified team.

Customer satisfaction is more important than employee satisfaction.

To be successful, we must all agree on our strategic objectives.

I know how I contribute to the goals of this company.

We need to develop more depth in our skill bank.

All employees here have their own ideas of what is important.

We share a common sense of purpose.

Expectations are clearly understood by everyone.

We need a clear employee development plan.

I have a clear understanding of how my work fits in with the work of others.

I feel comfortable talking to any manager here, including our president.

It is important for employees to feel comfortable talking with any level manager within the company.

We are a strong, dedicated team.

It is important that employees take initiative in determining their goals.

It is acceptable to challenge the status quo.

We need to take more risks as we move to a new level of success.

Teamwork only happens once in a while. I wish it happened more often.

We do not know how to work effectively as a team.

Listening is a high priority.

My issues are listened to with respect.

I get immediate responses to my questions.

Feedback takes too long to get.

We need to practice better listening as a whole company.

We treat our customers better than we treat each other.

We would be more successful if we tried new, creative ideas.

I wish we could all say what we really feel about things.

My ideas and contributions matter.

Employee achievement is not appreciated as much as it could be.

Conflict resolution is a skill we really need to work on.

Meetings are productive here.

People do not give effective feedback when there is a problem.

There is no clear employee development plan, but there should be.

Everyone is always busy, but we are not always productive.

We react rather than being proactive.

We need to be better at knowing our expectations.

Working in a positive environment is important.

There is a direct relationship between high morale and high productivity.

A strong sense of trust exists among the employees and leadership team of this company.

We work together to build an enthusiastic, rewarding, and positive work environment.

I trust our leadership team.

Personal goal achievement is more important than team success.

I understand what is rewarded at this company.

My manager communicates clearly and often with me.

I wish I had a clear picture of where we are headed in the next few years.

I believe that several people working as a team can achieve better results than by working individually.

Performance problems are dealt with quickly, fairly, and appropriately.

Some of our managers show favoritism.

We have depth in our workforce.

Good performance needs to be recognized more often.

Listening is a top priority here.

Important information is not shared enough to keep me "in the loop."

Innovative thinking should be rewarded more often.

I wish communication were stronger in both directions—up and down the chain.

I clearly understand the limits of my decision-making authority.

Mistakes are forgiven and seen as learning opportunities.

I wish there were a stronger effort to see mistakes as learning opportunities.

Disagreements about goals or processes often lead to personal attacks and defensiveness.

We operate in a "silo" mentality rather than a team mentality.

We are able to discuss disagreements openly, reaching creative solutions to our problems.

We conduct effective meetings with positive outcomes.

We celebrate success!

We need more cross-training to strengthen our workforce.

I like the camaraderie we share as a team.

I could be more effective in my job if my manager's expectations of me were clarified.

I need more training in order to perform my job as well as I would like.

I have all the information accessible to me to do my job well.

My manager is willing to go to bat for me.

It is important to offer career development opportunities for employees.

I understand and support the core values of this company.

To achieve our vision, we need to communicate more effectively at all levels.

Morale is affected by the lack of communication here.

Everyone is on the same page in terms of our strategic goals and objectives.

It is best to avoid conflict at any cost.

I wish I could share ideas I have about ways to do things differently.

I trust my team members with information.

Introduction
to the Editor's Choice Section

The Editor's Choice Section is a collection of contributions that simply do not fit into one of the other three sections: Experiential Learning Activities; Inventories, Questionnaires, and Surveys; and Articles and Discussion Resources. In the past we have had to reject exceptional work that did not meet the criteria of one of the sections or did not fit in one of the categories. The Editor's Choice Section allows us to publish these unique items that are useful to the profession, rather than turn them down.

Due to the mere definition of the section, it is difficult to predict what you may find. You may anticipate a potpourri of topics, a variety of formats, and an assortment of categories. Some may be directly related to the training and consulting fields, and others may be related tangentially. Some may be obvious additions and others may not. What you are sure to find is something you may not have expected but that will contribute to your growth and stretch your thinking.

Suffice it to say that this section will provide you with a variety of useful ideas, practical strategies, and creative ways to look at the world. The material will add innovation to your training and consulting knowledge and skills. The contributions will challenge you to think differently, consider a new perspective, and add information you may not have considered before. The contents of this section will stretch your view of training and consulting topics.

The 2005 Pfeiffer Annual: Consulting includes three Editor's Choice items this year: an activity, advice to consultants in the form of an article, and a list of ways to select group leaders.

Activities

Corporate Meeting: Building Understanding of the Vision,
by Doug Campbell, John Howes, Carrie Reese, and Saundra Stroope

Ensuring that all employees understand the organization's vision and how they can support it is critical to success. This activity presents an original process to accomplish that. Although it does not follow the typical ELA process, we wanted our *Annual* readers to have this activity in their toolboxes.

26 Ways: Selecting Team Leaders, by Robert Alan Black

As facilitators we often need to select leaders for group activities. This list of twenty-six provides you with a new idea every week for the next six months!

Article

Advice to a Protégé, by Kristin J. Arnold

Kristin's successful consulting practice is the source for twenty-two tips for building a successful consulting business.

Corporate Meeting:
Building Understanding of the Vision

Summary

These structured presentations and discussions allow participants in a large group setting to build a better understanding of the company or department vision statement and their role in achieving it.

Goals

- To identify essential components of the organization's or group's vision.

- To increase participants' awareness, understanding, and knowledge of the vision.

- To motivate participants to stay focused on the vision and the actions needed to achieve it.

Group Size

Total number is unlimited, but breakout sessions should be limited to groups of 20 to 45 participants.

Time Required

Approximately 4 to 6 hours. The total timeframe will depend on the number of breakout sessions conducted.

Materials

- Flip charts and markers for each breakout group.

- Presentation slides and handouts specific to the organization, if desired.

Physical Setting

A room large enough for the intended group size, and breakout rooms that will seat 20 to 45 people.

Facilitating Risk Rating

Low to moderate.

Prior to the Event

1. Meet with the senior leadership team, review the company or department vision statement, and identify the three to five essential components of the statement for the upcoming year. Focus on projects that best illustrate the vision and identify learning objectives for each component area that include key messages employees and/or managers should understand. Identify subject-matter experts who are knowledgeable about what's currently happening in the company or industry with respect to each component of the vision and who can speak effectively about that component. Contact the person and arrange for him or her to lead a breakout session at your workshop. Identify a facilitator/recorder for each breakout session from among the population of participants.

    ### Sample Vision Statement

    In line with PacifiCorp's corporate vision, Power Delivery's goal is to be a modern, efficient, regulated utility that provides reliable service and increasing returns to our shareholders over the long term. We must run the business as efficiently as possible, which in turn will allow us to recover costs through the regulatory process.

    ### Sample Breakout Sessions

    Breakout Session 1: Regulatory update: Recovery of costs through the regulatory process

    Breakout Session 2: Investment in the business in line with corporate vision

    Breakout Session 3: Priorities and controls on spending

    Breakout Session 4: Modern and efficient utility

    Breakout Session 5: The results of "sticking to it": Reliable service/ efficiency

2. Provide each subject-matter expert an overview of the goals of the workshop and the anticipated audience members and instructions to prepare a presentation that focuses specifically on his or her assigned component. Each presentation should include significant events that have occurred in the last year, what's going to be happening in the coming year, and specific information for participants about actions they can take to help make this part of the vision a reality, as well as key information they can communicate to others to help them understand the vision. Instruct presenters to design their presentations to be as interactive as possible and to allow about 10 to 15 minutes for questions and answers afterward.

3. Invite participants to the event and announce the presentation topics in advance to encourage them to come up with questions.

4. Meet with subject-matter presenters and practice a "dry run" presentation with the facilitator/recorder for that session. Incorporate any additional feedback into the presentation.

During the Event

1. *Opening presentation:* The senior executive welcomes participants and reminds the audience of the company vision statement, explains why it's important to the company, why it's important that the participants understand it, and how they can help communicate it to everyone on their team and in the company.

2. *Overview:* At this point, you (the facilitator) describe the agenda and the components of the vision chosen for breakout sessions and why they were chosen. Also explain that any components not being focused on today are still important. Introduce the subject-matter experts who will speak during the breakout sessions, explain the length and logistics for each session, and encourage participants to ask questions during the event.

3. *Breakout sessions:* Each subject-matter expert presents on the assigned component of the vision. Allow participants to choose which topics they wish to attend, allowing time for them to attend several. (It is a good idea to move among the breakout groups to watch for any problems or issues that come up.) During each presentation, the facilitator/recorder for that group writes all questions asked, groups them into common themes, and lists comments on a flip chart.

4. *After the presentations:* Bring everyone together and ask the following questions:

   - Based on what you heard today, how can you help us achieve the team or organization's vision?

   - What additional information or support do you need to help you achieve the vision?

   - What risks do you see in meeting any part of the vision? What challenges might your team face in meeting this part of the vision?

   - How could you overcome these risks and/or challenges? What would the biggest cynic on your team say about this? How could we respond to that person?

   - What projects are you currently working on that could help us meet a particular part of our vision?

   - What are the key initiatives happening in your department that support this vision?

5. *Closing summary:* The senior executive restates the company or department vision and reemphasizes some key points, summarizing the learning from the day. Explain that presentation slides used by each subject-matter expert and notes from the sessions will be sent to participants to help them spread the knowledge and understanding of the vision to their teams. Close the session by thanking the participants and speakers, especially the senior executive.

After the Event

1. Summarize notes from each session and send presentation slides and a summary paragraph explaining each presentation on the specific portions of the vision to participants after the event.

Variations

- Add a theme for the event, if desired.

- Allow participants to submit questions prior to the event.

- After the breakout sessions, rather than facilitating questions in a large group, ask participants to work in small groups or with a partner and discuss the debriefing questions.

- During the closing summary, ask participants to share one or two key things they learned during the day.

Submitted by Doug Campbell, John Howes, Carrie Reese, and Saundra Stroope.

Doug Campbell *is an organization development manager at PacifiCorp with twenty years of experience in organization development and training and development. Currently, he is an internal consultant specializing in organizational interventions such as large group interventions, talent management, team development, organizational assessments, culture and climate change, strategic planning, and leadership, coaching, and development. He has a bachelor's degree in organizational communication and an advanced certificate in ODHRM from Columbia University, Teachers College.*

John Howes *currently leads the organization development, leadership, and training (business skills, management/leadership development, and computer skills/IT systems) departments for the Power Delivery business, the largest business unit of PacifiCorp. He has earned a doctorate in industrial and organizational psychology from Colorado State University. Since completing his Ph.D., he has held progressively larger leadership positions focused on organization development, selection and assessment, labor relations, and training at various companies, including Sprint, AlliedSignal, Honeywell, and PacifiCorp/Scottish Power.*

Carrie Reese, APR, *has nearly fifteen years of experience in public relations, marketing communications, and employee communications. During her career, she has produced award-winning communications programs for a variety of companies, associations, and nonprofit organizations. She has worked at PacifiCorp since 2001 and is an accredited member of the Public Relations Society of America.*

Saundra Stroope, PHR, *is an organization development consultant at PacifiCorp with fourteen years of experience in human resources, team development, coaching, organizational assessments, talent management, training, and management and leadership development. She has earned a master's degree in human resources management and a bachelor's degree in psychology from Texas A&M University and has been published in two previous* Pfeiffer Annuals.

26 Ways:
Selecting Team Leaders

Summary

Use this quick exercise for picking someone to lead the group.

Goals

- To provide an interesting way to help participants select a leader for an exercise.

- To increase the energy in a group/team.

Group Size

Any size grouped in clusters of 3 to 12 people.

Process

1. Before finalizing any activity that requires a leader, tell the group that they will select a leader for their group for the next exercise.

2. Use one of the twenty-six ways listed below.

3. Vary the choices throughout the session. You may hand out copies of the list for them to choose from or simply call out individual items yourself.

   a. Put names on cards and draw them out of a hat, bag, or box.

   b. Pick the one who played the most sports in school.

   c. Choose someone who won a contest in school.

   d. Take someone who had a 4-point average at least once in school.

e.   Ask a person who held an elected office (school or community).

f.   Find out who has the most collections.

g.   Ask who owns the oldest rock-and-roll record in the group/table/team.

h.   Find someone who has been to Disneyland or Disney World the most or least.

i.   Choose someone who water skis.

j.   Pick a mountain climber.

k.   Decide who has the longest home address.

l.   Cut a deck of cards—highest or lowest.

m.   Choose the person who has seen the most movies in the past twelve months.

n.   Select alphabetically by family name.

o.   Choose the person who has the most siblings.

p.   Find whoever has traveled to the most countries.

q.   Ask whose hometown is closest to A or Z in the alphabet.

r.   Choose someone who likes prunes, broccoli, tofu, or another unusual food.

s.   Select someone who has been in the least number of states.

t.   See who has a birthday closest to the day's date.

u.   Find the person who has the oldest coin in pocket or purse.

v.   Pick the person who has had French fries most recently.

w.   Pick whoever owns the most computer games.

x.   Select whoever has the most unique hobby (choice of team).

y.   Do a quick test to see who knows the most state capitals.

z.   Ask who has held the most jobs.

You may also wish to have the groups generate their own list of ways to choose.

Submitted by Robert Alan Black.

Robert Alan Black, Ph.D., CSP Founder and President of Cre8ng People, Places & Possibilities, is a creative think-ing consultant and award-winning professional speaker who specializes in the S.P.R.E.A.D.ng™ of Cre8ng™ and Creative Thinking throughout workplaces around the world. Each year he speaks at many executive develop-ment institutes, conferences, and conventions in the United States, Canada, Turkey, and South Africa. He has written seventeen books, including BROKEN CRAYONS: Break Your Crayons and Draw Outside the Lines, *and over three hundred published articles.*

Advice to a Protégé

Kristin J. Arnold

Summary

This article provides suggestions derived from the author's own successful consulting business. The twenty-two pieces of advice cover a wide range of areas, including how to get started, how to keep your finances in order, hiring, taking care of yourself, visioning, mentoring, and some nitty-gritty details that you can apply to your daily consulting activities.

Over the years, I have been asked by many consultants to share my insights in building a successful independent consulting practice. One particularly bright fellow asked me to write my ideas down on paper. What follows is a potpourri of ideas. Some are my own, some are borrowed from others, and all have some relevance to my consulting practice. Who knows? Maybe these ideas have some relevance to your business!

1. Do What You Love . . . but Realize It's only 10 to 50 Percent of Running Your Business

Let's face it, you started consulting because you are good at what you do and clients value your expertise. But you are a business that requires much more than technical competency, including marketing, sales, finances, information technology, administration, research and development.

Smart consultants recognize that they will never become fully proficient in all aspects of their business. Instead, they surround themselves with those who have specific expertise or experience. They either hire needed expertise, purchase talent through a contractual arrangement, or beg their friends to help out!

2. Define "Success" and Describe Your "Vision" for the Future of Your Consulting Practice

Everyone wants you to be successful. So take time to define what "success" means to you and your long-term goals. Before you know it, five years will pass. Have you progressed toward your long-term goals or "vision"? Do you consider yourself to be "successful"? If you don't know where you are going, any road will get you there! So follow Stephen Covey's advice to "begin with the end in mind."

3. Share Your Dream/Goals with Others

Share your vision, dreams, and goals with trusted advisors, such as your friends, advocates, employees, and great clients. They will help you achieve them. You'll be surprised at how they can help connect the dots from where you are now to where you want to be in the next few years. Opportunities will open up for you simply because others are able to keep an eye open for you as well!

4. The Secret for Success Is. . .

In his book, *How to Survive Among Piranhas*, my dear friend, Dr. Joachim de Posada, shares a wonderful story that I will always treasure:

> Joachim was the opening speaker at a major fundraiser in Key West to collect donations for the victims of Hurricane Andrew. Another top-notch speaker, Ted Nicholas, author of the bestseller *How to Form Your Own Corporation Without a Lawyer for Under $75.00*, talked about his secret for success. When Ted was going to share his "secret" with the audience, the moderator, Gary Halbert, stopped him and told him to write the secret on a piece of paper. Gary placed the paper inside an envelope and proceeded to auction off the envelope with the secret sealed inside. The final offer was $1,500, purchased by a gentleman from Indiana. A few years later, Joachim was working in Indiana with the same fellow. Before he went to the airport to return home, Joachim asked him for the secret. The man opened his drawer, took out the envelope, and showed him the secret. It said, "Whatever you want in life, just ASK for it."

5. Find Mentors and Use Them

Isaac Newton once said, "If I have seen farther than others, it is because I was standing on the shoulders of giants." There are plenty of successful consultants you can tap on the shoulder and derive incredible knowledge from. Terry Sjodin and Floyd Wickman have a great book for both mentors and protégés: *Mentoring: The Most Obvious Yet Overlooked Key to Achieving More in Life than You Ever Dreamed Possible.* Check it out.

6. Have a Plan and Update It Quarterly

Each year, I escape to Cancun, Mexico, to rejuvenate my soul and my business. As I dream about the upcoming year, I create a plan for all the things I want to do for the next year. (For gosh sakes, as a consultant, we should practice what we preach, so do a little strategic planning, will you?)

More importantly, I take that overall master plan and chunk it down into three-month plans. You see, I can work with three months. One year is just too daunting considering I don't know who I will be working with, what my cash flow will be, or what my interests will be. Just as Goldilocks discovered the porridge that was "just right" for her, creating and following a quarterly plan suitable to the way in which you work will keep you in line with your larger goals.

7. Set Up Systems. Have Key Processes in Place and Improve Them

Everything you do of a recurring nature should have a "system," process, template, or form that supports that activity. For example, if you always write a thank-you note to someone who refers business to you, capture what you did and what you wrote, so you don't forget it!

My consulting practice has several "process guides" that document every critical business activity from how we go about creating demand through invoicing the client to ensuring we met our objectives. Each employee (including me) is required to keep the process guide updated. Each week, we review one process for simplicity and efficiency.

In the unlikely (or unfortunate) event that the person who knows how to do that particular activity is no longer available, anyone can pick up the process guide and figure out what to do (of course, not nearly as lovely as the process "owner," but it will do in a pinch!).

8. Know the Numbers . . . Unless You Don't Care About Cash Flow or Making Money

There are some critical numbers you should look at on a monthly basis:

- *Billables:* What did you bill out this month—either in time increments (hours/days) or money? Are you above or below goal?

- *Expenses:* What were your expenses this month? Are you above or below goal?

- *Quick Ratio:* Current assets divided by your current liabilities should be at least one (or greater) to one. This basically means you have more cash on hand than bills to pay. A good thing for a business.

- *Current Ratio:* All your assets divided by all your liabilities should be at least one (or greater) to one. If your business goes belly up, you'll have enough assets to cover all of your business debt.

- *Accounts Receivable:* You will always have some invoices that are outstanding. Know your "typical number" and stay within that range. Make sure people pay you within a reasonable amount of time and that you don't pile up a bunch of invoices that go unnoticed (this is especially true with small invoices for books and other small ticket items).

9. Report Progress (the Numbers) to Yourself and/or to Others

Nothing keeps you more focused than a monthly progress report that objectively tells you what is going on in your business. Personally, I keep five progress reports:

- *Activity Report:* The business you generate is directly proportional to your business development activity. Track the number of outbound calls, emails, direct mail pieces, networking meetings attended, proposals submitted, work completed, etc. Don't track everything; just track the one, two, three activities that generate the most business for you. Then be zealous about meeting your target numbers.

- *Pipeline Report:* How much work is on the horizon? Statistically, you know you won't land everything in your pipeline (Do you know what your closing ratio is?), but you need to keep the pipeline "full."

- *Profit and Loss Report:* Look at the top line: Did you generate the sales you projected? Bottom line: Did you cover all your expenses?

- *Balance Sheet:* Make sure your assets outweigh your liabilities (see quick and current ratio above).

- *Research and Development Report:* Make sure you devote enough time to your professional growth and development.

The specific content and format will vary depending on your consulting practice, but make sure your reports are simple to keep and easy to interpret. Better yet, create a visual display and share the results with your trusted advisors!

10. You Are in Business to Make Money First, and Then to Do Great Things

Many consultants are motivated by a greater good and eschew the idea that money is their primary motivator. However, money puts beans and weenies on the table and provides creature comforts for you and your family. By making sure your basic needs are taken care of, you can focus on the greater good and do even greater things with your business.

11. Unless This Is a Hobby, Pay Yourself Something

Many independent consultants pay themselves when there is money in the bank. Instead, pay yourself something every pay period. It may be a pittance, but you'll feel better about yourself and your business when payday arrives. Then at the end of each month or quarter, give yourself a "bonus" based on the gross revenues collected (versus billed).

And don't forget to pay your federal, state, and local taxes. Even if you don't have the money, find it.

12. You Will Want to Retire Someday, so Start Saving Now

Put at least 10 percent (if not more) aside in savings. Maximize your IRAs. Open up a SIMPLE IRA or tax-deferred retirement account. Hire a great financial planner to make recommendations on your entire portfolio and an able accountant to keep you out of trouble with Uncle Sam.

13. Everything Will Cost or Take Twice as Much Time as You Thought

Until you have been in business for a long time, you will woefully underestimate the amount of time it will take or the final costs. For example, it will take you twice as long and twice as much money to create and print your marketing materials, host a marketing breakfast, put together a website, etc. Ergo, budget twice as much time and twice as much money. If you come in under schedule and budget, then you have a reason to celebrate!

14. Be Prepared to Buy What/How Much You Need, Just When You Need It

Overhead and excess expenses can kill a new consulting business. Try to distinguish between a "need" and a "want." For example, you believe you "need" a new color laser printer to print out some cool handouts for your customer. Do you really need a laser printer or is there another way you can accomplish the task? For example, you can take the job to a local quick service printer or even to a fellow consultant who has a color printer! If you get a bit creative, you may not really need that printer after all.

But let's say you can mentally justify that you really need a color laser printer. Have you explored your options or will you grab the first one you see at the local computer store? If you really need it, you have been thinking about it for a while. (I have rarely needed to make a buying decision at a moment's notice.) When the time comes to buy a printer, you should know exactly what and where to buy it.

15. Beware of Purchases for Ego's Sake

A close corollary to number 14 above, watch out for purchases just because they make you feel good. Discretionary purchases fall right to the bottom line. Make sure you spend money to serve your business, not your ego.

16. Delight Your Clients . . . It's What Makes You Special and Why They'll Keep Coming Back

Go out of your way to help them . . . give a tad bit more than they expect. In the rare event you make a mistake, admit it, recover, and learn from it. Don't forget to keep in touch with your clients periodically, just to say hello or share some nifty information (not to sell them something).

17. Hire Eagles

The cookie maker, Debbie Fields, makes it a point to hire "eagles" or the best people she can find. Sure, you can hire minimum wage employees, but you'll get minimum productivity, simply because they don't know what to do. Hire people who already have the expertise to propel you to new heights versus drag you down.

18. Invest Time, Energy, and Training in Your Employees

Even when you hire eagles, they still need some care and feeding. Invest in a solid orientation plan, acquaint them with your business, and let them know your expectations. Offer training to bolster or supplement their current skill set. Whatever you do, don't just turn 'em loose on your business. You (and your employees) are doomed for failure. Invest in the relationship and they'll be able to soar in no time!

19. Surprise! They Will Leave You Some Day

Yep, eventually, they will move on and all that time, energy, and training will go out the window . . . unless you required them to maintain a process guide that captures their key learnings and procedures!

20. Get Out of Your Office

Hiding in your office won't get you clients. In order to meet clients, you must get out of your office! You must be able to network and sell yourself. If you don't know how to network, read Susan RoAne's book, *How to Work a Room*, and Jeffrey Fox's *How to Become a Rainmaker*. Then get out there and do it!

21. Take Time Off Every Once in a While

It's easy to get sucked into the office vortex, especially if your office is in your home. Try to have consistent working hours, take weekends off, and schedule holidays. Dan

Sullivan, in *The Great Crossover*, emphasizes that you need free time to rest and rejuvenate. He insists that "the more free time that entrepreneurs take, the better their results. . . . The most productive time is the period of ten days immediately following a stretch of Free Days—you return to work with a new perspective, a higher energy level and very probably a breakthrough." We all need breakthroughs, so take a vacation every once in a while.

22. Make a "Great Things" Book for Bad Days

Everyone has a bad day. When you run into a string of bad days, it's nice to turn to a book of "Great Things," a scrapbook of thank-you notes, certificates, articles, deliverables that you're proud of. It is a keepsake that reminds you why you are in this business, even while enduring a rough period.

So there you have it. Nothing too earth-shattering. Just a few words of wisdom from another consultant buddy. Just remember: Trust your instincts and remember to have fun!

References

Biech, E. (1998). *The business of consulting.* San Francisco, CA: Pfeiffer.

Covey, S. (1989). *The seven habits of highly effective people.* New York: Simon & Schuster.

De Posada, J. (2003). *How to survive among piranhas.* Bloomington, IN: First Books Library.

Fox, J.J. (2000). *How to become a rainmaker: The rules for getting and keeping customers and clients.* New York: Hyperion.

Gitomer, J. (2000, May 8). Debbie Fields, quoted in *Inside Business.*

RoAne, S. (2000). *How to work a room.* New York: HarperResource.

Sjodin, T., & Wickman, F. (1996). *Mentoring: The most obvious yet overlooked key to achieving more in life than you ever dreamed possible.* New York: McGraw-Hill.

Sullivan, D., Smith, B., & Neray, M. (1994). *The great crossover.* Toronto, Ontario, Canada: The Strategic Coach, Inc.

Kristin J. Arnold, CPF, CMC, CSP, *helps corporations, government, and nonprofit organizations build high-performance teams. She specializes in facilitating executives and their teams as well as training others to facilitate teams to higher levels of performance. An accomplished author as well as a featured columnist in the Daily Press, she is regarded as an expert in process and team development. She graduated with high honors from the U.S. Coast Guard Academy and earned her MBA with an emphasis on marketing strategy from St. Mary's College in California.*

Introduction

to the Inventories, Questionnaires, and Surveys Section

Inventories, questionnaires, and surveys are valuable tools for the HRD professional. These feedback tools help respondents take an objective look at themselves and at their organizations. These tools also help to explain how a particular theory applies to them or to their situations.

Inventories, questionnaires, and surveys are useful in a number of training and consulting situations: privately for self-diagnosis; one-on-one to plan individual development; in a small group to open discussion; in a work team to help the team to focus on its highest priorities; or in an organization to gather data to achieve progress. You will find that the use of inventories, questionnaires, and surveys enriches, personalizes, and deepens training, development, and intervention designs. Many can be combined with experiential learning activities or articles in this or other Annuals to design an exciting, involving, practical, and well-rounded intervention. Each instrument includes the background necessary for understanding, presenting, and using it. Interpretive information, scales, and scoring sheets are also provided. In addition, we include the reliability and validity data contributed by the authors. If you wish additional information on any of these instruments, contact the authors directly. You will find their addresses and telephone numbers in the "Contributors" listing near the end of this volume.

The 2005 Pfeiffer Annual: Consulting includes two assessment tools in the following categories:

Groups and Teams

Evaluation of Performance in Team Presentations, by Ira J. Morrow

Organizations

Organizational Citizenship Behavior Inventory: A Conceptual and Validation Analysis, by Biswajeet Pattanayak, Rajnish Kumar Misra, and Phalgu Niranjana

Evaluation of Performance in Team Presentations

Ira J. Morrow

Summary

This paper presents and discusses the use of two instruments developed to provide teams with structured and constructive quantitative feedback regarding their performance in presentations that are frequently required in educational or work settings. The content of the instruments is described in detail, and suggestions for using and adapting the instruments to maximize team reflection, insight, and skill development are given.

Requiring the preparation and delivery of presentations by teams to colleagues has become a common feature of life in both work and educational settings. In educational settings, this requirement is based on the assumption that students need as much practice as possible in this important, and frequently stressful, activity, that employers expect some degree of expertise in this area, and that one's upward career movement can be facilitated by demonstrated skill in this area or hampered by the lack of such facility. Typically, students receive a grade from their instructor on their performance on this task, as well as some additional feedback. In some cases, audience members may be asked to provide their feedback as well. Unfortunately, the impact and value of such feedback, either from instructors or from classmates, may be attenuated by lack of familiarity with how to provide informative and constructive feedback to presenters. Instructions to classmates in the audience to provide anonymous feedback to a presenter often result in vague and general comments of minimal use to the recipient, such as, "It was interesting," "I enjoyed it," "Good work," "Nice effort," "Keep up the good work," or "Your slides looked great." In this paper we present and discuss two instruments that have been developed and used successfully in management classes to facilitate and improve the feedback process and student learning associated with presentations. These instruments offer a structured and uniform framework that all parties, the audience, the instructor or facilitator, and the presenters themselves can use for providing detailed, specific, in-formative, constructive, developmental, and quantitative feedback to presenters. Suggestions for modifying the instruments for use by individual presenters rather than teams are also provided.

Description of the Instruments

Team Presentation Assessment (Instrument 1)

The Team Presentation Assessment consists of a set of criteria used for the evaluation of performance in team presentations. Such criteria can, of course, be adapted by each instructor, trainer, or facilitator to better suit his or her own instructional needs. The assessment consists of fifteen such criteria, including mastery of topic, apparent effort, preparation/rehearsal, relevance/interest, organization of material, coordination between sections and members, time management, teamwork, audience involvement/participation, audience rapport, inviting/fielding questions, clarity/communication skills, outline quality, visuals quality, and impact/persuasiveness. Two of these items (coordination between sections and members, and teamwork) pertain specifically to team presentations, and the rest of the items are applicable either to team-oriented or to individual presentations. For individual presentations therefore, the instrument can be used after the elimination of these two items. Each item is followed by a traditional five-point Likert-style rating scale ranging from 1 = far below standards, to 3 = neutral or undecided, to 5 = far above standards. Additional space is provided at the end for open-ended comments.

Theory Behind the Team Presentation Assessment

The items included in the Team Presentation Assessment reflect the criteria that audiences are likely to make natural but implicit and global use of in evaluating the effectiveness and quality of presentations that they are exposed to. The assessment separates and makes explicit these implicit and global criteria in order to enhance the quality and helpfulness of the feedback that presenters receive from their audiences. The criteria are consistent with the skills that good presenters are supposed to demonstrate, as discussed in skills-oriented management books (e.g., Whetten & Cameron, 2002).

Administration of the Team Presentation Assessment

To maximize the effectiveness of the Team Presentation Assessment, instructors and facilitators should provide it to presenters and discuss it several weeks prior to their presentation, perhaps as early as the first session of the course or training program, when requirements and expectations are being discussed with the class. This will provide presenters with a clear and precise sense of the criteria that will be used to evaluate their performance and will enable presenters to orient their efforts accordingly. When the assessment is being distributed, instructors or facilitators should lead an in-depth discussion of the meaning of each criterion. This can include reference to specific examples that illustrate relative degrees of effectiveness on the criterion, as well as recommendations for how to improve performance on the criterion.

To illustrate how this discussion might proceed, we will focus here on several criteria, beginning with the one that presenters generally have the most difficulty with, namely, encouraging audience involvement/participation. A discussion of this criterion could begin by asking presenters how they can make presentations more involving for their audience. Presenters may offer several ideas, such as using visual aids. This could lead to a discussion of the use or misuse of visual aids in presentations and may lead to the point that, although visual aids are useful, they do not necessarily enhance audience involvement or participation. Frequently, presenters must take other steps, such as asking the audience questions. This can lead to a discussion of different ways that presenters can ask questions, including asking rhetorical questions to get audience members more engaged with the material, asking for a show of hands in response to questions, asking questions of selected members of the audience, or putting questions in writing in the form of a survey to be administered to the audience several sessions prior to the presentation, followed by feedback and discussion of the results with the class. Examples of each of these techniques can be provided. Other recommendations for enhancing audience involvement that could be discussed and illustrated include having presenters role play certain scenarios relevant to the topic, combined with asking the audience questions at certain points about what is being acted out, or dividing the audience into groups for the purpose of discussing a short case or engaging in an exercise related to the topic and then soliciting input from the groups that have been formed.

The criterion of coordination between sections and members generally warrants further elaboration as well. Instructors could indicate here that, although team members may decide to do some of their work alone, the final presentation should be coordinated into an overall coherent package. Hence, the subtopics should be related to each other, visuals should have a certain uniform appearance rather than looking as if they were made by three or four different people, team members should appear to be familiar with each other's material, the first speaker should introduce the entire team, and each speaker should seamlessly "pass the baton" to the next speaker. Regarding the criterion of time management, presenters can be reminded that they are being granted a precious resource, namely class or training time, and that they are expected to make full and effective use of this gift.

It is this author's practice to set a time limit for presentations and to inform presenters in advance that their presentations will be timed by an electronic device that will buzz when the established time limit is reached. (Having an electronic timer perform this function enables the instructor to concentrate on the presentation rather than on a clock and to avoid the distasteful task of having to interrupt presenters in the middle of a sentence.) Presenters are told that, when the device sounds, they can finish their sentence if they are still speaking, but then must end the presentation and open the floor to questions.

The rationale for establishing a firm time limit is to keep all presenters playing on a level field by the same rules and to avoid students trying to impress the instructor or the class by going on much longer than the time limit, which can lead to things getting out of hand. Presenters are told that they should rehearse together in order to make sure that their presentations will not go over the limit.

On the other hand, presentations should not be too short either, suggesting a lack of effort and depth on the team's part and a failure to make adequate use of the gift of time that has been provided to them. Moreover, teams are told that each member of the team must present, not just the most fluent, articulate, or polished communicators, and that the amount of time each of them uses to present should be roughly equal. This is to make sure that each team member experiences the learning and developmental benefit of delivering a presentation before an audience. Hence, team members have some difficult balancing acts to attend to when it comes to managing their time.

Similar discussions about each criterion can ensue as the instructor sees fit, so that this assessment can actually form the basis for a course learning module on making effective presentations, in addition to serving as an evaluation, feedback, and personal development tool.

Scoring Process for the Team Presentation Assessment

The scoring for the Team Presentation Assessment is straightforward and direct, since the score for each item or criterion is simply what was provided by the respondent without any conversion of the score. However, since the five-point Likert scale refers to "standards" (as in far below, somewhat below, somewhat above, or far above standards), a discussion of what is meant by standards is in order. This author tells presenters that they may approach this rating scale from their own perspectives as to what is meant by standards and that they should use whatever experience they have had delivering and listening to other presentations to provide the frame of reference for handling this task. The instructor can point out that the problem of using different frames of reference in responding to a rating scale of this sort is certainly not unique to this instrument, but commonly occurs in other surveys, including most course evaluation instruments. Furthermore, if some audience members approach the rating task with an overly stringent frame of reference and others with a more liberal one, these are likely to balance out for the audience as a whole.

Finally, if several different presentations will be heard during the same session, audience members can be advised to provide an initial set of ratings after each presentation and told that these can be modified after they have the benefit of having heard more than one presentation—allowing for an enriched frame of reference.

Aside from having audience members complete the instrument and the instructor make use of the same instrument, presenters should be asked to rate themselves on the same assessment at the conclusion of their own presentations and to keep their self-ratings separate from the audience ratings that will be provided to them. The instructor can point out that this will enable the team to make fruitful comparisons between how they have been evaluated by the audience and how they evaluated themselves. This instructor points out that he will not ask to see the raw scores provided by the audience, but rather that some overall summary information will be provided by the team to the instructor before the next session. The summary information that is requested from each team derives from the second assessment, which is described and discussed in the next section of this paper.

The Team Presentation Assessment Worksheet (Instrument 2)

The second instrument, the Team Presentation Assessment Worksheet, provides presenters with a structured format for tabulating, performing further calculations on, and reflecting on the feedback they received from their audience on the Team Presentation Assessment. Thus, the Assessment Worksheet is to be completed by the team of presenters for submission to the instructor or facilitator at the next class or training session. The raw scores needed to complete this instrument are simply the set of ratings submitted to the team by the audience on the Team Presentation Assessment described above. The criteria included on the Assessment Worksheet exactly match the criteria on the first assessment (again with the possibility of eliminating two criteria—coordination and teamwork—if used by individual presenters rather than by teams). Additional open-ended items calling for organizing the data, interpreting its meaning, and reflecting on the team's performance are provided as well, and these are described in greater detail in the description of the scoring process below.

Theory Behind the Team Presentation Assessment Worksheet

The logic and rationale for the Team Presentation Assessment Worksheet is simply to help presenters complete the learning process by encouraging team members to take a closer look at the feedback that has been provided to them by their audience. This worksheet sends an important message to presenters, namely that your job as presenters is not finished simply because you have "exited the stage" and completed the active part of the presentation. Your additional mission as a team of presenters is to do all you can to improve your performance as team members and as presenters, by getting together yet again to carefully digest and reflect on the gift of feedback that has been provided by the audience.

The value of receiving feedback from others in order to improve future performance is widely accepted in the management and learning literature (e.g., Luthans, 1998; Whetten & Cameron, 2002). This worksheet affords team members the opportunity to carefully consider concrete, detailed, quantitative, direct, and specific feedback from their audience about their performance, to determine how they themselves felt about the presentations and their performance as a team, and to reflect on how their self-assessments compare to the ratings received from their audience and from the instructor or facilitator. Thus, this worksheet provides the basis for improving presentations and team skills and enriches the learning and skill-building value of the presentation experience. Moreover, presenters have an opportunity to develop a more realistic self-image (Haney, 1992) by thinking about and trying to account for differences or similarities in the way they perceived their own performance versus how their performance was perceived by others. Some presenters may see, for example, that they have been overly harsh in judging their own performance as compared to the ratings received from the audience. Others will see that they have been overly generous in evaluating their performance compared to their audience, and others will see that their self-perceptions are consistent with others' evaluations. This in turn can lead to fruitful discussions about why self versus others' evaluations are either consistent or not and about the premise that in organizations reality is socially determined and that perceived reality is what matters. Hence, if self versus others' performance ratings are inconsistent, presenters must consider why this is so and what, if anything, they would like to do about it. In the case of the team under-rating itself compared to its audience, perhaps team members need to consider the possibility that they are performing better as a team of presenters than they believe and that an upward adjustment of their self-perceptions is in order. On the other hand, when the team has overrated itself compared to its audience, perhaps team members need to consider ways to more effectively convey their self-perceived competence to their audience. In any case, the process of working together on the Team Presentation Assessment Worksheet and discussing intra-team score similarities or differences, as well as self versus audience instructor ratings, can further strengthen the team, build cohesiveness, and serve as a vehicle for sharing concerns and suggestions for improving skills. These outcomes can provide additional benefits, particularly to teams that will continue working together on other projects.

Administration of the Team Presentation Assessment Worksheet

Each team of presenters should be given one copy of the Team Presentation Assessment Worksheet, and teams should be encouraged to meet as soon as possible to perform the necessary calculations (none of which require higher mathematics) and to have the discussions required to complete the worksheet. If the presentation was videotaped, the tape should be returned to the team for their use, and the team should be told to view it together before completing the worksheet. A due date for returning the worksheet to the instructor or facilitator should be provided. The reasons for and advantages of completing the Team Presentation Assessment Worksheet should be shared with the team to encourage them to complete this task thoughtfully.

The Scoring Process for the Worksheet

For each criterion, the presenting team is asked to calculate average (mean) scores and score ranges from the ratings provided by and collected from their audience. To help them focus on their developmental needs and their greatest strengths, they are asked to list those criteria scoring means 2.99 and below and those scoring means of 4.0 and above, respectively. Next, to help them focus on those criteria about which there was the least and greatest consensus from the audience, team members are asked to indicate the criteria with the largest and smallest range of scores, respectively.

Team members are then asked to calculate the sum of mean scores and the mean of mean scores, either of which can be thought of as a summary quantitative indicator of their team's overall performance on the presentation as perceived by their audience. All of the above calculations are then performed again in a parallel column, using the team's own self-evaluation scores. (If the presentation was delivered by an individual rather than by a team, these second calculations would just consist of the person's self-ratings.)

Team members are then asked to list those criteria that they over-rated (when compared to the audience's ratings) by 0.5 points or more or under-rated by 0.5 points or more, and they are asked to comment on the degree of correspondence between the audience's ratings and the team's self-ratings. They are also asked for their self-assessment of their overall team functioning and of their presentation's quality using the same five-point rating scale and to indicate their rationale for their scores. (This item can be revised for individual presentations.)

They are then asked to reflect on what the team did well and on how the team could have functioned more effectively. (These items too can be revised to suit individual presentations.) Finally, if presentations were videotaped, respondents are asked what they noticed about their performance from viewing the tape.

Reliability and Validity of the Instruments

The combined use of the two instruments discussed here is designed to provide a team of presenters with quantitative feedback from their audience about their performance and a structured format for making sense of the feedback. The feedback being assembled and interpreted by using these instruments consists of perceptions by a certain audience, at a given point of time, in a certain situation, upon hearing from a particular team of presenters, presenting on a certain topic or issue. They are not designed to measure more enduring or general personal or team qualities or traits that may be exhibited in other situations or before other audiences or with other team compositions. These instruments are designed solely for training, education, and developmental purposes. No contention is made that these instruments measure a single construct and so neither inter-item reliability nor construct validity is relevant. Since we could well expect that enduring teams will improve their performance from one presentation to the next, or that different audiences will respond to the same team differently, or that teams will alter their performance if even one member is changed, test-retest reliability is clearly not relevant either.

References

Haney, W.V. (1992). *Communication and interpersonal relations* (6th ed.). Homewood, IL: Richard D. Irwin.

Luthans, F. (1998). *Organizational behavior* (8th ed.). New York: McGraw-Hill.

Whetten, D.A., & Cameron, K.S. (2002). *Developing management skills* (5th ed.). Upper Saddle River, NJ: Prentice Hall.

Ira Morrow *has a Ph.D. degree in industrial-organizational psychology from New York University. He is currently associate professor of management at Pace University's Lubin School of Business in New York City, where he teaches M.B.A. students from around the world. He also consults in the field of human resources with an emphasis on management assessment.*

Team Presentation Assessment

Ira J. Morrow

Team Number: _____

Topic: _____

Date: _____

Name of rater (optional): _____

Instructions: Please rate the performance of the team you observed on the criteria below using the following range of scores:

1 = far below standards   4 = somewhat above standards

2 = somewhat below standards   5 = far above standards.

3 = neutral or undecided

For determining "standards" for the above range of scores, feel free to use your own individual frame of reference, based, for example, on comparing this presentation to others that you have seen here or in other settings.

Criterion	Score
A. Mastery of topic	_____
B. Apparent effort	_____
C. Preparation/rehearsal	_____
D. Relevance/interest	_____
E. Organization of material	_____
F. Coordination between members	_____
G. Time management	_____
H. Teamwork	_____
I. Audience involvement	_____
J. Audience rapport	_____
K. Inviting/fielding questions	_____
L. Clarity/communication skills	_____
M. Outline quality	_____
N. Visuals quality	_____
O. Overall impact/persuasiveness	_____

How could the presentation have been improved?

Additional comments:

Team Presentation Assessment Worksheet

Ira J. Morrow

Team number: _____

Team members: _____

Presentation topic: _____

Presentation date: _____

Instructions: Using the information from the Team Presentation Assessment forms collected from the audience and your team's self-ratings (kept separate from the audience's ratings), please perform the requested calculations and respond to the questions below. Your team should work together to complete this worksheet, which is to be submitted to the facilitator or instructor at the next class or session.

For each criterion listed below, calculate and provide four scores, as follows:

Score 1 = Audience's mean score (add together and divide
          by the number of audience members for an average)

Score 2 = Audience's score range

Score 3 = Team's self-rating mean score

Score 4 = Team's self-rating score range.

Criterion	Score 1	Score 2	Score 3	Score 4
A. Mastery of topic	_____	_____	_____	_____
B. Apparent effort	_____	_____	_____	_____
C. Preparation/rehearsal	_____	_____	_____	_____
D. Relevance/interest	_____	_____	_____	_____
E. Organization of material	_____	_____	_____	_____
F. Coordination between members	_____	_____	_____	_____
G. Time management	_____	_____	_____	_____
H. Teamwork	_____	_____	_____	_____
I. Audience involvement	_____	_____	_____	_____

Criterion	Score 1	Score 2	Score 3	Score 4
J. Audience rapport	_____	_____	_____	_____
K. Inviting/fielding questions	_____	_____	_____	_____
L. Clarity/communication skills	_____	_____	_____	_____
M. Outline quality	_____	_____	_____	_____
N. Visuals quality	_____	_____	_____	_____
O. Overall impact/ persuasiveness	_____	_____	_____	_____

Criteria with mean audience scores of 2.99 and below: _____

Criteria with mean audience scores of 4.00 and above: _____

Criteria with biggest range of audience scores: _____

Criteria with smallest range of audience scores: _____

Sum of audience's mean scores: _____

Mean of audience's mean scores: _____

Criteria over-rated by the team by 0.5 points or more (compared to audience ratings): _____

Criteria under-rated by the team by 0.5 points or more (compared to audience ratings): _____

The team's comments on the degree of agreement between the audience's ratings and the team's self-ratings:

The team's self-assessment of the quality of the
presentation (on 1 to 5 scale used in rating form):   _____

Rationale for this rating:

The team's self-assessment of its overall effectiveness
as a team (on 1 to 5 scale used in rating form):   _____

Rationale for above:

What did your team do well in regard to this project?

How could your team have functioned more effectively on this project?

What did your team notice about its performance from viewing the videotape?

Additional comments:

Organizational Citizenship Behavior Inventory:

A Conceptual and Validation Analysis

Biswajeet Pattanayak, Rajnish Kumar Misra,
and Phalgu Niranjana

Summary

Industrial organizations have always been concerned with whether employee loyalty is an important characteristic to be rewarded or not. The debate still continues, and the word "loyalty" has been replaced with a more suitable term. Graham, Organ, and Van Dyne came up with a new concept they called "organizational citizenship behavior" (OCB). What it is and how it can be measured are tough questions to answer. Although Van Dyne has developed a measure of OCB, it reflects 360-degree feedback about citizenship behavior. The present authors define and measure organizational citizenship behavior for its applicability in an Indian context.

Organizations are designed around business processes, with each process divided into tasks and activities that, put together, form a job. The expectations of people about that job or position and how they perform them are referred to as role (Katz & Kahn, 1978). However, the individual also has to perform some tasks outside his or her role expectations. This is generally called extra-role behavior, defined as behavior that benefits the organization (and/or is intended to benefit the organization), that is discretionary, and that goes beyond existing role expectations (Van Dyne, Cummings, & Parks, 1995). This behavior is of four types: (1) organizational citizenship behavior (OCB); (2) pro-social organizational behavior (PSOB); (3) whistle-blowing (WB); and (4) principled organizational dissent (POD). The most researched among these is the concept of organizational citizenship behavior.

Organizational Citizenship Behavior

In 1983, Denis Organ and his colleagues were first to use the term organizational citizenship behavior (OCB) (Bateman & Organ, 1983; Smith, Organ, & Near, 1983). Then, drawing on the concept of "willingness to cooperate," Chester Bernard and Daniel Katz's (Bernard, 1983) distinction between dependable role performance and innovative and spontaneous behaviors, Organ (1988) defined OCB as individual behavior that is discretionary, not directly or explicitly recognized by the formal reward system, and that in aggregate promotes the effective performance of the organization. By discretionary, we mean that the behavior is not an enforceable requirement of the role or job description, that is, the clearly specifiable terms of the person's employment contract with the organization; the behavior is rather a matter of personal choice, such that its omission is not generally understood as punishment. This concept has also been characterized as constructive and cooperative extra role gestures that are neither mandatory nor directly compensated by a formal organizational reward system (Organ, 1988, 1990a, 1990b). In addition, Organ described such behaviors as having an accumulative positive effect on organizational functioning.

Subdimensions of Behavioral Tendencies

According to Inkeles (1969), the behavioral tendencies of people in society can be viewed as "active citizenship syndrome," comprised of three subdimensions, the first being loyalty, which reflects serving the interests of society and practicing the values professed by it. People who are loyal go out of their way to help others. The second subdimension refers to the obedience aspect, meaning a law-abiding person who respects the prevalent structures and processes within the society. Involvement in the society's current and related issues and helping it to overcome them is the third aspect considered to be important. In a similar vein, Aristotle also viewed citizenship as a role-related responsibility and therefore citizens needed to have a balance in all the aspects highlighted above.

Three Dimensions

Graham (1991) was of the opinion that OCB may be seen from a global perspective, and she took the opportunity of studying and implementing it in the industrial organization. According to Graham, three dimensions make up OCB: organizational obedience, loyalty, and participation. Organizational obedience reflects acceptance of organizational rules, regulations, and policies formulated with respect to organizational structure and processes. It can be observed in employees adhering to the rules and their punctuality in finishing work, their meeting deadlines, and their low rate of absenteeism. Organizational loyalty consists of admiring the leaders and their views and talking favorably about the company within and outside the organization. This can happen only when a person has internalized the values and norms prevalent in the organization and is guided by them in a most favorable way. The third dimension, organizational participation, reflects the eagerness and willingness to participate in the affairs of the organization, such as providing valuable suggestions to management to overcome a current or emergent problem. Such an employee is a keen observer of the organization's activities and works toward the welfare of the organization.

Although the rapid growth in theory and research undoubtedly has been gratifying to those interested in OCB, it also has produced some unfortunate consequences. To cite an example, Van Dyne, Cummings, and Parks (1995) have noted that much of the empirical research on OCB and the related concept of pro-social behavior and organizational spontaneity has focused more on what Schwab (1980) called substantive validity rather than on construct validity, that is, the literature has focused more on understanding the relationships between organizational citizenship behavior and other constructs rather than on carefully defining the nature of citizenship behavior itself. Following Schwab (1980), Van Dyne, Cummings, and Parks (1995) warned that, unless additional attention is directed toward more comprehensive theoretical explications of the constructs and their measures, we are in danger of developing a stream of literature that may prove to be of little value to the field in the long run.

In-Role Versus Extra-Role Behavior

Katz and Kahn (1966, 1978) distinguished between in-role behavior (behavior in accordance with formal role descriptions) and extra-role behaviors (actions above and beyond formal role requirements). According to their theory, formal and extrinsic rewards are based on in-role behavior, while intrinsic rewards accrue to extra-role behavior. Extra-role behavior arises from feelings of citizenship with respect to the organization. Thus, the employee-citizen performs certain activities on behalf of the organization to which he or she is committed without being formally required to do so.

Usually, OCB is defined as extra-role behavior that may benefit an organization or people within the organization, even when these behaviors are not part of a worker's formal job description or requirements, that is, people voluntarily choose to engage in OCB (Borman & Motowidlo, 1993; Organ, 1988; Organ & Ryan, 1995). Like volunteerism, OCB is a long-term behavior that typically involves proactive efforts to benefit others and takes place in an organizational setting. The fact that OCB is a voluntary, extra-role behavior does not mean that it goes unnoticed and unappreciated by an organization's leaders, that it has no impact on formal and informal evaluations of an employee's performance, or even that people are unaware of the benefits that might result from being a good organizational citizen. To the contrary, there is evidence that

OCB is noticed, that it does affect evaluations, and that workers know this (Allen, 1996; Borman, White, & Dorsey, 1995; Motowidlo & Van Scotter, 1994). However, we believe that people volunteer and engage in OCB because they want to, rather than because they are formally required to. Thus, the defining characteristics of OCB are not that it is pro-social and selfless, but rather that it is pro-social and voluntary.

Hence, OCB is not just the compliance of workers to a job description drawn in the organization; rather, it has been observed that people sometimes do perform more than what they are expected to do, which ultimately helps the organizations to enhance productivity. OCB research attempts to discover what makes employees engage in citizenship behaviors and how this can be used within the organization to enhance productivity. OCB is partly a function of the extent to which employees feel supported by the organization and have good relationships with their immediate supervisors and do not perform only to impress management (Jardine & Bagraim, 2000).

Early researchers were of the opinion that OCB may be considered as an extra role and as organizationally functional, and therefore can be considered as an organizationally relevant behavior. Although it is difficult to determine whether these behaviors will be related to individual performance vis-à-vis organizational performance and also how it is going to be rewarded, it needs to be understood (Graham, 1991; Van Dyne, Cummings, & Parks, 1995).

The Instrument

This inventory was designed after taking the above research into consideration. The authors also studied results obtained from an OCB instrument designed by Van Dyne, which resulted in 360-degree feedback. The inventory presented here was designed to elicit only one respondent's impressions of his or her colleagues.

Development of the Instrument

The instrument consists of statements to which the person responds using a 7-point scale. The degree to which each attribute is considered to be present in one's colleagues is then evaluated and scored. The instrument was tested by administering it to 365 executives working in the manufacturing industry selected on a random basis.

Administration

The instrument can be administered individually or in a group, irrespective of the departments of the respondents. Respondents are asked to fill in their scores based on their observations about how their colleagues in the organization behave.

Scoring and Interpretation

All items are rated on a 7-point scale and their scores summed for each factor/dimension. Negatively worded item scores are reversed. These are as follows: 2, 3, 5, 6, 11, 14, 16, 17, 27, 28, 29, 30, and 32.

All the other items are to be scored as shown below:

1 = strongly disagree

2 = moderately disagree

3 = slightly disagree

4 = neither disagree nor agree

5 = slightly agree

6 = moderately agree

7 = strongly agree

Reliability and Validity

The reliability of this instrument was calculated through variance method for internal consistency with a Cronbach Alpha of 0.87.

The item validity of the inventory was found through factor analysis to determine whether each item measures what it claims to measure. The items were selected on the basis of factor loading and the correlation coefficient (r) of each item with the total score. Two items had to be rejected because of low correlation values.

Discussion

The three factors that have emerged after factor analysis are as follows:

1. *Sharing and involvement attributes of the employees.* Sharing and involvement here represent the interactions between employees about organizational issues and how they can be solved through creative ideas. Two examples of looking for this dimension are Item 17, "My colleagues only attend work-related meetings if they are required to do so by their jobs" (and therefore do not want to waste their time in meetings) and Item 21, "My colleagues frequently make creative suggestions to co-workers about organizational improvements." The reliability estimate for this factor's Cronbach alpha is 0.77.

2. *Sense of organizational ownership.* Organizational ownership here represents the degree to which the individual is devoted to the organization and its resources and also performs his or her duties with full responsibility. This factor is represented by Item 1, "My colleagues represent the organization favorably to outsiders," and Item 12, "My colleagues are mentally alert and ready to work when they arrive each day." The reliability estimate for this factor's Cronbach alpha was 0.76.

3. *Professional competence of the employee within the organization.* Professional competence refers to the degree to which the individual performs his or her task and duty in meeting deadlines and performing to high standards to achieve organizational goals. This factor is shown by Item 11, a negatively worded item, "My colleagues do not meet all deadlines set by the organization," and Item 32, "My colleagues have difficulty cooperating with others on group projects." The reliability estimate for this factor's Cronbach alpha is 0.83.

Uses of the Instrument

The instrument can be used for determining what respondents think is the organizational citizenship behavior of colleagues on the three dimensions described above.

References

Allen, T.D. (1996). *Examining the effects of performance beyond role requirements: A field and laboratory study.* Unpublished Doctoral Dissertation, Knoxville, TN: University of Tennessee.

Bernard, C.I. (1983). *The functions of the executive.* Cambridge, MA: Harvard University Press.

Bateman, T.S., & Organ, D.W. (1983). Job satisfaction and the good soldier: The relationship between affect and employee "citizenship." *Academy of Management Journal, 26,* 587-595.

Borman, W.C., & Motowidlo, S.J. (1993). Expanding the criterion domain to include elements of contextual performance. In N. Schmitt, W.C. Borman, & Associates (Eds.), *Personnel selection in organizations,* (pp. 71-98). San Francisco, CA: Jossey-Bass.

Borman, W.C., White, L.A., & Dorsey, D.W. (1995). Effects of ratee task performance and interpersonal factors on supervisor and peer performance ratings. *Journal of Applied Psychology, 80,* 168-177.

Graham, J.W. (1991). An essay on organizational citizenship behavior. *Employee Responsibilities and Rights Journal, 4,* 249-270.

Inkeles, A. (1969). Participant citizenship in six developing countries. *American Political Science Review, 63,* 1120-1141.

Jardine, J.J., & Bargraim, J.J. (2000). *The relationship between perceived fairness at work and organizational citizenship behavior.* A University of Cape Town working paper.

Katz, D., & Kahn, R.L. (1966, 1978). *The social psychology of organizations.* New York: John Wiley & Sons.

Morgan, C.D., & Murray, H.A. (1938). Thematic apperception test. In H.A. Murray (Ed.), *Explorations in personality: A clinical and experimental study of fifty men of college age* (pp. 530-545). New York: Oxford University Press.

Motowidlo, S.J., & Van Scotter, J.R. (1994). Evidence that task performance should be distinguished from contextual performance. *Journal of Applied Psychology, 79*, 475-480.

Organ, D.W. (1988). *Organizational citizenship behavior.* Lexington, MA: Lexington Press.

Organ, D.W. (1990a). The motivational basis of organizational citizenship behavior. *Research in Organizational Behavior, 12*, 43-72.

Organ, D.W. (1990b). The subtle significance of job satisfaction. *Clinical Laboratory Management Review, 4*, 94-98.

Organ, D.W., & Ryan, K. (1995). A meta-analytic review of attitudinal and dispositional predictors of organizational citizenship behavior. *Personnel Psychology, 48*, 775-802.

Pattanayak, B., & Niranjana, P. (2002). Organizational citizenship behavior: A proposed hierarchical model for performing organizations. In B. Pattanayak, V. Gupta, & P. Niranjana (Eds.), *Creating performing organizations.* New Delhi: Response Books.

Schwab, D.P. (1980). Construct validity in organizational behavior. *Research in Organizational Behavior, 2*, 3-43.

Smith, C.A., Organ, D.W., & Near, J.P. (1983). Organizational citizenship behavior: Its nature and antecedents. *Journal of Applied Psychology, 68*, 653-663.

Van Dyne, L., Cummings, L.L., & Parks, J.M. (1995). Extra-role behaviors: In pursuit of construct and definitional clarity (a bridge over muddied waters). *Research in Organizational Behavior, 17*, 215-285.

Biswajeet Pattanayak, Ph.D., *is director, Institute of Business Administration & Training (IBAT), Business School of KIIT. Prior to joining IBAT, he was professor of OB & HRM in IIM Indore & Lucknow, NITIE Mumbai, and director, Indian Institute of Bank Management (IIBM) Guwahati. He is a Ph.D. and D.Litt. (post-doctorate) in industrial and organization psychology and Fellow of the All India Management Association (AIMA), New Delhi. He has written seventeen books.*

Dr. Rajnish Kumar Misra *is currently assistant professor in HRM and has over seven years of work experience in both industry and academia. Dr. Misra has published research papers in various reputed journals in the area of knowledge management and virtual organizations. He has his master's in human resource development and management and Ph.D. in organizational climate from Allahabad and Purvanchal University.*

Dr. Phalgu Niranjana *is currently assistant professor of organizational behavior and has three years' research and teaching experience. She has written fourteen research publications in national and international journals. She has also co-edited* Creating Performing Organization: An International Perspective of Indian Management. *She has her master's degree, a master's in philosophy in psychology, and Ph.D. in management from Utkal University, Orissa, India.*

Organizational Citizenship Behavior Inventory

Biswajeet Pattanayak, Rajnish Kumar Misra, and Phalgu Niranjana

Instructions: The statements listed below describe a variety of possible behaviors your colleagues might exhibit at work. By using the 7-point scale shown below, indicate the extent to which you agree or disagree that each statement accurately describes the behavior of your co-workers as a group. Place the appropriate number in the space next to each statement.

1 = strongly disagree	4 = neither disagree nor agree	5 = slightly agree
2 = moderately disagree		6 = moderately agree
3 = slightly disagree		7 = strongly agree

My colleagues. . .

_____   1. represent the organization favorably to outsiders.

_____   2. do not tell outsiders that this is a good place to work.

_____   3. do not defend the organization when other employees criticize it.

_____   4. promote the organization's products or services to potential customers or clients.

_____   5. would accept an offer of employment from a competing organization if it would mean more money (or other benefits).

_____   6. would not be willing to encourage co-workers to invest their own money in the organization if this were permissible and the organization needed it.

_____   7. rarely waste time while at work.

_____   8. produce as much as they are capable of producing at all times.

_____   9. always come to work on time.

_____   10. produce the highest quality work they can, regardless of the circumstances.

_____   11. do not meet all deadlines set by the organization.

_____   12. are mentally alert and ready to work when they arrive each day.

_____   13. follow work rules and instructions with extreme care.

_____   14. waste organizational resources (for example: supplies, time, space, money) as they work.

1 = strongly disagree	4 = neither disagree nor agree	5 = slightly agree
2 = moderately disagree		6 = moderately agree
3 = slightly disagree		7 = strongly agree

_____ 15. keep their work areas clean and neat.

_____ 16. miss work, even though they do not have a legitimate reason for doing so.

_____ 17. only attend work-related meetings if they are required to do so by their jobs.

_____ 18. share ideas for new projects or improved operations as widely as possible throughout the organization.

_____ 19. keep informed about all the organization's products and services (even those outside their own areas) so they can suggest them to potential users.

_____ 20. try to make their personal appearance at work as attractive as possible, and also appropriate to the setting.

_____ 21. frequently make creative suggestions to co-workers about organizational improvements.

_____ 22. use their professional judgment to assess what is right and wrong for the organization.

_____ 23. encourage management to keep their knowledge and skills up-to-date.

_____ 24. encourage others to speak up at meetings.

_____ 25. help co-workers to think for themselves.

_____ 26. keep well-informed about organizational issues in areas where their opinions might be useful to the organization.

_____ 27. do not push me or their superiors to perform to a higher standard.

_____ 28. do not pursue opportunities off the job for additional training that would help them to do a better job at work.

_____ 29. avoid taking on extra duties and responsibilities at work.

_____ 30. do not work beyond what they are required to do.

_____ 31. volunteer for overtime work when the organization needs it.

_____ 32. have difficulty cooperating with others on group projects.

OCB Scoring Sheet

Instructions: Place the score you gave each of the items in the appropriate box below. Then add the numbers in each column for a total score for that factor. If there is an asterisk after the item number, REVERSE the scores, that is, 7 = 1, 6 = 2, 5 = 3, 4 = 4, 3 = 5, 2 = 6, and 1 = 7.

After you have completed the scoring grid, look at the possible minimum and maximum scores for each factor to see where your own scores are in comparison. If you have scores close to the minimum possible, your perceptions of your colleagues' organizational citizenship behavior is quite negative. On the other hand, if your scores are close to the maximum, you believe your colleagues at work to be exhibiting good organizational citizenship.

Item	Score	Item	Score	Item	Score
24		8		29*	
23		10		30*	
19		12		32*	
21		9		2*	
26		15		3*	
22		14*		6*	
25		4		28*	
18		7		11*	
20		1		16*	
31		13		27*	
17*				5*	
Factor 1 Total		Factor 2 Total		Factor 3 Total	

	Factor	Minimum Score	Maximum Score
1	Sharing and involvement	11	77
2	Organizational ownership	10	70
3	Professional competence	11	77

Introduction

to the Articles and Discussion Resources Section

The Articles and Discussion Resources Section is a collection of materials useful to every facilitator. The theories, background information, models, and methods will challenge facilitators' thinking, enrich their professional development, and assist their internal and external clients with productive change. These articles may be used as a basis for lecturettes, as handouts in training sessions, or as background reading material. This section will provide you with a variety of useful ideas, theoretical opinions, teachable models, practical strategies, and proven intervention methods. The articles will add richness and depth to your training and consulting knowledge and skills. They will challenge you to think differently, explore new concepts, and experiment with new interventions. The articles will continue to add a fresh perspective to your work.

The 2005 Pfeiffer Annual: Consulting includes thirteen articles, in the following categories:

Individual Development: Life/Career Planning

Consultants on the Cutting Edge, by Barbara Pate Glacel

Communication: Clarity and Precision in Communication

Cultural Identity and Self-Concept: Implications for Influencing Others, by Phyliss Cooke

Communication: Coaching and Encouraging

Mentoring: Empowering Human Capital, by Mohandas K. Nair

Communication: Communication in Organizations

Managing Sideways, by Peter R. Garber

Problem Solving: Change and Change Agents

An Integrative Model for Leading Change in Organizations,
by Linda Russell and Jeffrey Russell

Groups and Teams: Group Process

What If We Took Teamwork Seriously? by W. Warner Burke

Consulting: Organizations: Their Characteristics and How They Function

A Structural and Behavioral Model of Human Resource Planning,
by A. Venkat Raman

Consulting: OD Theory and Practice

Evaluation, the Final Phase of Consulting, by Charles L. Fields

Consulting: Consulting Strategies and Techniques

Value-Added Diversity Consulting, by Tyrone A. Holmes

Consulting: Interface with Clients

The Write Stuff, by Richard T. Whelan

Facilitating: Techniques and Strategies

The Systemization of Facilitation, by M.K. Key

Leadership: Strategies and Techniques

Leadership Coaching: Avoiding the Traps,
by Jan M. Schmuckler and Thomas J. Ucko

Leadership: Top-Management Issues and Concerns

Corporate Values and Bottom-Line Performance: The Value of Values,
by Steve Terrell

As with previous *Annuals,* this volume covers a wide variety of topics. The range of articles presented encourages thought-provoking discussion about the present and future of HRD. We have done our best to categorize the articles for easy reference; however, many of the articles encompass a range of topics, disciplines, and applications. If you do not find what you are looking for under one category, check a related category. In some cases we may place an article in the "Training" *Annual* that also has implications for "Consulting," and vice versa. As the field of HRD continues to grow and develop, there is more and more crossover between training and consulting. Explore all the contents of both of these volumes of the *Annual* in order to realize the full potential for learning and development that each offers.

Consultants on the Cutting Edge

Barbara Pate Glacel

Summary

Several analogies come to mind when I think about how consultants must stay on the cutting edge. "Keeping up with the Joneses" is one such adage. Consultants are expected by clients to be the experts, but expertise can become old. If "the Joneses" are those in the know, and we're supposed to know, then how do we as consultants keep up? This article explores a variety of ways, suggested by top leaders in the field, that consultants can stay abreast of developments in their fields and keep themselves engaged and energized.

To find out answers to how consultants stay on top of their game, I asked other consultants. I sought out consultants, among them the best-of-the-best by reputation. I asked them: How do consultants get their own stimulus, training, and creativity? How do we learn new skills? Or are we like the shoemaker's children, teaching others and not stimulating ourselves? Over fifty top-notch consultants responded with their own good ideas for keeping up-to-speed in order to better help our clients. Here are the top ten good suggestions.

1. Love to Learn

One well-known leadership guru captured this idea by saying he would much prefer to be introduced as a thirty-five-year student of leadership rather than as an expert on leadership. When one defines oneself as the expert, then learning may become secondary. Good consultants must love to learn and continue lifelong learning. Recently, a graduate student interviewed me during her investigation into the value of a doctoral degree. She asked if my degree had provided me the knowledge and skills required to be successful in my career. My response surprised her: "Oh, I certainly hope not," I exclaimed. The idea that a degree completes the learning process and guarantees success is a naïve assumption.

Consultants who stay on the cutting edge create a conscious learning plan. Some choose a new theme each year and immerse themselves. They study it, speak about it, teach about it, and write about it. This plan then creates new areas of expertise in which to consult.

Several consultants emphasized the need for "think time." They clear their calendars and turn off their phones. When they fly, they do not bring work onboard, but they give themselves the space for free thinking. One consultant insisted that six hours of time each week should be devoted to continuing to learn.

Learning comes from reading widely and discussing topics with peers and with knowledgeable thought leaders. Listening to and learning from others who may disagree and who offer a diversity of perspective creates an opportunity to think outside the conventional boundaries of theory and solutions that have been offered in the past.

2. Know the Current Issues

With the incredible amount of information available in today's media-flooded world, keeping up-to-date should be easy. Many consultants believe just the opposite. The amount of information is overwhelming and often goes unused because there is too much to know. The best piece of advice I heard was to be selective.

Many consultants emphasized that merely receiving the newsletters and buying the books is not enough-one must actually read them. Novel idea, isn't it? The favorite magazines of top consultants include *Harvard Business Review, Fast Company, Fortune,* and *The Wall Street Journal.* Selective e-zines and newsletters may supplement that knowledge.

Cutting edge consultants must keep up with their own fields and also the business environments and issues of their clients. Knowing about the issues the clients are facing, whether technical, marketing, personnel, or strategic, adds to the knowledge and credibility of the cutting edge consultant. Client home pages are an excellent source of information about the client and its issues.

Hot topics of the day may be gleaned by wandering around the local bookstore. Take a look at the books on the nonfiction bestseller lists and browse in the business section. A review of the titles and tables of contents may be enough to provide the issues and allow the consultant to choose one title to read in-depth. A further topic search on Amazon.com or Barnesandnoble.com will provide a wider array of selections. This survey allows the consultant to refer clients to the latest books and articles on topics relevant to their needs.

Keeping up-to-date may mean more than books, articles, and websites. As corporate leaders get younger and consultants get older, the cutting edge consultant may need to relate to the client through other means, such as lessons learned from music and movies. Keeping up-to-date means understanding the world in which the client lives.

The cutting edge consultant also keeps up-to-date on the competition. The worldwide web provides an easy way to know about the competition. Just read the website brochures of other consultants offering similar services.

3. Seek Out Online Resources

The worldwide web is a treasure trove of resources. How did we exist without it? A sampling of favorite websites for cutting edge consultants include the following:

- www.Amazon.com

  Search for books on the topic of your choice or register your subject and receive notices when new titles are published.

- www.Utne.com

  This URL is described as the consultant's "reader's digest" on magazines and journals. Utne reprints the best articles from over 2,000 alternative media sources, presenting the latest ideas and trends. The provocative writing from diverse perspectives stimulates thinking.

- www.Google.com

  A Google search on any topic presents multiple websites about the topic; information may include URLs, articles, chat groups, organizations, and newsletters. If you click on "news" at the Google homepage, you have access to articles from the 4,500 newspapers and media sites that Google monitors continuously, getting up-to-the-minute information.

- www.humanresources.about.com/

  This human resource site offers articles, a forum, chat on topics of interest, a newsletter on current human resource issues, a guide to other human resource URLs, and even a job search service.

- http://picks.yahoo.com/picks/

  Yahoo Picks allows the consultant to register specific topics of interest and to receive either daily or weekly notices of interesting and sometimes useful information on that specific topic.

- http://dir.yahoo.com/new/

  The Yahoo bulletin board provides search options for current articles, websites, and information on specific topics.

- www.communispace.com

  Online communities, such as the one offered by Communispace, enable to-day's organizations to accelerate innovation, improve collaboration, extend learning, and share knowledge across time and geography faster than ever before. Consultants can join an online community of their peers or share in a community with their clients.

4. Stretch Yourself

Many of the consultants who offered good ideas for staying on the cutting edge suggest that stretching oneself to areas beyond one's core strength is key to keeping up with the best of the best. Getting out of one's comfort zone and learning about a new area exercises one's brain while demanding a certain rigorous plan of attack for learning and using the new material.

A novel way to learn a new field is to team up with an expert to do a joint project. When your area of expertise and that of your colleague are compatible, yet different, then both consultants learn and add value to the client.

Partnering with a client also allows the consultant to learn. By asking open-ended questions and listening deeply, rather than always providing answers, the consultant is able to immerse himself or herself in the client's world. When a client presents a new issue, the consultant may offer to work on it and learn as the project progresses.

Work with best-in-class clients, even if your effort is pro bono. These organizations tend to set the stage for new and innovative approaches to problems. Your participation gives you an opportunity to learn and enhances your credibility.

Taking a leadership role in one's professional organization provides direct access to information in the field as one plans conferences and newsletters. By leading this effort, a consultant gains both experience and information.

Stretching oneself beyond the comfort zone means taking a risk, but includes the other top ten suggestions to becoming—and staying—a guru.

5. Network Widely

A good piece of advice from a seasoned consultant was to keep current with one's colleagues, even when you don't need something from them. He spends time in airports and taxis calling his colleagues just to see how they are doing. Sometimes, he says, they keep waiting to hear the agenda topic. When they realize that it is a friendly phone call, they relax and have a great conversation. Later, when the consultant may need their professional assistance, they are eager to help.

Participate in professional organizations where you rub shoulders with others in your field. The most frequently named organizations by the cutting edge consultants I queried included American Society for Training and Development, Instructional Systems Association, National Speakers Association, Institute for Management Consultants, Entrepreneurs Exchange, Organization Development Network, Society for Human Resource Management, International Coach Federation, and the American Society for Quality.

Most professional organizations also operate special interest groups (SIG) that cater to individual topics of interest, introducing colleagues and sharing ideas and best practices.

Networking widely means networking with client groups or industrial groups representing one's clients. This allows access to real business issues that the clients face, as well as introducing the consultant to the personalities representing client organizations and associations.

Join or create a community of practice of colleagues where you are surrounded by the best-in-class consultants. A community allows for economical professional development, a forum for sharing best practices, a sharing of diverse thoughts, and the ability to survey each other, to learn together and work together while brainstorming cutting edge solutions to problems.

Stay in touch with former colleagues or clients who are in leadership positions within organizations. Network with them to understand what is happening inside organizations. Talk to employees and managers to understand all dimensions of the organizational impact of real-time problems that organizations face.

6. Participate in Professional Development Opportunities

While professional development is important, many consultants suggest that it is as helpful in rejuvenating and energizing oneself as well as for learning a new skill. Seminars on new tools and approaches may add to the consultant's toolkit. University courses may add more substantive or theoretical knowledge. Briefings by professional organizations and clients present the latest real-time issues. Conferences include top-name speakers from the business and academic communities to challenge the status quo and present "what if" scenarios.

A particularly effective professional development experience is to take a sabbatical from consulting and join an organization. A consultant who has actually been on the firing line, in addition to being an advisor, has more credibility and more expertise to offer a client. Serving a year leading a volunteer organization, or inside a client organization, or in a government agency provides knowledge and experience unavailable through reading or consulting.

Professional development should be an everyday effort. Meetings can include a time for learning opportunities such as sharing the main points of books and articles, experiencing a new training or consulting tool, or hearing a speaker. Many consulting firms or communities of practice hold annual retreats where the consultants meet off-site to think "outside the box" on topics not addressed every day. A favorite public offering for such mind-expanding development includes the programs offered by The Aspen Institute.

Every consulting engagement should be debriefed to learn professionally about what worked and what did not work. Three simple questions provide professional development specific to one's consulting activities:

- What went well that we want to continue?

- What went poorly that we want to discontinue?

- What did we not do that we should do next time?

7. <u>Have a Mentor; Be a Mentor</u>

You've heard the expression, "What goes around comes around." In the world of consulting, the cutting edge practitioners mentor others to do the same good work. As junior consultants become good at the practice, they need to seek out new mentors in new fields or with more experience. Then they must mentor others who come behind them. This continuous learning and passing on of best practices allows each individual to continue to learn and conduct new and exciting interventions.

Mentors are available in many places. They may be members of your professional organizations and trade associations. Perhaps they are competitors who are willing to share good ideas. Client organizations provide mentors who are line managers or internal consultants. A university professor or thought leader may be a mentor. Within firms, senior consultants may mentor junior consultants. And junior consultants with more recent theoretical study may mentor those who have become set in their ways.

The mentoring process builds one's network, increases one's credibility, nurtures the love of learning, keeps one on the cutting edge, and gives back to the profession.

8. <u>Write, Teach, and Speak</u>

A guru in the performance consulting process believes that writing is the best way to become crystal-clear in your thinking. She sends what she writes to others to seek their reactions, and she interviews others to collect diverse opinions and additional thoughts. The reactions of others, even if there are differences of opinion, allow her to "noodle" in her mind about her methodology, her technology, and her underlying theories that support her practice. Both by being open and by writing, she synthesizes diverse input and clearly explains her cutting edge ideas.

In similar fashion, teaching and speaking require a consultant to state clearly the seminal thought being conveyed. Students, who may know less theoretically, sometimes ask the proverbial "dumb" question that allows a consultant to refine and define the cutting edge principle even better than before. That kind of testing is invaluable before putting the idea in front of a client.

Speaking at professional conferences and association meetings may be challenging, as the consultant is presenting to peers who know the subject or have an opinion on the subject. By engaging in dialogue about the topic, one learns more and knows how to defend the cutting edge theory or design.

Several consultants suggested taking a sabbatical from consulting work and devoting time to writing and teaching. This may rejuvenate one's thought processes and applications to create new fields of work.

9. Create the Cutting Edge

A seasoned compensation consultant suggests that the very act of intelligent discussion causes unrest and intellectual fermentation. "Something may be brewing," he says, "so be the brewer." Staying current means that someone or something is causing a need—why not you?

Utilizing all the suggestions in this list allows the opportunity to throw out new ideas, create new needs, suggest new approaches, and chart the course for which cutting edge consultants are known.

An internationally known communications consultant suggests that consultants should look to primary research and survey data, even from different fields, and apply it to one's own expertise. She says that ideas transpose from one area to another more readily than one might think.

Team learning across disciplines or by utilizing opposing points of view can create new applications of knowledge or new solutions to old problems. A cutting edge consultant must have cutting edge solutions, not the same old bag of tricks.

10. Stay Attuned to Yourself

Just as a cutting edge consultant must love to learn, that consultant must love the work. When the work gets old and dull, or when the approaches become rote, perhaps it is time for a change. The cutting edge consultant must know and acknowledge what motivates outstanding performance. Why do you get up in the morning and go to your consulting engagement? What is your passion?

A consultant gives to others, and one cannot give what one does not have. So it is important to be attuned to one's own energy level and excitement about the practice. Cutting edge consultants learn to fill up their own tanks and feed their minds, bodies, and souls.

When the consulting becomes just work, it is impossible to stay on the cutting edge. Then it is time for a new direction, a rest, or a self-examination to discover one's new passion in life.

Dr. Barbara Pate Glacel *is principal of The Glacel Group of Virginia and Brussels, Belgium. She is author of a business best seller on teams. She works with individuals, teams, and organizations in the Fortune 500 and not-for-profit arenas. She has over thirty years' experience in executive coaching and leadership development at all levels of organizations. She is a well-known author and public speaker and has consulted in Europe, Asia, and South Africa.*

Cultural Identity and Self–Concept: Implications for Influencing Others

Phyliss Cooke

Summary

In an attempt to influence others, some consultants will try to forge connections with their clients or audience based on cultural factors. The consultant may have read or heard that, for example, Northern Europeans prefer some style of communications, whereas Asians prefer another. In this article, the author suggests that the concept of cultural identity is much more complex than that and offers several insights into the concepts of culture and self.

If you are attempting to influence others, the development of rapport in followers is most reliably built on the basis of shared humanity, not on shared cultural identity. Even within a specific cultural group, "cultural identity" is too complex and idiosyncratic to be a useful concept.

Certain human and social factors challenge many consultants as they attempt to influence clients. Through experience, I have come to appreciate the significance of certain "insights" regarding these factors that, at first, may seem obvious.

Insight #1: The Fallacy of "Cultural Identity"

To attempt to understand, relate to, or influence others in terms of their "cultural identities" is impossible. There is as much diversity within any cultural grouping as there is without.

Much of my recent work has been with Asian and Native American clients. The primary focus of my work has been on my clients' issues with "cultural diversity" and its impact on business practices and relationships in the workplace. There are many cultural stereotypes of Native American peoples, e.g., that they offer few visual cues as to their emotional states, are reluctant to engage in direct or confrontational dialogue, are reluctant to make eye contact, do not pay attention to schedules, are unwilling to state personal opinions, and identify strongly with their familial and tribal affiliations. Many of these stereotypes are attributed to Asian people, as well. I have learned that these are not necessarily accurate or reliable indicators of whom or what I might be interacting with.

You might attempt to establish rapport with another person or group by assuming that you are culturally similar or dissimilar, but both assumptions are flawed, and neither approach will be successful.

Understanding the concept of cultural identity requires one to also understand the processes through which it developed. To assume that one must understand or share another's "culture" in order to establish rapport is to ignore the evidence that its ability to influence a relationship is directly proportional to the choices made by the individuals involved.

No one "belongs" to a cultural group automatically. Belonging is a very personal matter. Even in closely knit societies, there are individual differences among members, and there are those who are labeled "rebels" because they refuse to accept some or all of the prevailing norms.

Furthermore, for individuals with multiple cultural influences (e.g., Asian-Americans, Hispanic-Americans, African-Americans, and others in our global society), there is a plethora of influences, values, norms, and behaviors from which to choose. Each person's cultural identity is unique, complex, and consists of factors only partially defined, with the influences among these factors ranging from strongly compelling and predetermined to weakly influencing or weakly acknowledged. The creation of an individual's cultural identity involves both conscious and unconscious processes. Only the individual in question can shed light on his or her cultural identity.

Insight #2: Self-Concept

Self-concept is the foundation of each person's identity, including the person's cultural identity. In order to understand others, one must first relate to them as individuals.

Self-concept is developed through conscious and unconscious decision processes drawn from a variety of potentially influencing factors, such as family affiliation, lineage, or status; national or geographic origin; racial or religious heritage; political philosophy; education; profession; and personal causes or interests with which the individual identifies. These "anchors," the foundations of our self-concepts, are chosen (consciously or unconsciously) at points in our lives. Each person's basic personality, as well as his or her "culture" and life experiences, shapes his or her assumptions, perceptions, interpretations, and reactions—both emotional and behavioral.

Although necessary for healthy psychological well-being and in order for the individual to be able to function effectively in society, these developmental processes are complex and completely idiosyncratic. There is no simple way to interpret the significance of individual factors.

In trying to understand human nature and human behavior, I have found it helpful to begin with our basic animal instincts. For example, one of the most relevant of these is that humans are herd animals. We are most receptive to those whom we perceive to be similar, familiar, and, therefore, "safe." Perceived differences alert us to possible danger. The importance of visual cues, nonverbal behaviors, and first impressions to the process of establishing rapport is well-represented in behavioral science literature. As we begin our work with clients, we need to pay more attention to these factors, rather than paying attention to more abstract concepts.

Another basic animal instinct is that we are hierarchically oriented, that is, we are predisposed to seek our place within a group. We accord a higher level of status and authority to, and accept dominance from, those whom we perceive to deserve them.

Although these phenomena are well-documented, the attributes of status are not always obvious or consistent from situation to situation, nor is there consensus among individuals as to which factors merit status.

Each person in each situation presents an opportunity to stumble or to succeed in establishing rapport. The most important factors in any interpersonal encounter are the interpretations and the decisions that are made by the individuals involved.

I am not attempting to minimize the differences between humans and other animals or to diminish the significance of our spiritual nature or the importance of beliefs, heritage, lineage, race, geographic origin, historic events, ceremonies and rituals, language, or any of the other aspects that figure so prominently in the understanding of self-concept. I am proposing that the process of attributing importance to such factors is or should be a rational one, a process that can be completely under each person's control. I oppose the view that one's self-concept is fixed from birth, based on known or established factors, immutable, or part of one's basic nature.

In spite of our instincts, we are also capable of forming individual beliefs about who we are, whom we are related to, the significance we place on those relationships, what we want, and whom we will support or be influenced by. All these factors are subject to our review and to change, should we choose to redefine ourselves.

Insight #3: Who We Are

We are who we decide to be, regardless of the facts of our lives. For example, a person may grow up thinking that he or she is of Anglo-Saxon heritage and may develop a self-concept based on that belief. If this person later discovers that he or she has a grandparent of another heritage, the impact of that new factor can be either positive or negative. The person may choose to deny it, to disregard its significance, or to embrace it and explore the newly discovered heritage as a way of redefining his or her self-concept. It all depends on how the person views the new information and what he or she decides about the effect it will have.

Much of what influences us appears to function at the unconscious level, yet the conscious nature of the process is one of the most dramatic ways in which humans differ from animals.

I have found that only when my self-concept (including whatever cultural identity I have) is uncluttered by factors to which I alone have ascribed meaning can I relate to others as a fellow human being; only then can my attempts to lead or influence others be received as intended.

Insight #4: The Relevance of "Facts"

If a person has not incorporated specific facts or influences into his or her self-concept or identity, those will not be relevant to establishing rapport with that person.

As consultants, our goal is to influence others. Our attempts will not succeed unless we are first able to establish rapport.

When I work with Native American and Asian clients, it is apparent that my ethnic heritage differs from theirs. I am of Swedish descent, with blonde hair and blue eyes. My grandparents were born in Sweden, and my parents were born in the United States. Who would be able to predict from these facts anything about my self-concept?

When asked to tell about themselves, many people will respond by stating where they were born or where they live. I lived in one state until I reached adulthood, and I have lived in another state for more than two decades, yet I do not "identify" myself in terms of either. It would not occur to me to define myself in that way. Even though, for some others, the place where they were born or currently live may be a very significant factor, my self-concept is not significantly influenced by these factors. If someone is attempting to relate to me or influence me, it will have to be based on other factors.

Insight #5: Developing Followers

You cannot successfully lead without developing followers, and people cannot be influenced successfully unless they decide to accept the influence.

As consultants, we frequently address issues that, on the surface, seem to relate to cultural diversity and conflict resolution. Improving relationships, practices, and processes are our typical goals. There are many theories to guide us in these endeavors. What has not been well established is how to begin these processes based on a human connection. So, what are the implications for those of us who attempt to consult on cross-cultural issues, to be resources to persons who are "different" from us, or to influence others in general?

Insight #6: Establishing Rapport

The best way to establish rapport with others is in terms of our strongest shared factor: our humanness.

If I am to be accepted by others as a resource, if I am to succeed in leading them or influencing them, they must accept the premise that we share an important human nature and that it will be the basis of our relationship, by our mutual choice. Although the "who" I am attempting to relate to may or may not be completely knowable, most humans have the capacity to relate to another on the most basic (and contactful) level: their shared humanity. I believe that this level of relating is what we observe during times of great crisis and human tragedy—when the people from different "cultures" realize and acknowledge their shared human identity and decide to make sacrifices to ease the suffering of others or to accept help from others who are different from them.

This conscious decision process also is apparent when "cultural hatred" is passed from generation to generation and "cultural wars" and "ethnic cleansing" are carried out, based simply on group attitudes toward historic wrongs or what is believed to be rightful geographic boundaries. The only hope for influence in these situations is to unlock the mystery of how individuals can gain control of their behavior through reasoning and conscious choice—through selection of self-images based on rational thought and shared humanity.

Conclusion

Although it may be tempting (and seemingly simpler) to try to deal with groups of people based on broad generalizations, the fact is that this sort of thinking is rarely effective. The six insights presented in this article should help consultants (and others) learn to be more thoughtful in their endeavors to influence others.

Phyliss Cooke, Ph.D., *is a licensed clinical psychologist and consultant in private practice. She has previously been a senior consultant and dean of the intern and master's degree programs in HRD for University Associates/Pfeiffer & Company as well as an instructor at Kent State University. She is the author or co-author of numerous articles, instruments, and experiential learning activities.*

Dr. Cooke currently works with clients in the public and private sectors. She has worked for a variety of Native American clients in the U.S. and Canada and with clients in Australia, New Zealand, Singapore, and Hong Kong, focusing on cultural issues related to business practices and skills training. Dr. Cooke also is an adjunct faculty member in the Industrial and Organizational Department of the School of Psychology at Capella University.

Mentoring:
Empowering Human Capital
Mohandas K. Nair

Summary

Today's competitive organizations need employees with knowledge and skills to accept multiple roles and to excel in them. Fortunately, this human capital is available in-house. However, the individuals themselves are often not aware of their capabilities. This article suggests that an organization, through an institutionalized mentoring program, can enable its employees to discover the competencies within them. Through a process of understanding and action, the aware individual can power the organization to achieve excellent results in whatever it reaches out to do.

Competing for Customers

Change, as we all know, is a fact of life. Rapid development in products and services has led customers to demand the best. Competition enables them to get the best value for whatever they choose. If we want them to choose our products and services, we will have to provide this best value.

Competition for customers forces organizations to be "lean and mean." This means improving productivity and quality through the use of fewer resources. In the case of human resources, it translates into the need to use fewer people while simultaneously improving the abilities of the survivors. The survivors will have to improve their ability to perform: take initiative, be more creative, manage all resources more effectively, lead people and teams, and so on. To do this, individuals will have to improve their competence and capability along a wide spectrum of activities.

The Human Capital Dimension

To satisfy, delight, and earn the commendation of customers, organizations have to bring out the best in themselves through their processes. Since people drive all the processes, organizations have to get the best out of their people.

Every individual working in the organization should be a self-starter. He or she should be an intrapreneur, organize work in line with corporate goals, work in teams, lead and manage people as required, manage his or her own budget, spot opportunities, innovate, and move quickly to obtain results. The emphasis should be on self-management rather than on supervision.

The above concept is in line with the requirements of modern organizations. They require that better decisions be made more quickly to be more responsive to customer demand and competitive activities. Efficient use should be made of all resources—people, material, information, money, and so on. Organizations want people to dream, create, and invent new ideas and processes to not only satisfy customer needs but also to bring these dreams to reality. They require efficiency in the delivery of goods and services and the maintenance of a high level of quality in all their processes. They want their people to be in a continuous learning mode and to create a culture of continuous learning and development.

However, the majority of employees are not up to this critical organizational need. It is not because they lack potential to handle these tasks. It is because of a lack of awareness of their own ability to perform at high levels of effectiveness. There is also a lack of inspiration to reach out for the new and the challenges confronting them in their daily activities. Most of them need to be driven initially before they can get into their own drive.

Organizations recruit people to undertake various assignments so that the different processes that make up their work are handled satisfactorily. Individuals who are taken into the organization are brought in for their perceived skills to discharge their roles satisfactorily. Provided individuals are satisfied with the rewards and the environment provided by the organization, they would give their best depending on their own perception of their capability and competence. This effort may be sufficient to enable handling of normal activities, which help the organization maintain its basic processes. To face new challenges, temporary, one-off learning is usually provided through training programs. However, for new, more challenging assignments, the organization often looks outside for resources. The current resources are not "good enough."

Looking Within

Today's excellent organizations need high-performing individuals. They may not be readily available in the market—or not at a cost affordable to the organization. This would hinder the organization's plans to be the best in its area of activity. However, these competencies are available within the organization itself, among its incumbent employees. Each person has, over his or her life, logged in experiences and competencies that are not in current awareness. Occasionally, when in need, people utilize these skills and learning unconsciously. Since they are not conscious of this fact, they do not realize they have these abilities. Using an iceberg metaphor, the individual's awareness of his or her capability is only the tip of the iceberg. According to Sydney Harris, "Ninety percent of the world's woe comes from people not knowing themselves, their abilities, their frailties, and even their real virtues. Most of us go almost all the way through life as complete strangers to ourselves."

Once we help individuals to look introspectively and dive into their unconscious to start rediscovering themselves, we find an amazing treasure chest of capabilities just waiting to be tapped. However, the individuals cannot do this on their own. They need help. The process will take time and a lot of patience and persistence. This is where a mentor can help. By being a sounding board, friend, philosopher, and guide, the mentor can slowly and patiently help an individual on his/her road to self-discovery. With the individual slowly opening up, the organization can hope to start a process of learning and discovery, which will enable it to maximize the potential of its human resources. Employees, in turn, can become the instruments to drive powerful changes to enable the organization to become the best in its sphere of activities.

Establishing a Mentoring System

The Mentor

A mature person who has experienced life, in industry or elsewhere, can be a source of confidence and support to an individual to guide him/her through situations where he/she lacks adequate confidence. This mentor can help the mentee (the individual being mentored) take adequate risks to reach out to assignments and roles he/she does not believe he/she can handle. Playing various roles, depending on the situation—a coach, guide, guardian, networker, trainer, teacher, counselor—the mentor can help the mentee challenge him/herself to keep raising the bar.

A mentor encourages mentees to discuss their thoughts and ideas. Mentors help mentees to look at issues differently and encourage them to take calculated risks, guiding them on what should or should not be done or how to prepare before taking the plunge. Mentors are only cheerleaders; they do not interfere in the decisions mentees take as they work toward solutions. Mentors point out mentee strengths and encourage mentees to take advantage of opportunities in cases where they believe mentees have a high probability of success. To quote a Chinese proverb, "A single conversation across the table with a wise man is worth a month's study of books."

Advantages of Mentoring

Ordinary development programs, through training or education, do not provide adequate inputs in developing a fully rounded person—a prerequisite for building self-driven, mature, and motivated individuals. They can only fill up gaps in skills, knowledge, and attitudes. Also, they have a fairly temporary impact on the individual. With mentoring, however, there is continuous feedback, enabling the individual to focus on his or her development.

The System: Formal or Informal

The mentoring system can be formal or informal. An informal process in which there are no specific guidelines and where employees seek out their own mentors is an ideal system, as there is a natural pairing between a mentor and a mentee. The probability of success in achieving objectives is also better than in a formal system, as both parties have willingly entered into the relationship and are likely motivated. However, the process is left to chance and people may or may not work toward building the system in the organization.

A formal system, although in a way a forced situation, could also benefit an organization. The opportunity to institutionalize the system in the organization allows the organization to show the importance of the mentoring process. If the system becomes an embedded part of the organization's culture, then individuals will automatically reach out for the roles of mentor and mentee, as they will be seen as an important part of the organization's structure and ethos. This will ensure the success of the process, and the organization will benefit.

Making the Effort

The goal of mentoring paints a rosy picture of an organization reaching for and succeeding in maximizing the potential of its members. The path to this is not an easy one to tread. Like all efforts to change human behavior, this effort too is going to be difficult. It will require persistence and a gentle touch. When two individuals from two different hierarchies come together, with a third (the mentee's boss) thrown in, the equations are not going to be simple. These equations are going to be at the heart of a successful mentoring program.

Some Thoughts on System Implementation

There are no formulas or quick fixes for implementing a successful mentoring program. However, the program has a much better chance of success if some of the following are taken into consideration:

- The mentee is the customer and so drives the program. Unless the mentee wants to learn, grow, and change, the process will not work. Thus, the mentee has to be in control. This is hard on the mentor sometimes. As the senior member of the pair, there is often a need to control the process. The mentor has to understand that he or she has to be in the picture only when the mentee has a need. The mentor can offer comments and guidance only when he or she has judged the mentee as not having understood a particular issue, thought, emotion, or action.

- The organization should have a formal implementation system in place. There could be a governing body to review the system periodically and to mediate in any issues that arise, like a dispute between the mentor and the line manager of the mentee.

- The mentoring system should be institutionalized. The mentor role has to be accorded respect and a focus in the appraisal system. New employees should be encouraged to select mentors, preferably with the help and support of their line managers. During the appraisal of the mentee, the line manager should be encouraged to discuss the mentee's progress with the mentor.

- A "Mentoring System Manual" could provide information on the system. Some topics would include operation, the ethical code of practice, the structure and staffing, guidelines, and so on. This manual should be available to all members in the organization and should be provided to new employees during orientation.

- The mentee should be allowed to choose the mentor. Being either a mentor or a mentee should be voluntary activities.

- The mentor and the mentee should agree to the objectives of the assignment. Both parties should be extremely clear about this issue. If necessary, senior personnel could facilitate a clarification exercise wherein the objectives and the boundaries are discussed and written down. The goals might initially be narrowly focused, but could later be expanded, depending on the need.

- Once the process begins, the mentor and mentee should interact naturally. The primary onus on making the relationship effective will lie with the mentor.

- The mentor's approach should be tempered according to the mentee's characteristics: values, motivation, ability to achieve and succeed, maturity, etc. The mentor might take a more active role when the mentee is all at sea and work from a distance when the mentee has a high degree of maturity.

- Trust between the mentor and the mentee is paramount. Without trust, the relationship will not be sustained, and there will be no output from the process.

- The mentor, mentee, and the mentee's manager form a triad. The relationships among the three are very delicate. The mentor is a facilitator who helps the manager in the development process of his/her subordinate, the mentee. But the mentor cannot take over the manager's role or the mentee will suffer. The mentor and the manager should occasionally discuss the developmental needs of the mentee. The mentor may make suggestions for challenging assignments to enable the mentee to develop capabilities through experience. The mentee may be briefed on these meetings as appropriate.

- If the value systems of the mentor and the mentee are very different, the mentoring process will not proceed well. These values might include compliance with laws, honesty and credibility, treatment of employees, customer relationships, social attitudes, and so on. Rather than forcing the relationship if differences are great, it is better that the relationship be dissolved. If differences are minor, they may be overcome through discussion.

- The mentor should help the mentee develop a concept of excellence. This should be both for him- or herself and as an organizational goal and be a continuous theme in all meetings between the two.

- A good mentor does not provide answers. He/she asks questions, enabling the mentee to reach his/her own conclusions and to make appropriate decisions. The mentor cannot make decisions for the mentee. The mentor, using common sense, can help the mentee consider the risks inherent in various choices.

- The mentor should not have unrealistic expectations of the mentee. He/she must understand the major strengths and weaknesses of the mentee and help the mentee in proportion to his/her mental capacity. The focus is always on the number and nature of the options available to the mentee.

- The mentor's role is not to criticize, even constructively. He/she does not judge the achievement of the mentee, but enables the mentee to understand his/her own actions and, in the process, make his/her own judgments.

- The mentor, by participating in the journey, helps the mentee to improve and to "move on." He/she joins the mentee in the search for a practical and common-sense approach to the risks.

- The mentor and the mentee embark on the journey with open minds. Various issues will confront them along the way, and only the two of them can work on those issues. The focus will be on the journey, rather than the destination. As the journey progresses, the relationship between the mentor and mentee develops in terms of trust, compatibility, friendship, etc. A lot will depend on the openness with which the two approach their relationship.

- The mentor is not in the shoes of the mentee. Thus, the mentor cannot provide solutions. He/she can only help the mentee to discover his/her latent potential. The mentor can provide another perspective or perspectives about the issues.

- The number of mentees under a mentor will depend on the capability of the mentor. Mentoring should not be "work" (and definitely not stressful work). The mentor has to be calm and collected all the time. He or she must provide positive inputs to the mentee to build the mentee's confidence in his or her ability.

- There are various stages during an average work life. For most people, right up to the age of fifty, they are concentrating on building a career or business or making money to save for the future. In their fifties, people want to give back to society what they have learned from life. This is the time to involve them in the mentoring process. However, ensure that the mentor chosen really wants to help make a difference.

- The organization should consider hiring mentors if needed. They could first tap individuals who were formerly associated with the organization as employees, major customers, consultants, suppliers, etc. Freelance trainers, consultants, educators, and so on could also be of immense help.

The mentor can assist the mentee throughout the empowerment process as the mentee works toward greater autonomy and responsibility, including the following aims:

1. Have the desire to change and improve.

2. Have confidence in own ability to "do it."

3. Take up greater ownership of the assignment.

4. Learn more skills to handle a broader spectrum of activities.

5. Accept credit for achievements along the way.

6. Take on even more demanding work with higher risks.

Conclusion

Empowering themselves to accept greater responsibility is not an easy process for the majority of employees in an organization. This is primarily because of lack of confidence in their own ability. They are not aware that they have the necessary "stuff" to be a success. A mentor has the capability to help such individuals believe in themselves and put in maximum efforts to make a success of whatever they set out to achieve.

Resources

Clutterbuck, D. (2001). *Everyone needs a mentor.* London: Chartered Institute of Personnel and Development.

Doyle, B., & O'Neill, V.N. (2001). *Mentoring entrepreneurs: Shared wisdom from experience.* Cork, Ireland: Oak Tree Press.

Mohandas K. Nair *freelances as an HRD consultant and trainer. He has an engineering background, and his early work was in industrial engineering. He is an author of two books:* Thoughts to Live By *and* Management: From the Experts. *His vision is "to make a positive impact on every person I meet and 'touch' and in the process make them aware of their potential."*

Managing Sideways

Peter R. Garber

Summary

With the advent of both flatter and matrix organizations, it would seem that organizations would find better ways to communicate goals and create synergies across the organization. However, it's still not unusual to find planning and goal setting structured in a top-down manner. In this article, we explore the concept of managing sideways—also known as horizontal alignment—which is designed to take full advantage of an organization's strengths and synergies to increase efficiency and better meet organizational goals.

Managing sideways may sound more like something that might cause you to be off balance rather than an effective management technique. But managing sideways can help you discover ways to achieve your business objectives and help your organization reach its greatest potential. Managing sideways can help you improve communications, teamwork, resource utilization, and synergy in your organization.

Most managers view their responsibilities vertically, as in Figure 1, tending to think in terms of whom they report to and who reports to them. There is nothing incorrect in this view of a manager's role in an organization. After all, there must be boundaries for everyone's span of control. Even the manager of an entire business can only pay attention to a finite number of factors that influence the organization's success.

But what about all the things that fall between these vertical views of accountabilities and responsibilities? The many things that can "fall between the cracks" of these vertical slices cause tremendous waste and inefficiency. This causes millions, even billions, of dollars to be lost as common goals and potential synergies between these vertical slices of the organization go without attention or action.

Who is in the best position to see these lost opportunities? The answer is that anyone in the organization has the potential to realize these opportunities if they look in all directions rather than just their own vertical reporting relationships. It's all a matter of looking in the right places.

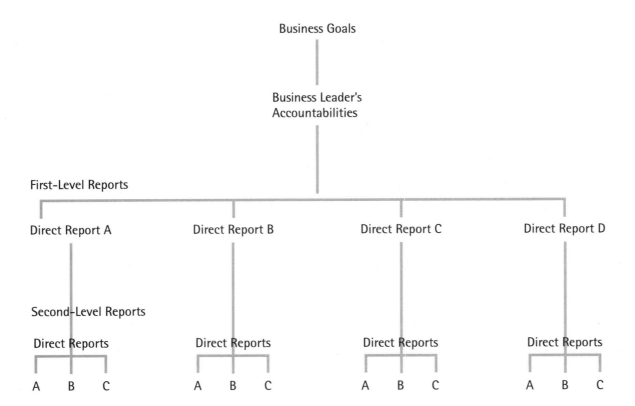

Figure 1.   Traditional Vertical Accountability

Setting Goals

Before we can explore how to increase efficiencies and synergies within an organization, we need to explore one of the driving factors in any organization: its goals.

Typically, a cascading goals alignment exercise takes place annually in an organization to ensure that the leader of the function's goals, or a subset thereof, is incorporated into each direct report's goals and their direct report's goals. The leader is typically energized to provide the resources to achieve and maintain these goals, particularly if the goals have been initiated by the leader. Leaders can also eliminate obstacles that may become barriers to others achieving these goals.

In this way, the leader of the function ensures that his or her accountabilities are the focus of everyone in every level on his or her reporting chart. Unfortunately, this review of accountabilities often is limited to the vertical reporting relationships in an organization, which is too bad, since a great deal of the natural momentum of the organization gets lost in these vertically aligned goals. This same downward push in a typical top-down hierarchy does not exist horizontally, however, and it is in this horizontal alignment that greater efficiency and success can be found.

Horizontal Alignment

Horizontal alignment refers to all of the potential synergy that exists across the organization as opposed to only thinking in terms of vertical reporting relationships and accountabilities. By managing horizontally, rather than exclusively vertically, you can find synergies that otherwise would remain undiscovered. There is a tremendous amount of positive momentum and gains that can be achieved by this broader perspective of the organization.

Benefits

Creating horizontal synergy creates a more collaborative organization focused on solving shared goals and objectives across the organization as well as up and down. It is in this culture and climate that an organization can be best aligned to meet its organizational goals. Instead of vertical slices of the same organization working autonomously, employees will begin to work together as a team, searching for ways to better enable one another to achieve shared goals. Resources will be more readily shared, communication will improve, and a greater sense of teamwork and collaboration will prevail throughout the organization. Different parts of the same organization will begin to communicate more thoroughly and effectively. This will help to develop both better working relationships and continuous improvement of the various interconnected processes within the same reporting relationship organization.

Instead of silos, with each faction working independently, this management approach can help everyone begin to work more interdependently.

Application

By looking more closely for these horizontal alignments throughout your organization, you may find you need to create new ways to cut across the organization. Finding this horizontal alignment and synergy can be particularly important in today's new matrix organizations. Having multiple reporting relationships can make goal prioritization extremely confusing and counterproductive. Identifying these horizontal alignments in a matrix reporting organization can make goal attainment less frustrating and much more possible. Gaining consensus among everyone involved in a matrix reporting situation can make what once appeared to be unconnected and possibly even competing goals now become more cohesive and achievable.

As can be seen in Figure 2, finding this horizontal alignment between the various functions in this business can have significant potential benefits. For example, by having Sales/Marketing, HR, Production, and R&D working together in a synergistic manner,

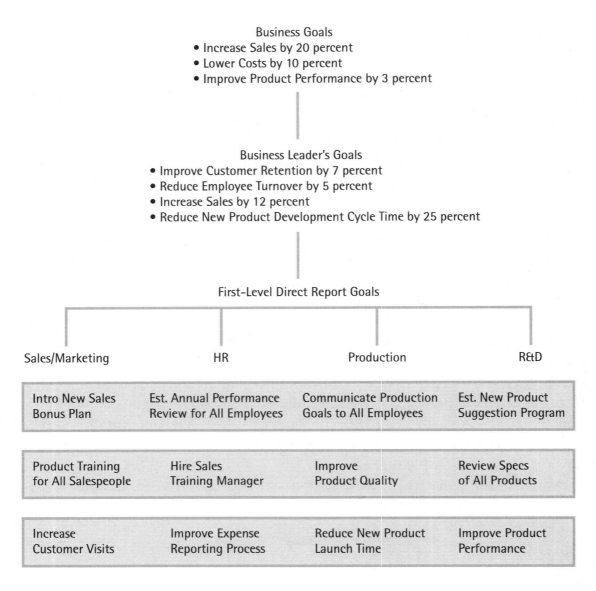

Figure 2. Horizontal Alignment

one of the business leader's overall goals—reduce employee turnover by 5 percent—can be better achieved. Rather than each of these departments autonomously trying to meet this goal, finding or even creating horizontal alignment among these functions greatly improves the organization's ability to achieve or exceed this goal. Each function contributes in different ways to this goal, adding its own unique contribution to the common objective.

Summary

In summary, there are seven steps to managing sideways.

1. Understand the vertical alignment in the organization first.

2. Organize goals that can be viewed horizontally at each level in the organization.

3. Look for commonalities in the goals and accountabilities in each level of the organization.

4. Highlight these shared or common goals and find ways that these goals could be worked on across the functional areas of the organization.

5. Create a list of shared goals and stakeholders in the achievement of these goals.

6. Arrange for a meeting or series of meetings with these stakeholders to share these common goals and create horizontally oriented action plans to achieve these goals.

7. Conduct follow-up meetings to track progress to achievement of these horizontal goals.

Peter R. Garber *has been working as a human resource professional for the past twenty-five years. He is currently manager of Equal Employment Opportunity for PPG Industries, Inc., headquartered in Pittsburgh, Pennsylvania. Garber is the author of a number of business books and articles, including his most recent book,* Giving and Receiving Performance Feedback. *He has been a contributor to* Pfeiffer Annuals *for the past ten years.*

An Integrative Model for Leading Change in Organizations

Linda Russell and Jeffrey Russell

Summary

We live in a time in human history that is increasingly being defined by tumultuous change: the rapid pace and scope of technological innovation, dramatic demographic and cultural shifts, the global economy and marketplace, the fundamental restructuring of our social systems and community, environmental degradation, evolving definitions of the "family," and the workplace.

The rapidity and depth of these changes compel leaders, organization development specialists, and training professionals to look for strategies and approaches that will help people more effectively understand and deal with these changes. This paper presents a model for understanding the emotional impact of change on individuals, which, in turn, can help us find a healthier, more productive response. It also offers insights into the actions that change leaders, OD specialists, and HRD professionals can take to guide people through the emotional journey of change.

The Nature of Change

Change disrupts the status quo. It breaks the momentum and continuities that represent the steady streams of our lives and organizations. Change "shocks" us out of our comfortable complacency and moves us into discomfort. This disruptive nature of change is true even for change that we perceive as positive and useful for us.

The dictionary defines change as "to make the form, content, or future course of something different from what it is, or from what it would be if left alone" and "to transform or convert." In both definitions, the heart of change is movement, transition, and discontinuity. Although a given change may be necessary for survival, it still fundamentally tampers with something stable that has been carried along by momentum.

It is, however, the nature or character of change (more than its definition) that concerns us here. When we are attempting to lead change in our organizations, we must understand its character. For when we understand its fundamental nature and its effects on those impacted by a change, we are more likely to be better prepared for the inevitable challenges it creates for our organization—and for us as change agents.

Two aspects of change's nature profoundly influence the course of change in an organization and its effects on others (Russell & Russell, 1998):

1. Change and the forces for change introduce disruptions that can significantly diminish both the organization's and the individual's capacities to envision a clear and positive future. The more disruptive a change is to the status quo, the greater it diminishes our capacity to envision the future, and the more likely it is that it will have a negative effect on our personal and organizational self-confidence, competence, morale, and overall self-esteem.

2. The path of change is unpredictable. The leaders of any given change may think they know where the change they are introducing will lead them, but there are always unintended consequences when you disrupt a stable system. As the rule of unintended consequences postulates, you may get a lot more than you expected—and none of what you had hoped for.

Effective change leaders quickly realize that the change they are introducing must undergo its own change in order to respond to emerging issues, customer and employee reactions, financial realities, pressing deadlines, and a host of other environmental, competitive, investment, and organizational pressures. In spite of a change leader's efforts to think strategically and effectively manage the change process, the path and destination of change is unknowable. Once initiated, a given change will follow its own path, which means that people other than the change leader will inevitably influence its future. The change leader's work, then, involves staying engaged throughout the change process by providing ongoing direction and guidance and actively working with others to shape the change as it evolves.

The unpredictable nature of change also has a significant impact on stakeholders—those whose lives are influenced by the change. Just when people think that they understand an impending change and how it is likely to affect them, the path that the change takes alters. When this happens, the common emotional response is anxiety, frustration, anger, and even a sense of having been betrayed by the organization and its leaders.

It's clear from our research that a key challenge for change leaders is to recognize this inherent nature of change—its potential for disruption and its unknowability—and then to work with this nature rather than against it. When change leaders accept and work with these characteristics of change, they are likely to experience less frustration and stress while increasing the chances that the change they promote will achieve the intended results for the organization and its stakeholders.

Exploring the Emotional Impact of Change

When a change initiative falls apart, it is usually due to a failure by change leaders to truly understand—and subsequently respond to and effectively manage—the significant emotional impact that a given change is likely to have on organizational stakeholders. The most effective change leaders recognize that a change of any size or shape has an emotional consequence for those asked to implement or live with a new direction.

In recent years a number of researchers and organization development authors have explored the effects of change on people. Beginning with Elizabeth Kübler-Ross's (1969) five-phased death and dying model (denial, anger, bargaining, depression, and acceptance), such authors as William Bridges (1991) (endings, neutral zone, new beginnings), Daryl R. Conner (1992) (stability, immobilization, denial, anger, bargaining, depression, testing, and acceptance), Flora/Elkind Associates (Scott & Jaffe, 2004) (denial, resistance, exploration, and commitment), and Daniel Oestreich (2001) (comfort and control, shock and denial, chaos and confusion, facing a new reality, and adapting and learning) have tried to describe the emotional toll that change can have on people. Each has identified patterns in the human response to change that suggest a near universal reaction that follows a predictable emotional journey.

Figure 1 represents an integrated model that seeks to blend together both our own consulting work in organizational change and the common themes from these ground-breaking authors. Our model presents a simple, clearly defined sequence of what we have found to be the most common human responses to change.

As Figure 1 indicates, when change is introduced into an organization, the once stable system moves from a place of stability and order (where everything is fixed, well-defined, and certain) toward disintegration (dis-integration, the absence of integration) and chaos (where there is an absence of explicit structure, definition, or certainty). As this changing system—with its structures, rules, and parameters now in flux—moves through instability and, eventually, toward a gradual return to stability and order, there is usually a significant and negative impact on those who work within this churning system. Understanding and dealing with this impact—an impact that follows a natural, inevitable, and predictable emotional journey in the face of disruptive change—is the focus

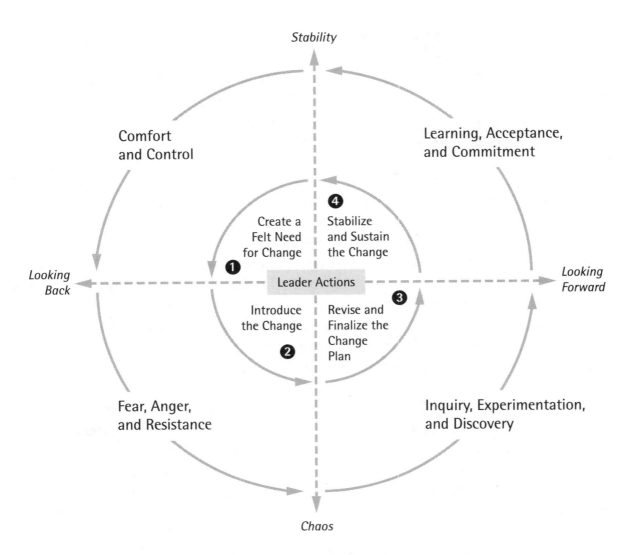

Figure 1.   Model for Change

of this paper. Beginning with Comfort and Control and ending with Learning, Acceptance, and Commitment, understanding this journey will help change leaders and OD and HRD professionals to better deal with the array of responses we see in others—and even ourselves—when confronted by change.

Phase 1: Comfort and Control

To introduce a change within a stable system or organization, the change leader must first Create a Felt Need for Change. As noted within the inner circle of leader actions in Figure 1, in this initial step of leading change, the leader introduces a destabilizing force while confronting the emotional roadblocks of comfort, control, and a sense of complacency. In the first phase of their emotional journeys through change—a place characterized by stability and certainty—people generally feel comfortable, safe, and in control of their lives. There is order and structure in their environment. They understand where they fit in and what's expected of them. Even if they are dissatisfied with the status quo, it is at least a familiar place. Their dissatisfaction is at least an unhappiness that they know. One key characteristic of this stage of the change journey is an attempt to hang on to the traditions and comforts of the past. This "clinging" to the way the world is is a major barrier to both personal and organizational growth.

At this stage, the greatest challenge for the change leader is simply to get people to wake up, to move them out of their comfort zones. That's why the actions called for in this stage involve giving people a reason to move. The effective change leader must create conditions in which people begin paying attention to the forces driving change and which are influencing the organization and its future success. For real change to take hold, people must first feel the need to move out of comfort and control, give up their attachments to the status quo, and respond to the forces that pose a perceived threat to their own long-term security, satisfaction, and health and to that of their organization.

Phase 2: Fear, Anger, and Resistance

Once someone realizes the need for change (whether begrudgingly or enthusiastically), he or she is soon plunged into the next emotional phase: Fear, Anger, and Resistance. This phase of the journey, marked by the absence of stable and comforting structures and combined with a nostalgic longing for the past, leads people to feel anxious and uncertain—as well as angry and fearful. These emotions surface because people have been forced to forsake that which they knew to be true about the organization and their roles within it. They have been told that the old dependable and reliable ways of the past and present are inadequate for the challenges of the future. Suddenly, the world is a more insecure and uncertain place.

How should leaders respond? Those who are leading a change should not be surprised by the fear, anger, resentment, and resistance that emerge. People are angry and fearful because much of what they knew to be true is no more and because they're not really confident about what should be true in the future—much less where they fit into this uncertain future. Preparing for this response is the change leader's first responsibility; the second is to listen to and empathize with employees' anxieties and fears; and the third is to integrate stakeholder issues, fears, and concerns into the design of the change itself.

In Introduce the Change as a follow-along to Create a Felt Need, the change leader offers specific solutions to the forces that are driving the need for change and the dilemmas on the road ahead. In creating a felt need for change, the leader suggested that the status quo wasn't adequate for meeting these challenges. By introducing ideas, approaches, and methods that address these dilemmas and challenges, the leader is offering a way out of the anxiety and confusion that results when people experience a felt need for change. The leader proposes new structures to fill the void created by the disintegration of the old.

As part of the leader's task of guiding stakeholders through this phase of their emotional journey, change leaders will need to explore what employees believe they are likely to lose under the new structures, rules, and methods. Both anger and fear emerge when people perceive that a change forces them to give up too much of what they value while gaining too little. People become fearful because they imagine that they will lose something that is important to them and angry because this is being taken away. These are natural and inevitable reactions.

To help manage these emotional responses, change leaders must acknowledge the perceived losses posed by change. As they begin to introduce new structures to replace those left behind, leaders must also listen to employee concerns, anxieties, fears, and doubts about the future and the new way of working. Change leaders must either try to convince people that the losses aren't likely (change their perceptions) or try to offset the perceived losses with new benefits and opportunities that stakeholders are likely to realize from a change.

William Bridges (1991), in his landmark book *Managing Transitions,* writes about the endings that change creates for people. He suggests that acknowledging what has ended for people, what they are losing, and what they are fearful of are essential leadership actions for this phase. With employee fears and anxieties reduced or at least compensated for (by an equivalent benefit or gain), the change leader can begin shifting attention to the last of the emotions in this phase: resistance to new ideas.

Although, to the change leader, a given change is seen as addressing the challenges ahead and an essential ingredient in the organization's future success, others are likely to see the change quite differently. Those who are asked to accept and implement the new methods or approaches may experience these so-called "solutions" as disruptive and threatening. Hence the emergence of resistance—the reluctance or even refusal by some employees to think, work, or act in a new way.

As with the other emotional responses to change, resistance is a natural and inevitable reaction when employees are asked to move in a new direction. Resistance is part of each person's cognitive autoimmune response: An internal process tests a change to determine the level of perceived threat that the change represents. If the perceived threat is low, the person is more likely to work through his or her reservations and concerns and accept the change fairly quickly. But if the change is perceived as a significant threat to the self and "business as usual," all of the person's systems can move into a "fight or flight" response. This is true even when we initiate a positive change that affects our lives (for example, getting married). Even when we make a change of our own free will, we are likely to experience some level of internal resistance (for example: "Getting married is great! But I'll be giving up some of my autonomy").

People tend to resist change because they . . .

- Fear the loss of something that they value.
- Lack trust in the motives of those leading the change.
- Fail to understand the change and its impact on their role, their work, their future.
- Fear a loss of control or influence over their future.
- Remember a negative experience with past change initiatives.
- Are change-averse.
- Disagree on the need for change or in the solutions offered to solve the "problem" behind the change.

Figure 2.   Why People Resist Change

Effective change leaders recognize that some level of resistance goes with any change and take proactive steps to better understand and deal with its causes early on in the process. As suggested in Figure 2, these causes can range from perceived losses and disagreements on the merits of the ideas behind a change to a lack of trust in those leading the change to people having change-averse personalities. Successful leadership strategies in response to resistance involve communicating the vision behind the change; listening to people's concerns, anxieties, and fears; establishing a trusting relationship; offsetting perceived losses with gains; and inviting people to "co-create" the change's vision.

Involving others in helping to design the change itself accomplishes two of the change leader's primary objectives in the change process: It tends to reduce employee resistance while, at the same time, actually refining and improving the intended change. When people are invited to help craft a change, they make it better by bringing their practical, in-the-trenches perspectives to bear on the proposed ideas. This increases the likelihood that the "great idea" proposed by the leaders can actually be implemented at the front line. And by inviting resisters with concerns and complaints to suggest changes to the change itself, its design is not only strengthened, but it is also left with the designers' "fingerprints," thereby reducing the intensity of their autoimmune responses. It is harder to reject something wholesale that you've had a part in developing or designing.

Phase 3: Inquiry, Experimentation, and Discovery

As people's anxieties, fears, and perceived losses are listened to and addressed in the change process, and as they begin to take part in designing the change itself, people move from focusing on the past to focusing on the future. They choose, consciously or unconsciously, to begin making the change work for them personally and for the organization. In turning toward the future and striving to make the change work for them on their own terms, people in this phase of the emotional journey help construct new structures and systems to replace those that were torn down as the system moved into chaos and instability.

This new phase in the emotional journey—Inquiry, Experimentation, and Discovery—is still an unstable and chaotic time, but one that is shifted toward the positive. In this phase, employees work to ensure that they experience positive outcomes by taking charge of how the organizational change plays out in their own work. They look for answers to such fundamental questions as where they are going, what they are expected to do, what they need to learn, and what rewards are available. As they explore answers to these questions—and with proper guidance—people in this phase find increasing levels of clarity, stability, and focus. The chaos gradually begins to subside with the emergence of new stabilizing systems and structures that result from the experimentation and discovery that occur in this phase of the process. Along with the dissipation of chaos and the emergence of a new structure and stability, in this phase people experience a gradual lessening of anxiety, fear, self-doubt, and uncertainty.

Leaders and OD/HRD professionals can be most helpful to people in this emotional phase of the change process when they Revise and Finalize the Change Plan to integrate the ideas generated by people who are discovering solutions to the challenges brought on by the forces for change.

Within this leadership response, leaders must provide both direction and support to those experiencing the change. When they provide direction, leaders remind people of the vision behind the change, its long-term goal, and why achieving this vision is important. When they provide support, leaders acknowledge the continuing frustrations with the ambiguity of the change and with not having ready answers to important questions. Support also involves giving people freedom to discover their own answers and to begin testing out these answers as they move forward. It involves answering questions truthfully (saying what we know and what we don't know), providing frequent updates on the progress of the change, facilitating one-on-one and group discussions about issues surrounding the change, acknowledging people's hard work in helping make the change happen, and celebrating accomplishments along the way. Finally, by continuing to incorporate the insights and ideas of others into the change's vision and plan, the plan is strengthened. When this occurs, the evolving change plan is more readily accepted by those experiencing the change.

Phase 4: Learning, Acceptance, and Commitment

If change leaders and those experiencing the change can effectively manage the chaos, anxiety, and frustration of the preceding phase, people will naturally move into the last phase of their emotional journey: Learning, Acceptance, and Commitment. In this phase people begin to see that the change—which has been tested, shaped, and molded by their own actions and the actions of others—is beginning to lead to tangible and positive results. They continue their search for answers to the challenges posed by the forces for change and the change itself as they enter this phase. And, as with the previous phase, the solutions they discover become integrated into their thoughts and behaviors as well as into the change plan itself.

The learning that occurs in this phase, sparked by the chaos and confusion of the change process and the need to restore direction and stability, is the first sign of a strong emotional commitment to the change. For the first time, people who may have initially resisted the proposed change begin realizing the promised opportunities and benefits.

The insights and solutions that employees learned in the Inquiry, Experimentation, and Discovery phase become integrated into an emerging definition of their new workplace roles, functions, and behaviors. They see other evidence that, despite how difficult the transition to a new way of working might have been, the change is starting to produce results that effectively respond to the internal or external challenges that precipitated the change in the first place.

Leaders can be most helpful during this phase by working to Stabilize and Sustain the Change. Leader actions to stabilize the change include encouraging and supporting employee learning and celebrating their successes and accomplishments. Celebrating the desired behaviors and rewarding the successes people are beginning to experience encourage people to continue taking actions that sustain the change. In this phase change leaders and OD/HRD professionals must build or strengthen organizational systems, structures, policies, and procedures that reflect the desired change and that reinforce the desired employee behaviors. These can include new methods for goal setting and performance management, reward systems that provide incentives for the desired behaviors, information systems that give people the data that they need when they demonstrate the new behaviors, training programs that teach people the skills and knowledge required by the change, and the appropriate tools and equipment that people need to achieve their newly defined goals.

Although the leader's efforts have helped guide people into and through the change to achieve the vision behind the change and arrive at a better place, the relentless process of environmental challenge and organizational change continues. For just as the organization's leaders and employees sit back to enjoy the positive results from their hard work (and perhaps because of this "sitting back"), people will inevitably begin a gradual drift into the early stages of Comfort and Control. And the cycle begins again!

Regaining stability in a better place—a place where the change has led to significant improvements in the organization's health and effectiveness—is a good thing. Wise leaders, however, recognize that there is danger in the comfort and complacency of organizational success. This is the paradox: Efforts that change leaders take to stabilize and reinforce the new ways of thinking and working may subsequently reduce employee openness to new ideas, further improvements, or the next needed change. Effective leaders understand that an organization that endures over the long term can never rest. While they must take action to stabilize the change and provide a place to help people reintegrate themselves into their new roles and functions, leaders must also prepare employees for the next change—and the inevitable journey through the change process.

Ten Governing Assumptions About Organizational Change

The change model introduced in this paper is based on ten fundamental governing assumptions about change, about how people respond to the forces of change, and how leaders can best influence the choices people make in the face of change. We want to make these assumptions explicit so you can better understand both the origin of our model and how to apply it in your own organization.

Our assumptions about change and how to lead people through it successfully include the following:

1. *Change is inevitable; growth is optional.* Change is simply part of the human experience. It is ever-present and inescapable. While people can't turn their backs on change, they do have the ability to turn their backs on growth and learning. And the absence of growth and learning leads to decline and obsolescence.

2. *Change is difficult because it moves people out of their comfort zones.* When we're in the Comfort and Control phase, we feel safe; we know the territory. Change that moves us out of our comfort zone is like sitting on a tack: we have to stand up in spite of our desire to take it easy. Change introduces pain as a catalyst to move away from comfort, control, and complacency.

3. *People don't resist change as much as they resist being changed.* There will always be some level of resistance to any change, but the more we involve people in a hands-on way to help define the change, the less they will work against it. When people design their own change, they recognize their own genetic fingerprints. Their immune response systems say, "Hey, it's okay. I still may not like this change, but I recognize part of me in the change."

4. *Resistance to change occurs for a reason.* It emerges due to inadequate communication, the loss of something of value, mistrust of the motives or goals of change leaders, anxiety about an uncertain future, disagreements over the design of the change, or the temperament of the person affected by a given change (change-averse versus change-embracing). Successfully dealing with resistance means understanding its origins.

5. *People respond to change differently, based on their personalities, histories, personal visions, and perceptions of the surrounding environment.* The lesson from this assumption? Make room in your change process to help people move through change starting

from wherever they are. Don't assume that everybody starts at the same place or moves at the same pace. In fact, some of your staff may be way ahead of you.

6. *You can't change people; only they can make the choice to change.* Change leaders and OD/HRD professionals can, however, try to influence the choices people make in the face of change.

7. *The complexity and size of a change matter.* The more complex and expansive a change, the greater the level of potential disruption, the higher level of likely resistance, and the greater the need for ongoing two-way communication. People desire continuity in their lives, and complex change often fundamentally alters both their sense of self and their hope for the future.

8. *You can never communicate too much during a difficult and complex change.* If people don't have information, they will make it up (and their version is usually far more Draconian than yours will ever be). Keep information flowing before, during, and after a change. Clear information channels help people work together, know what's ahead and what to expect, track the progress they've made, constructively vent their frustrations, and prepare themselves for the next change.

9. *Resilience enables people to thrive during a change.* Those who fare best in the face of change have the characteristic of resilience—the capacity to bounce back after a shock or setback. Effective leaders embody this attribute in their own lives and help their staff develop it in their lives. Resilience includes such characteristics as being self-assured, having a clear personal vision, being flexible in the face of uncertainty, being proactive, having interpersonal competence, being socially connected, having problem-solving skills, and being proactive.

10. *Leaders don't control change; they guide, shape, and influence it.* Once initiated, change follows its own nonlinear path in response to uncertainties, reactions from the system, and guidance from the sidelines. The lesson? Rather than focusing their efforts on tightly controlling a change, leaders should instead focus on giving it order and structure, being open to new directions to the change, and guiding the change as it evolves. Give direction, provide incentives, and give people the freedom to explore.

Conclusions

Introducing a change in an organization elicits inevitable and predictable responses in those who are affected by the change. As a change creates instability in the organization or system, people start an emotional journey that begins from a place of Comfort and Control; moves through Fear, Anger, and Resistance; then Inquiry, Experimentation, and Discovery; and, finally, Learning, Acceptance, and Commitment.

Change leaders have a responsibility to understand this journey and to take the appropriate actions to help people first begin the change journey (by creating a felt need) and then to guide them successfully through the pain of change toward a healthier place—one that meets the initial challenge presented by the forces for change.

Introducing a change successfully requires that change leaders, organization development specialists, and HRD professionals learn this integrated change model and then take the steps they need to take to make change happen.

References

Bridges, W. (1991). *Managing transitions.* Reading, MA: Addison-Wesley.

Conner, D.R. (1992). *Managing at the speed of change.* New York: Villard Books, Random House.

Kübler-Ross, E. (1969). *On death and dying.* New York: Simon & Schuster/Touchstone.

Oestreich, D. (2001). *Our star.* Redmond, WA: Oestreich Associates.

Russell, J., & Russell, L. (1998). *Managing change.* Dubuque, Iowa: Kendall/Hunt, CUNA and Affiliates.

Russell, L., & Russell, J. (2003). *Leading change training.* Washington, DC: ASTD Press.

Scott, C.D., & Jaffe, D.T. (2004). *Managing change at work* (3rd ed.). Boston, MA: Crisp.

Jeffrey and Linda Russell *are co-directors of Russell Consulting, Inc., of Madison, Wisconsin. For more than fifteen years, they have provided consulting services in such areas as leadership, strategic planning, change implementation, employee surveys, organization development, and performance coaching. Their clients include Fortune 500 companies, small businesses, nonprofit organizations, and government agencies. Their most recent book is* Leading Change Training *(ASTD Press, 2003). They publish* Workplace Enhancement Notes.

What If We Took Teamwork Seriously?

W. Warner Burke

Summary

A great deal of time is spent talking about the importance of teams and teamwork. Yet it appears that little occurs or, if it does, the effects are not long-lasting. This article addresses why teamwork is less than 100 percent effective and what must be taken into consideration in order for it to be more effective.

Recently I witnessed something rare, an exceptional event. Six ad hoc teams in an organization presented the results of their work. For six months, each team of seven people had labored diligently on a significant problem or issue for its company. A final off-site event (two previous training and progress-report type off-site meetings had occurred) was held to hear each team's report and to make decisions regarding its recommendations. While there was some variance in the results of performance across these six teams, on the whole their work was impressive and rare compared with most such activities in organizations. They had accomplished much in spite of the fact that all team members had to maintain their regular, normal responsibilities during the six-month period; that is, the teams' work was in addition to each person's daily job responsibilities.

Typical Teams

No doubt all of us have seen if not been a part of a task force with similar responsibilities over a similar period of time. What made this event exceptional?

Before considering the exceptions, however, a brief word about what was not special about these teams. First, each team was given the task of studying a company-wide problem or issue that had been in existence for quite some time; that is, it had been a lingering problem but had never really been addressed. It was time, if not past time, for something to be done. Each team tackled a different problem/issue; thus, there were six different tasks. There is nothing special about these team assignments. Organizational executives often compose task forces to take on such assignments.

Second, the teams were composed of individuals from different functions and business centers within the company. Composing task forces representing a cross section of the organization is common. Third, the team size of seven members was about right for the types of tasks. Again, nothing new here; task forces and similar groups are often about seven, plus or minus two members.

Exceptional Teams

What, then, was special and exceptional regarding the work of these teams?

First, each and every team member at the end stated publicly what he or she had learned. In most cases, each person said something about being challenged, stretched. Yes, there was overlap among some forty statements, yet there was a sufficient number of unique expressions to make these statements ring with credibility.

Second, as stated above, the quality did vary somewhat from team to team, but the lowest performing team among the six would make most executives in most organizations happy.

Third, the teams were diverse, not only representing a cross section of the company but with a mix of genders and ethnicities in each group as well. We preach diversity, and should in my opinion, yet a diverse mix of people who achieve high performance is no small accomplishment.

Exceptional Outcomes

Why was this a special event, an exceptional outcome?

The most important reason was the fact that each team had a highly challenging and compelling goal. The outcome of each team's work would potentially have a significant impact on the future of the company. Katzenbach and Smith (1993) claim that high-performing teams are rare. Moreover, what they argue is that a challenging goal is an absolute necessity for high performance.

A second reason was the immediate feedback and impact of the work. After each team had presented, all others answered a brief questionnaire rating, among other things, the feasibility of the team's recommendations. Then the team met in private with the CEO to discuss its recommendations. Next, the CEO met in the main room with two representatives from the presenting team and with his key executives in a "fishbowl" setting to decide on the recommendations. In other words, immediate action, one way or the other, was taken on each team's recommendations.

Another reason for this exceptional work in teams was the fact that these events were part of and integral to a larger change effort for the entire organization. The teamwork, even though ad hoc, was not an isolated set of events.

And, finally, there was pressure to perform well. Each group presented to members of the other five teams—their peers—as well as to the top executives of the company.

Effective Teamwork

We talk and talk about the value of teams and teamwork, but little real, effective teamwork occurs or, in any case, if achieved at all only lasts for a brief period (Burke, 1995). Why is this so? Among myriad reasons, here are a few that stand out:

1. We have seen and experienced such mediocrity, why bother?

2. Working as a member of an ad hoc team means attending yet another series of boring meetings.

3. Teamwork takes time, and we have so much individually to do that team participation requires such a sacrifice.

4. While there may be a chairperson for the team, real leadership is often lacking, with a consequence being a lack of clarity, unresolved conflicts, and eventual feelings of imposition and resentment.

5. And perhaps most important of all, who cares anyway? The team may work hard to produce good results, but the likelihood is that insufficient attention will be paid to its work.

To increase the effectiveness of teams, we must take teamwork seriously, that is, we must pay careful attention to such matters as:

- Goals: making certain they are challenging.

- The context within which the team's work will occur: ensuring it is part of some larger effort tied directly to organizational mission and strategy rather than an isolated event.

- Team composition: making certain the teams have the unique talent required for the task; the proper mix of people, i.e., experience and personality; and the right number of members, which, of course, should be a function of the nature and complexity of the task.

- Results: how the team's outcomes will be considered and treated, particularly with respect to decision making for the organization.

- Recognition: how the team's work will be evaluated and recognized by management, especially the CEO.

These five considerations are not exhaustive by any means but represent some of the most important matters to address to increase the odds in favor of team effectiveness.

References

Burke, W.W. (1995). Organization change: What we know, what we need to know. *Journal of Management Inquiry, 4*(2), 158-171.

Katzenbach, J.R., & Smith, D.K. (1993). *The wisdom of teams.* Boston: Harvard Business School Press.

W. Warner Burke, Ph.D., *is the Edward Lee Thorndike Professor of Psychology and Education at Teachers College, Columbia University, where he has been since 1979. He heads the graduate programs (M.A. and Ph.D.) in social-organizational psychology. He combines his academic life with practice and is currently working with Barclays Bank, GE, and a couple of nonprofit organizations. In August 2003, he was the first recipient of the Academy of Management's new Scholar-Practitioner Award, and in October 2003, he received the Organization Development Network's Lifetime Achievement Award. His latest book is* Organization Change: Theory and Practice.

A Structural and Behavioral Model of Human Resource Planning

A. Venkat Raman

Summary

In this article, a conceptual model is proposed, summarizing the influence of structural configuration of an organization, as well as the resultant behavioral outcomes, on planning for human resources in an organization.

Human resource professionals, who may consider human resource planning as a complex quantitative calculation, will be able to understand the context in which organizational factors influence employee turnover, absenteeism, demand for additional staff, and ability of the organization to attract quality employees and the consequent effects of these factors on performance, productivity, profitability, and organizational restructuring.

Human resource planning is generally considered to be a quantitative calculation (in the form of estimations and projections of demand and supply) carried out by the line managers based on the business plans. Human resource managers typically consider the concept of human resource planning in terms of behavioral outcomes such as employee turnover, absenteeism, retention, recruitment needs, etc. This article explores how the concept of human resource planning should be understood as an outcome of interplay among the structural configuration of an organization and the subsequent impact on management systems, behavioral dynamics, performance and productivity, and profitability, leading to organizational restructuring, in a cyclical manner.

In the first part of the article, a conceptual model in the form of a flow chart is presented, illustrating both empirically verified relationships as well as hypothetical relationships between the various dimensions stated in each of the boxes. (See Figure 1.)

In the second part of the article, evidence from research literature is provided to substantiate the conceptual model.

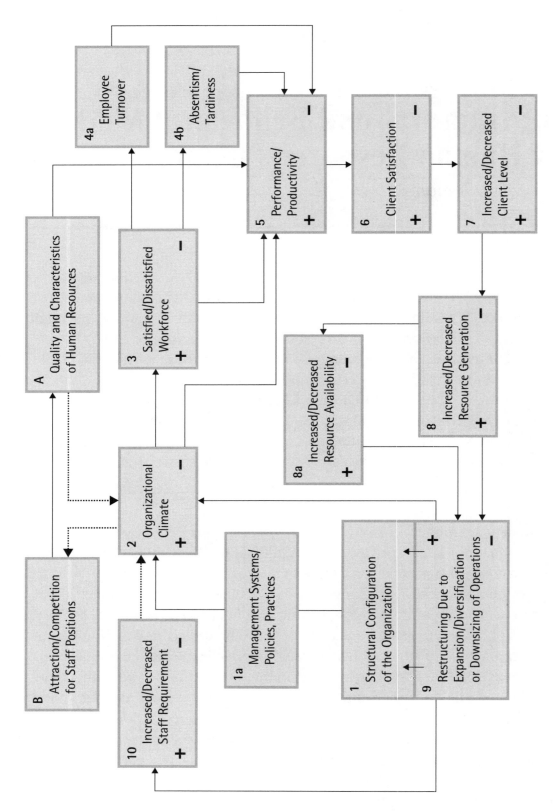

Figure 1.   Structural and Behavioral Model of Human Resource Planning

A Structural and Behavioral Model

Every organization structures the internal configuration of its work activities into certain hierarchical and administrative subsystems, depending on the functional requirements, environmental contingencies, technology employed, and the resources available (Box 1 in the flow chart). The structural configuration of an organization (measured in terms of size, complexity, formalization, etc.) determines the management systems, policies and practices (Box 1a). Such policies are clearly intended to manage the resources, including the human resources, in an efficient manner. Management systems, more specifically the human resource policies and practices, are likely to impact the behavioral dynamics of people working in an organization.

One of the most widely used measurements of behavioral outcomes (of organizational structure and management systems) is "perceived organizational climate" (Box 2). Organizational climate is how the organizational incumbents perceive various attributes, events, practices, and procedures of the organization or subsystems in terms of types of behavior expected and rewarded. Organizational climate could be either positively perceived (+) or negatively perceived (–). It is well-established that perceived organizational climate influences job satisfaction among the employees (Box 3). However, there may not be any causative or direct relationship between the climate and job satisfaction. For example, an employee may perceive the organization to be a good place to work (+ climate), but may be dissatisfied (– satisfaction) with the job. Similarly, an employee may feel that the organization is not a good place to work (– climate), but may be highly satisfied (+ satisfaction) with the job. Dissatisfied employees (–) are more likely to either leave the organization (resignation or voluntary turnover) (Box 4a), or resort to absenteeism (dissatisfied and yet unable to leave the organization) (Box 4b). Perceived organizational climate combined with employee satisfaction level induces improved performance and overall organizational productivity (Box 5). Positively perceived climate (+) and satisfied employees (+) are more likely to perform better (+), and are likely to be more productive, than those who are dissatisfied. It is presumed that negatively perceived climate (–) and/or dissatisfied employees (–) would likely lead to weaker performance and reduced productivity. Here the notion of productivity and performance needs to be understood from the overall organizational perspective rather than as an individual outcome. Productivity and performance could also be reflected in the form of client (customer) satisfaction (Box 6). Client satisfaction will determine the volume of clientele (Box 7). Higher levels of client satisfaction (+) lead to an increase in clientele (+); client dissatisfaction (–) leads to a decline in clientele (–). Client satisfaction/dissatisfaction may affect the organization's profitability (or resource generation) (Box 8). More satisfied customers, and the resulting increase in clientele, lead to greater profitability (+).

It is hypothesised that increased profitability (+) leads to the following:

1. Availability of adequate resources (Box 8a) (+). Resource availability induces the organization toward expansion, diversification, and other such growth-oriented business plans (Box 9). This could be termed as positive restructuring (+).

2. A positive restructuring of the organization (growth), creating more functional units and administrative subsystems. Not only does the structural configuration of the organization undergo a change, but it also necessitates commensurate changes in the management systems and policies (e.g., control and coordination mechanism, increased formalization of work flows, etc.).

3. Management policies in a growing (positively restructuring) organization could create conducive working conditions in the form of increased rewards and incentives, better career opportunities, job enrichment, etc., which could lead to positively perceived organization climate. And the consequent effects complete a virtuous cycle.

4. Positive restructuring, and the resultant expansion and diversification, could lead to demand for more employees (+) (Box 10). Demand for more staff increases the career avenues and promotional opportunities for the existing employees, thus inducing a positively perceived climate of opportunities.

5. However, the capacity of the organization to attract prospective employees (new employees) will depend on the perceived image of the employer and on the organizational systems and management policies (Box B). It is assumed that some organizational climate variables could be proxy measures for "perceived image of the employer."

6. A larger number of applicants provides a greater opportunity for the organization to hire better quality employees (Box A). It is assumed that the quality and characteristics of the new employees may influence (1) the quality of organizational climate, through organizational socialization, new skill sets, and values, and (2) organizational performance and productivity.

It is further hypothesised that declining (–) profitability (Box 8) leads to the following:

1. Shortages of resources (– resource availability) (Box 8a), which lead to downsizing in the form of sell off, closures, or divestments of certain business units. This could be termed as negative restructuring (–) (Box 9).

2. Negative restructuring (downsizing) necessitates commensurate reduction in functional units and administrative subsystems. It also necessitates changes in the management systems and policies (e.g., rigid cost control, less autonomy for managers, centralization of decision making, etc.).

3. In a negatively restructuring organization, employees may face career stagnation, reduced incentives, uncertainties, etc. Due to such constraining management practices, employees may perceive a less favorable (negatively perceived) organizational climate. The consequent effect of negatively perceived organization climate completes the vicious cycle.

4. Negative restructuring and the resultant downsizing could lead to surplus workforce, necessitating retrenchment of the employees (–) (Box 10). Employee retrenchment generally leads to widespread discontentment, further influencing the negatively perceived organizational climate.

5. Even if the organization wishes to hire new employees, the number of prospective job applicants may be less than desired due to the perceived constraints in management practices and less favorable organizational climate (Box B).

6. A limited number of applicants may lead the organization to either repeat the recruitment effort (expending resources) or to hire lower-quality applicants (Box A). Hiring under-skilled or low quality employees in turn leads to undesirable consequences such as increased training costs and attitudinal and performance problems.

The conceptual model presented here is partially supported by research literature, which is reviewed in the following section.

Research to Support the Model

Organization Structures

Mintzberg (1979) defined the structure of an organization as the way labor is segmented into task activities and the methods used to coordinate these activities. Organization structure emanates from the interplay of the organization's context, purpose, size, resources, technology, environmental dependencies, and ownership (Scott, 1992). There has been a wide range of opinion among the organization theorists regarding the structural configuration of organizations, ranging from a traditional bureaucratic model to a contingency model. Mintzberg (1991) argues that there is no one blueprint for an effective organization structure and that organizations must build their own structures using established forms or combining them.

Structural Variables

Studies on organizational structure have taken either an "anatomical" view, (i.e., age, size [number of employees], ownership, hierarchies, division of labor, span of control, differentiation, etc.) or an "operational" view, (i.e., centralization, formalization, standardization, etc.). Some researchers have also recognized the need for inclusion of psychological subsystems in organization structure (Kalleberg & Van Buren, 1996; Schminke, Cropanzano, & Rupp, 2002; Sommer, Bae, & Luthans, 1997).

Derek Pugh and his associates (1968) developed three dimensions that are widely accepted for measuring organization structure: (1) structuring of activities, i.e., degree of employee behavior that can be specified through routines, procedures, and formal written records, degree of specialized roles (specialization or complexity), degree of standard rules and procedures (standardization), and the degree of instructions and procedures (formalization). Specialization is also referred to as differentiation or complexity, which can occur both horizontally and vertically. Vertical complexity refers to the levels in the organizational hierarchy, while horizontal complexity refers to the division of labor or the number of differentiated functional units at the same hierarchical level; (2) concentration of authority (centralization), i.e., the extent to which authorized decision making discretion is concentrated at the top or outside the organization; and (3) control of the work flow, i.e., the extent to which control of the work activities is exercised by individual judgments or by impersonal procedures (processes).

In summary, size, complexity, formalization, and centralization are the four most critical factors reflective of organization structure, and they are closely interdependent.

Structure and Organizational Outcomes

According to Kalleberg and Van Buren (1996), the difference in management practices and employee benefits between larger and smaller organizations—in terms of their earnings, fringe benefits, promotion avenues, and autonomy—could be influenced by (a) product-market characteristics, (b) labor market characteristics, (c) relationship between the organization and its institutional environment, (d) structure of the organization, (e) unionization, (f) job characteristics, and (g) quality and skill of the workforce.

Size is also positively associated with employees' striking and absenteeism (Marginson, 1984). A decline in organizational size could stimulate both structural changes and stability (McKinley, 1993;), increase centralization, and destabilize the organization's existing formal and informal control mechanisms (Tushman & Romanelli, 1985).

Complexity and formalization also induce certain organizational outcomes. More complexity means more departments and more managers and a smaller average span of control. Formalization and centralization are strongly correlated to productivity, quality, efficiency, and organizational adaptability to environmental contingencies (Burns, 1995; Glisson & Martin, 1980).

Structure and Behavior

Structure is a method of regulating behavior in order to achieve a common purpose in a coordinated manner (Scott et al., 1981). The attitudes most frequently measured with respect to organization structure are perception of organizational climate, job satisfaction, alienation, interpersonal relations, and cooperation. The behavioral outcomes that have been studied in relation to structure include absenteeism, turnover, labor disputes, and performance.

While emphasizing the influence of structure on employee perceptions of organizational features, Turnipseed (1990) offers the following argument: "Seldom are administrators correct in assuming that organization structure or their management tactics are working in the manner in which they are intended. In fact, the appropriateness of their activities may not be the key issue. Rather, the perceptions of the employees should be the crucial concern—it does not matter which management actions or organization structures are right and which are wrong—it is the employees' perceptions of them which triggers their responses" (p. 249). "Often visible difficulties that trouble management, such as interpersonal problems among employees, high turnover, low productivity, excessive grievances, and low quality work, are not the problems, but rather, symptoms of a greater hidden problem. [Organizational] climate assessment is useful in identifying [and evaluating the wide range of work-related] phenomena, which can be the underlying cause of the easily observed symptoms" (p. 260).

Size, centralization, and formalization as structural factors have been shown to consistently and effectively influence climate, and perceived fairness and justice (Burke & Litwin, 1992; Schminke, Cropanzano, & Rupp, 2002; Sommer, Bae, & Luthans, 1997). In fact, the relationship of centralization and formalization to climate assumes a central focus in an OD model. Management practices and structural features of an organization both influence the climate, in both manufacturing and service sectors. Human resource management practices have been found to strongly influence the climate for service (Schneider, Wheeler, & Cox, 1992).

Organizational Climate

Climate can be defined as how the organization's incumbents perceive the events, practices, procedures, and types of behavior that are expected and rewarded (Schneider, 1990). Schneider characterized the concept of climate as follows:

- A set of perceptual measures that are primarily descriptive rather than evaluative;

- The level of inclusiveness of items, scales, and constructs are macro rather than micro;

- The units of analysis are attributes of the organization or specific subsystems rather than individuals; and

- The perceptions have potential behavioral consequences.

Litwin and Stringer (1968), pioneers in research on organizational climate, illustrate three distinct approaches to the study of climate: (1) the perceptual measurement of individual attributes; (2) the perceptual measurement of organizational attributes; and (3) the multiple measurements of organizational attributes by combining perceptual and more "objective" measurements.

According to Schneider and Reichers (1983), climate arises out of structural characteristics of an organization. Secondly, selection—attraction and attrition of individuals—produces homogenous organizational membership, resulting in similar climate perceptions. Individuals seek and are sought out by organizations to ensure an appropriate match between individual and organizational characteristics.

Climate is not good or bad, but positive or negative. Depending on the value structures of the organization, various climates can exist, such as a climate for productivity, service, innovation, or safety (Schneider, Wheeler, & Cox, 1992). Conceivably, more than one climate might co-exist within an organization.

Climate Outcomes

Climate is positively associated with organization-level outcomes (productivity, firm performance, quality of output/services, creativity) as well as individual-level outcomes (ability to initiate changes in a team, role conflict, commitment, job satisfaction, absenteeism, willingness to leave the organization) (Isaksen & Lauer, 2002; Jansen & Chandler, 1994; Ostroff, 1993).

Schuster (1986), in a study of the 1,000 largest industrial and three hundred largest non-industrial firms in the United States, found a significant relationship between employee-centered management practices (motivational strategies) and financial performance of the firm. Schuster et al. (1997), in a five-year quasi-experiment on a Canadian firm (using fifteen dimensions of employee perceived work environment) found strong evidence that "the improvement in motivation, morale, and commitment . . . has led to significantly improved organizational performance (i.e., financial performance)" (p. 223).

When employees describe their workplace as one of service-focused routines and rewards, customers also reported receiving high-quality service. General measures of human resource climate are also related to customer perceptions of service quality and customer satisfaction (Paradise, 1991; Schneider, 1990; Schneider, Wheeler, & Cox 1992; Tornow & Wiley, 1991).

Organizational Climate–Job Satisfaction

Innumerable research studies have clearly indicated that organizational climate influences individual satisfaction and job satisfaction among employees, both in business organizations as well as service organizations.

According to Shugars et al. (1991), construct of job satisfaction is influenced by three primary factors: (1) work characteristics—both the actual and perceived features of the job and its rewards; (2) worker attributes—demographic characteristics, emotional well-being, and personality factors; and (3) non-work factors—social interaction, family life, and general life satisfaction.

Age, gender, marital status, education, first job, personality-job-organization congruency (PJO fit), and pre-employment expectations are important demographic factors in affecting satisfaction levels. Ostroff (1992) suggests that organizations that desire satisfied employees can either select employees with a predisposition to be satisfied or create a work environment that facilitates satisfaction, or both.

Job Satisfaction

Outcomes

The literature on job satisfaction suggests that one of the major reasons for the keen interest in this area is the widely held view that job satisfaction influences two kinds of consequences: (1) behavioral outcomes (negative consequences such as grievances, absenteeism, intention to quit, actual turnover, and the subsequent cost to organization) and (2) performance-related outcomes, such as productivity, quality, and cost of operations (Mitra, Jenkins, & Gupta, 1992; Mobley, 1982; Tett & Meyer, 1993).

Turnover often results in additional costs for recruitment, selection, and training and adversely affects the quality of services in service organizations, reduces productivity, and impairs group cohesion (Cascio, 1991). Lee and Mitchell (1994) propose that job satisfaction and job alternatives are the key antecedents to employee turnover. The relationship between job satisfaction and turnover will be strong during periods of low unemployment (high opportunity) and weak during the periods of high unemployment (Carsten & Spector, 1987). According to Campion (1991), only dysfunctional turnover is considered bad for the organization, for example, the loss of good performers that the organization would require and who will be hard to replace. The consequences depend on the productivity of the former employee relative to the new employee, cost differences (in salary) between the employees, and the cost of the transactions (termination and recruitment).

There are several reasons why turnover rates of an organization should receive more attention. Accurate forecasting and planning of an organization's human resource requirements includes both an awareness of turnover rates and a strategy for keeping turnover rates at a desired level.

Performance

Research has shown that employees who are satisfied with their jobs are more likely to be productive (Tett & Meyer, 1993). Shugars et al. (1991) contend that numerous studies exploring the association between overall job satisfaction and job performance have found a consistently significant correlation between the two. Ostroff (1992) finds that organizations with more satisfied employees tend to be more effective than organizations with less satisfied employees. Ostroff further contends that most research examining the relationship between satisfaction and performance has been done solely on individuals within organizations. However, it is likely that a study of satisfaction and performance at the organizational level would show that organizations that have more satisfied employees are more productive and profitable than organizations where employees are less satisfied. The satisfaction-performance relationship at the organizational level may be stronger than the relationship at the individual level. Both human relations and human resource approaches suggest that organizational productivity is achieved through employee satisfaction. Therefore, the outcomes of job satisfaction should be viewed at the organizational level rather than at the employee's individual performance level alone.

Performance, Organizational Effectiveness, Structural Change, and Human Resource Planning

It is assumed that organizational effectiveness leads to increased volume of production, sales, or clientele (in case of service organizations). However, there is a lack of consensus as to what constitutes a valid set of organizational performance and effectiveness criteria. Many investigations rely on indicators, such as financial turnover or overall firm rating (Arthur & Cook, 2003; Schuster et al., 1997). But there seems to be agreement that multiple criteria are needed for a more comprehensive evaluation of an organization's effectiveness; these criteria may include financial performance, productivity/efficiency indicators, employee stability, customer base, and corporate image.

It is hypothesised that organizational productivity and performance, in the form of profits, provide additional resources for the organization. Availability of additional resources would provide an opportunity for the organization to expand, diversify, or provide new and more products/services. This growth would inevitably lead to structural changes and administrative reorganization. Structural changes will have an effect on the behavioral outcomes of employees. For example, if the organization expands, it could lead to creating a more positive human resource climate in terms of promotions and career opportunities. Structural changes may not only influence the consequent behavioral outcomes but also generate additional manpower requirements, leading to labor market interface. The organizational climate, which is a result of structure, is assumed to create the attraction capabilities of the organization.

Having high-quality employees alone does not assure an organization of better performance. Traditional hierarchies must be transformed in the organizations in which individuals know more, do more, and contribute more, meaning a management system that creates and sustains this environment (Schuster et al., 1997).

As stated earlier, when organizations diversify, grow, or expand they also adopt more complex structures and tend to become more bureaucratic. A decline in organizational size/growth can also stimulate structural change and stability. During decline, resources become scarce. Resource scarcity frequently results in competition and conflict among organizational members. Thus, decline can destabilize an organization's existing formal and informal control mechanisms and motivate it to alter its administrative structures (Tushman & Romanelli, 1985). Organizational decline, when combined with a conservative reaction to this decline, will generate a powerful centralized decision-making structure, and managers may be reluctant to give up this enhanced power. Even if managers are willing to change, limited resources may prevent their doing so (Baker & Cullen, 1993).

Organizational changes in the form of organizational restructuring may have implications for the psychological well-being of organizational members, given the potential for uncertainty that may accompany changes (Howard & Frink, 1996).

Apart from the behavioral outcomes of restructuring discussed earlier, structural changes could also generate negative human resource outcomes. Structural redesign is achieved through elimination of managerial personnel, flattening the organization structure (for increased information flows and improved decision making), optimization of personnel utilization (optimizing the productive work time), downsizing, and layoffs (Walston & Kimberly, 1997).

When organizations restructure as a result of growth, more employees will frequently be needed. Internal labor supply alone may not be sufficient to fill the vacant positions, thus necessitating further recruitment from external sources. It is assumed that various organizational factors (including work environment) would influence the supply level (i.e., number of applicants) from the external labor market, acting as an attraction element. However, obtaining needed employees may be more difficult for larger employers, because they have more vacancies to fill. It is also said that large employers seek to reduce high recruitment costs by hiring better-qualified workers (Oi, 1983). A related argument assumes that large organizations might attract high-quality workers because they provide better job rewards and a more elaborate sorting and selection mechanisms (Evans & Leighton, 1988).

However, from the individual's point of view, many organizational factors (other than rewards, opportunities for career advancement) may influence their decision to go to work for a particular organization. Schneider (1987) proposes that people select employers based on the "fit" they perceive between themselves (e.g., their personality) and relevant organizational attributes (e.g., climate). The notion of person-organization fit has been highlighted by Chatman (1989) to include the "congruence between the norms and values of organization and values of persons" (p. 339). Organizational norms and values are reflected in perceived climate and personal values (Day & Bedeian, 1991).

Rynes and Barber (1990) suggest that organizations can proactively select and mold organizational characteristics, such as the ability to pay, business strategy, culture, and values as a strategy to attract those considered most desirable in the labor force. For example, the pay incentives can be modified to best suit the current desires of the labor force, thus creating an individual-organizational fit to attract desirable applicants. It is likely that those organizational characteristics that are easily observable and are likely to affect applicants' impressions of organizations would be most likely to influence applicant attraction to organizations.

Conclusions

The conceptual model and the research literature supporting the model provide a comprehensive understanding of the dynamics of structural and behavioral variables on planning for human resources in an organization. The model also brings forth new research propositions, in the form of hypothesized relationships between certain variables in the flow chart.

References

Arthur, M.M., & Cook, A. (2003).The relationship between work-family human resource practices and firm profitability: A multi-theoretical perspective. *Research in Personnel and Human Resource Management, 22,* 219-252

Baker, D.D., & Cullen, J.B. (1993). Administrative re-organizational and configurational context: The contingent effects of age, size, and change in size. *Academy of Management Journal, 36*(6), 1251-1277.

Brown, C., Hamilton, J., & Medoff, J. (1990). *Employers large and small.* Cambridge, MA: Harvard University Press.

Burke, W.W., & Litwin, G. (1992). A causal model of organizational performance and change. *Journal of Management, 18,* 523-545.

Burns, L.R. (1995). Medical organization structures that promote quality and efficiency: Past research and future considerations. *Quality Management in Health Care, 3*, 10-18.

Campion, M. (1991). Meaning and measurement of turnover: Comparison of alternative measures and recommendations for research. *Journal of Applied Psychology, 76*(2), 199-212.

Carsten, J.M., & Spector, P.E. (1987). Unemployment, job satisfaction, and employee turnover: A meta-analytic test of Muchinsky model. *Journal of Applied Psychology, 72*(3), 374-381.

Cascio, W. (1991). *Costing human resources: The financial impact of behavior in organizations.* (3rd ed.). Boston, MA: PWS-Kent.

Chatman, J.A. (1989). Improving interactional organizational research: A model of person-organization fit. *Academy of Management Review, 14*, 333-349.

Day, D.V., & Bedeian, A.G. (1991). Predicting job performance across organizations: The interaction of work orientation and psychological climate. *Journal of Management, 17*(3), 589-600.

Evans, D.S., & Leighton, L.S. (1988). Why do smaller firms pay less? *The Journal of Human Resources, 24*, 299-318.

Glisson, C.A., & Martin, P.Y. (1980). Productivity and efficiency in human service organizations as related to structure, size, and age. *Academy of Management Journal, 23*(1), 21-37.

Howard, J.L., & Frink, D.D. (1996). The effects of organizational restructure on employee satisfaction. *Group & Organizational Management, 21*(3), 278-303.

Isaksen, S.G., & Lauer, K.J. (2002). The climate for creativity and change in teams. *Creativity and Innovation Management, 11*, 74-86.

Jansen, E., & Chandler, G.N. (1994). Innovation and restrictive conformity among hospital employees: Individual outcomes and organizational considerations. *Hospital & Health Services Administration, 39*(1),63-80.

Kalleberg, A.L., & Van Buren, M.E. (1996). Is bigger the better? Explaining the relationship between organization size and job rewards. *American Sociological Review, 61*, 47–66.

Lee, T.W., & Mitchell, T.R. (1994). An alternative approach: The unfolding model of voluntary employee turnover. *Academy of Management Review, 19*, 51-89.

Litwin, G., & Stringer, R. (1968). *Motivation and Organizational Climate.* Cambridge: MA, Harvard University Press.

Marginson, P.M. (1984). The distinctive effects of plant and company size on work place and industrial relations. *British Journal of Industrial Relations, 22*, 1-14.

McKinley, W. (1993). Organizational decline and adaptation: Theoretical controversies. *Organization Science, 4*, 1-9.

Mellow, W. (1982). Employer size and wages. *Review of Economics and Statistics, 64*, 495-501.

Mintzberg, H. (1979). *The structuring of organizations.* Englewood Cliffs, NJ: Prentice Hall.

Mintzberg, H. (1991). The effective organization: Forces and forms. *Sloan Management Review, 32*(2), 54-68.

Mitra, A., Jenkins, G.D., & Gupta, N. (1992). A meta-analytic review of the relationship between absence and turnover. *Journal of Applied Psychology, 77*(6),879-889.

Mobley, W.H. (1982). *Employee turnover: Causes, consequences and control.* Reading, MA: Addison-Wesley.

Oi, W.Y. (1983). The fixed employment costs of specialized Labor. In J. Triplett (Ed.), *The measurement of labor cost.* Chicago, IL: University of Chicago Press.

Ostroff, C. (1992). The relationship between satisfaction, attitudes and performance: An organizational level analysis. *Journal of Applied Psychology, 77*(6), 963-974.

Ostroff, C. (1993). The effects of climate and personal influences on individual behavior and attitudes in organizations. *Organizational Behavior & Human Decision Processes, 56,* 56-90.

Paradise, C.A. (1991). Management effectiveness, service quality and organizational performance in banks. *Human Resource Planning, 14,* 129-140.

Pugh, D.S., Hickson, D.J., Hinings, C.R., & Turner, C. (1968). Dimensions of organization structure. *Administrative Science Quarterly, 13,* 65-105.

Rynes, S.L., & Barber, A.E. (1990). Applicant attraction strategies: An organizational perspective. *Academy Of Management Review, 15,* 286-310.

Schminke, M., Cropanzano, R., & Rupp, D.E. (2002). Organizational structure and fairness perception: The moderating effects of organizational level. *Organisational Behavior and Human Decision Processes, 89*(1), 881-905.

Schneider, B. (1987). E = f(P,B): The road to radical approach to person-environment fit. *Journal of Vocational Behavior, 31,* 353-361.

Schneider, B. (1990). The climate for service: An application of the climate construct. In B. Schneider (Ed.), *Organizational climate and culture.* San Francisco, CA: Jossey-Bass.

Schneider, B., & Reichers, A. (1983). On the etiology of climate. *Personnel Psychology, 36,* 19-40.

Schneider, B., Wheeler, J.K., & Cox, J.F. (1992). A passion for service: Using content analysis to explicate service climate themes. *Journal of Applied Psychology, 77*(5), 705-716.

Schuster, F.E. (1986). *The Schuster report: The proven connection between people and profits.* New York: John Wiley & Sons.

Schuster, F.E. et al. (1997). Management practice, organization climate and performance: An exploratory study. *Journal of Applied Behavioral Science, 33*(2), 209-226.

Scott, W. (1992). *Organization: Rational, natural and open-system.* Englewood Cliffs, NJ: Prentice Hall.

Scott, W., Mitchell, T.R., & Birnbaum, P.H. (1981). *Organization theory: A structural and behavioral analysis.* Chicago, IL: Irwin.

Shugars, D.A., Hays, R.D., Matteo, M.R., & Cretins, C. (1991). Development of an instrument to measure job satisfaction among dentists. *Medical Care, 29*(8),728-744.

Sommer, S.M., Bae, S.H., & Luthans, F. (1997). The structure-climate relationship in Korean organizations. *Asia Pacific Journal of Management, 12*(2), 23-36.

Tett, R.P., & Meyer, J.P. (1993). Job satisfaction, organizational commitment, turnover intention and turnover: Path analysis based on meta-analytic findings. *Personnel Psychology, 4*(2),259-293.

Tornow, W.W., & Wiley, J.W. (1991). Service quality and management practices: A look at employee attitudes, customer satisfaction and bottom-line consequences. *Human Resource Planning, 14,* 105-116.

Turnipseed, D.L. (1990). Evaluation of health care work environments via a social climate scale: Results of a field study. *Hospital & Health Services Administration, 35*(2), 245–263.

Tushman, M.L., & Romanelli, E. (1985). Organizational evolution: A metamorphosis model of convergence and reorientation. In L.L. Cummings & B.M. Staw (Eds.), Research in organizational behavior (pp. 171-222). Greenwich, CT: JAI Press.

Walston, S.L., & Kimberly, J.R. (1997). Reengineering hospitals: Evidence from the field. *Hospital & Health Services Administration, 42*(2), 143-163.

A. Venkat Raman, Ph.D., *is a senior lecturer in the Faculty of Management Studies (FMS), University of Delhi, India. He teaches courses in human resource management and health services management. He has wide-ranging experience providing training and consulting and conducting research in HRD, organizational restructuring, TNA, and strategic analysis of corporate and health care organizations.*

Evaluation, the Final Phase of Consulting

Charles L. Fields

Summary

Too often in the rush to complete a project, when conducting an evaluation, only the hard numbers are reviewed. Yet there is much more to be examined, and that information can provide useful learnings for both consultants and their client organizations. In this paper, through the use of an extended example, the various elements of evaluation are explored and an explanation is provided for their worth.

Flawless Consulting, by Peter Block, is one of the foundational works on internal consulting skills. In it, Block describes the five phases of consulting: Contracting, Discovery, Feedback, Implementation, and Evaluation. He stresses that the implementation phase is the point of consultation. Consultants act as social architects to design the plan using an engagement strategy.

Evaluation is telling the story of the consultation, particularly of the implementation phase. As the work ends, we look at what was achieved. To most people it means, "Did we meet or exceed the plan?" We evaluate with the mindset of the economist ("What did it cost?" and "What did it contribute to the bottom line?") and the engineer ("Was it on time?" and "Did it improve efficiencies?").

But the evaluation phase is more than that. It is about the results of our stewardship of the organization's assets and resources. Stewardship is about taking accountability, meaning, "I personally choose to commit to the success of the whole business without barter or promise of return."

The intent of evaluation is to tell the story of what we did (implementation) with the resources we were given. The questions are "In completing this work, as stewards of the organization's assets, what was the fruit of our labors? What did we create together? What is its impact on the world around us? What did we learn?"

An Evaluation Example

I want to explore evaluation through a story about a mandate to reduce travel expenses. It covers the planning, implementation, and evaluation of the results achieved. From it there are several observations that we can use in evaluating other work.

The Story of "Cutting Expenses by 15 Percent"

About the end of September, the senior vice president (SVP) of finance advised the senior management team (president and all SVPs) that travel expenses were growing and would jeopardize the year-end results and the earnings per share if something didn't change. The team promptly sent out a directive to all field directors to cut travel expenses by 15 percent before the end of December.

The question facing Chris, a regional director, was "How do we cut travel expenses 15 percent over the next three months and keep up the service commitments to the customers?" He initially planned to send out the usual email to all regional people telling them to reduce travel expenses wherever possible.

However, even though he still was considering sending the email, Chris asked me to help him with a brainstorming session for his management team. His goal—to generate some other ideas on how to reduce expenses. He agreed to meet with me to plan the brainstorming session. During that meeting, I asked Chris. . .

1. "If you were a field engineer, what would be your reaction to an email to hold down travel expenses?" He remembered his reactions from when he was in the field, a combination of anger, cynicism, and frustration. He held off on the email, but hoped that I would help him craft a meaningful one later.

2. "Where are you currently—under or over budget?" He was slightly under budget overall and knew that he still had to cut 15 percent from travel.

3. "Where is the money going? Who's spending the most?" He wasn't sure and referred me to two work reports from Corporate IT and Regional Accounting, both based on expense accounts. Neither report was in a useable format. They gave only monthly raw data, people identified only by code numbers, no year-to-date data, and nothing summarized.

Getting Useful Data

Chris and I discovered that no one used the corporate work reports. IT faithfully generated and distributed these reports monthly at a cost of about $150,000 a year. We also learned that many regions and branches had bootleg systems that reprocessed the IT reports into a useable format. Chris was considering such a system for next year.

Engineering had an adversarial relationship with IT, and Chris was reluctant to approach them to change the format of the report. We did approach Lee, the individual who produced the report, and asked what it would take to reformat the reports for the northeastern region. To Chris's surprise, Lee said that it would be a simple task and he just needed to know how Chris wanted it formatted. After that, Lee would have the report in twenty-four hours. Chris gave Lee the format, and we had the report the next day.

The Brainstorming Session

Chris convened a meeting of his management team to address ways to cut expenses. The reports showed individual data, summary by supervisor, and summary by region. They showed that the supervisors and a few field engineers were generating most of the expenses!

One supervisor, Jerry, averaged more expenses than the others. He said that this was because he was responsible for the regional training and generally charged the expenses for rooms, meals, and A/V equipment on his travel expense account. Chris told the team that training expenses were allocated to the training budget, not to travel. The region was significantly under budget in training. Most of Jerry's expenses were reallocated to training.

The other supervisors said that much of their travel wasn't needed. Some of the newer supervisors admitted that they still weren't comfortable being supervisors. They weren't sure why and how things worked. So they would schedule a coaching trip with their engineers. (Engineers felt they were being over-coached and wished the supervisors would stay in the office.) While the supervisors were out, their office work suffered and they constantly struggled to get things done. They worked out a way to still spend time in the field and back each other up. They reduced their travel and had better results when they did.

The engineer with the most expenses traveled three to five days a week. Most of the customers he served were nearly two hundred miles from his home. The first question was, "How do we get him to cut his expenses yet serve these customers?"

Chris realized that he could move the engineer at a one-time cost (chargeable to relocation expenses) and reduce the ongoing travel expenses. The obvious question was, "Will he move to that area?" When asked about a move, the engineer immediately said yes. He confided that he was considering resigning from the company. The issue was his time away from home. He loved the work, but constant travel had strained his marriage. He moved his family before the end of the year.

Results

Chris accomplished all this in less than thirty days. The results began to show on the October reports and, by the end of December, Chris had reduced the regional travel expenses by nearly 20 percent. He never sent the email.

Here's an evaluation of Chris's results as seen by the economists and engineers:

- They were satisfied and happy.

- They are only interested in a single line item—the travel expenses.

- The S.M.A.R.T. goal was 15 percent reduction by Dec. 31—roughly ninety days; Chris achieved nearly 20 percent and had results in thirty days. He exceeded the goal.

What We Should Measure

To me, Chris's story shows a broader picture of what he accomplished. When we think about the impact our work has on the world around us, there's even more to consider.

We usually only consider the financial and operational aspects of an implementation plan. We measure the planned versus actual results in terms of money, time, and deliverables. These measures are developed as goals in the implementation plan. They would include things like the following:

- Staying within or below the specified budget;

- Completing the work on, or before, a specified date;

- Improving customer service;

- Improving work processes; and

- Increasing quality.

These metrics become the standards for measurement of the success of the financial and operational part of the implementation plan. The plan is, at its very best, still a guess, yet to be tested by reality. And when we only evaluate planned versus actual, we are really asking, "How good was our guess?"

The following sections explore some of the areas we need to evaluate.

What Changed During the Project?

We also need to tell the story of the changes that occurred. Many times the plan gets changed. We need to track those changes and the impact they had on the outcomes. This is not to justify or focus blame for results not achieved. It allows us to learn, to become better planners on the next project.

Changes will occur due to internal factors . . . things we didn't anticipate during the planning. And due to external factors . . . events caused by someone else or by outside circumstances. Here are some things to consider:

- What changes occurred over the life of the project?

- What was their impact on the financial and operational goals relative to actual results?

- What caused the changes to occur?

What Did We Impact?

Unfortunately, we are frequently content to just consider the changes and then stop there. There is much more to the picture. Our plans impact many things. We need to tell those stories as well. Here are a few to think about:

1. *Service and Relationships:* To commit to the success of the business means that we serve others. Others include those inside the company, vendors or suppliers, and customers. We are called to build and nurture relationships with all those involved. Meeting the plan, yet damaging relationships, is not a mark of success. We need to ask, "How are our relationships?"

2. *Our Culture:* This is the environment in which we work. This means that by our conversations and actions we will sustain the existing culture, or we will be creating a different one. If we believe in being authentic, we need to ask, "To what extent did our actions encourage others to take accountability, to become stewards of the organization's assets?"

3. *Organizational Beliefs:* Each project must examine its outcomes relative to the corporate beliefs. Work that meets a fiscal goal, yet is contrary to core beliefs, is not successful. It tears at the heart of the organization. We need to ask before each project begins, "To what extent will this project live out our core beliefs?" Later, part of our evaluation is to ask again, "To what extent did this project live out our core beliefs?"

4. *The Greater Community:* We live and work in a community. Our presence is in towns, cities, states, and nations. What we do impacts them. Being accountable means caring for their well-being as well as the organization's. Although most of our work may have little effect, we do have to consider the impact of what we're doing on this greater community.

All four of these areas tell the broader story of the project. We rarely consider these things when planning. We primarily focus on the fiscal and operational goals.

What Did We Learn?

Another part of the story concerns what we learned. We learn from our experiences, individually and collectively. This is part of our development, our growth. Some things worked; some did not. We need to collect what we learned in completing the work. We also need to tell others what we learned so that it can help them in their work.

If we are in the role of consultants, we want to collect our learnings regarding the consulting model we followed. What did we try? What worked? What didn't work? What would we do differently? What became clearer for us? To what extent did we live out stewardship, accountability, and engagement?

Who Evaluates the Results?

A better question is "Who tells the story?" The people who live the experience are the ones to tell the story. They are the ones who make the promises and commitments during implementation. They do the work, nurture the relationships, and have the intimate details of what happened.

I realize that there are others who have an interest in the results. There's the customer who received the service and the boss or manager who provided the assets and resources. For management, the story helps them see the fiscal and operational results, understand the impact of the work on the organization, discover what the people learned, and make decisions for the future.

CAUTION!!! There is a very real trap here. In many evaluations our desire is to justify what we did, NOT tell the story. Justification is about "being enough"; it's about trying to satisfy others. "Am I enough?" "Did I do enough?" We want to be justified by what we have done and we want to know that it was enough.

This need to be justified is aggravated by pressure from management to demonstrate our contribution to the company's success. Then we support that pressure by trying to justify our individual contribution to meeting the plan or impacting the bottom line. Such efforts work only to build internal competition and not community. Stop before you hurt yourself and the community. It takes the whole community to serve the customers. Remember—even the Lone Ranger had Tonto.

When Do We Evaluate?

Early and often! Evaluation is not just something that you do at the end of the work. It's ongoing, it's at the end, and it's in the future.

First will be our periodic meetings—times when people convene to discuss the work. Each meeting is an opportunity to take stock of how it's going and make any changes necessary. Whenever you meet, in addition to the usual talk about fiscal and operational progress, individually and collectively ask yourselves questions like the following:

- What promises have I made that I have kept . . . not kept?

- What doubts and concerns do I have about this project?

- What has become clearer as the work progresses?

- What are the tough conversations that I've been avoiding?

- What strengths and contributions do we see in each other?

Most projects have times for regularly scheduled status meetings called to check the fiscal and operational progress of the work.

Next, we want to complete a formal evaluation at the end as a summary showing what was achieved.

And finally, we'll want to evaluate over time. We must deliberately look back and see how our efforts impacted the organization. Do the first follow-up in thirty days. It's long enough to get some results and soon enough to catch mistakes or bad habits. Then decide what future follow-ups are needed.

The Tools of Evaluation

There are the usual tools of most projects. Things like documentation, financials, budget reports, status reports, and a final project report. These tell part of the story, but not the whole story. Keep a personal journal for recording the meetings, questions, conversations, and events of the project. Use powerful questions to spur thinking and debate. Later, harvest the journal to help you tell the story of the work and what was accomplished.

Creating the Story

If your role in implementation was social architect, your role in evaluation is journalist. You're telling the story of the work. Remember to keep the context simple, direct, and from the heart. Tell the good, the bad, the ugly, and the indifferent. If you need a format, try something like this. . .

1. Call a meeting of those who were involved to create the story.

2. Bring any documentation and personal journals.

3. Start by using powerful questions to provoke thinking and help guide the conversations. Here are some examples:

   - What happened (good or bad) that we didn't expect?

   - Given the outcomes we achieved, what would we have done differently at the beginning?

   - What would we have paid more attention to during the project?

   - What changes would we make in the ways we did the planning, handled the logistics, used the resources, etc.?

   - What did we achieve that we didn't expect?

   - What can we do to sustain what we've done?

4. Have each person respond to the questions and tell his or her stories.

5. Have someone keep notes and then write a simple story about the project. Here's a simple outline for the story:

   - Summary.

   - The impact on service and relationships, the culture, organizational beliefs, and the greater community.

   - Learnings.

   - Strengths and contributions we want to acknowledge.

   - Schedule for the first follow-up.

   - Financial and operational results in terms of the implementation plan.

You're probably wondering if you should do this on every project or work assignment. You'll find on smaller or shorter assignments it goes faster and changes the way you think. So why not?

Revisiting Our Example

There's still a nagging question, "Was the project successful?" After all, isn't this the whole point of evaluation? I've never liked that question. It's too narrow, too "yes-or-no" focused. Let's ask that question of Chris's work to reduce expenses.

"Yes, he was." He reduced the travel expenses by more than 15 percent by December 31.

Yet there were other outcomes. As a group we never really talked about the other results. We never told our story. It was a few years later before I began to recognize the significance of that simple task of cutting expenses 15 percent. Here's a broader picture.

Financial and Operational

- Chris reduced expenses by over 20 percent.

- Results were seen in thirty days.

- The new performance reports cost less and became widely accepted and used. This resulted in a substantial cost savings over time.

- Over time, the bootleg systems disappeared (savings in time and money later realized).

Relationships

- This was the beginning of a new relationship with IT. Over the next year, Engineering and IT grew closer together. The old adversarial relationship was replaced by one of partnership.

- The relationship between the supervisors and their engineers improved. Coaching trips became more meaningful and appreciated.

- The engineer didn't leave the company.

Corporate Beliefs

- The field engineers designed the new reports. This was the corporate philosophy of empowerment being lived out.

- Senior management was not involved.

Learnings

- The regional management team hadn't really acted as a team. That changed.

- A creative approach can work. They began to change how they solved problems as a group.

- New supervisors weren't as literate about the business as they thought.

- Chris's stress levels dropped. (I learned later that he had been experiencing health problems related to stress. He felt that he was alone and had to solve all the problems of the region.)

So was Chris successful? To me the real questions are, "What did they learn?" and "What did they impact?" These are questions of growth and development, of community and accountability.

The next time you're involved in an implementation, think about ALL the aspects that you'll want to measure, not just the financial and operational goals. Tell the whole story. It's your choice.

Charles L. Fields *created The Fields Company after nearly twenty years at HSB Group, where he gained experience in management positions in training, consulting, engineering, and claims. He was always in a line operation, even when functioning in HR/OD roles. His consulting practice includes working with organizations in creating sustainable change, strategic thinking, leadership development, building and restoring relationships, and innovation and creativity. He is affiliated with Peter Block and Designed Learning Inc. as a senior consultant.*

Value–Added Diversity Consulting

Tyrone A. Holmes

Summary

America in the 21st Century is one of the most culturally diverse societies on earth. We are more likely than ever to find ourselves in organizations where people have significant differences in terms of race, ethnicity, religion, gender, nationality, and sexual orientation. Because of this, formal diversity initiatives have become prevalent. Many books and articles have been written on the benefits of diverse organizations and the steps we can take to manage diversity, but few have focused specifically on the consultant's role in facilitating successful interventions (for example, see Carnevale & Stone, 1995, Carr-Ruffino, 1999, Jackson & Ruderman, 1995; and Hayles & Russell, 1997).

This article introduces a Diversity Consulting Model that can be used by internal and external consultants to add value and improve the client's position via performance-based diversity initiatives. It also describes the activities of successful diversity consultants and illustrates the role we must play to make these programs successful.

According to a study by the Society for Human Resource Management (SHRM) and *Fortune* (2001), over 75 percent of surveyed organizations have engaged in some type of diversity activity or initiative. In a follow-up study four months after the events of 9/11, SHRM and *Fortune* (2002) reported that over 97 percent of responding organizations said their investment in diversity programs would either stay the same or increase. Whether it is training, recruitment, career development, or community outreach, it is clear that more and more organizations are implementing diversity programs and will continue to do so. Because these organizations often use internal or external consultants to facilitate these initiatives, it behooves us to clarify the specific steps that should be taken to ensure success and to identify the actions that consultants can take to add value to the process.

Although the goals of diversity programs can greatly vary from one organization to the next, there are several steps that should be a part of every initiative. The Diversity Consulting Model proffers five questions that must be answered in order to facilitate interventions that have a measurable impact on individual and organizational performance:

1. What are your opportunity areas?

2. What are the benefits of enhancing these opportunity areas?

3. What are your goals and how do they connect with organizational objectives?

4. How will the goals be achieved?

5. How will we measure success?

What Are Your Opportunity Areas?

The first step in facilitating a performance-based diversity process is to identify opportunity areas where the organization can benefit from an emphasis on diversity. Intervening in one or more of these areas can help an organization empower diversity. Empowering diversity consists of systematic, proactive steps taken to create organizational environments in which members accept, respect, and effectively utilize the diversity found within as a source of added value. Such environments recognize the benefits of diversity, include culturally diverse members as full participants, reflect the contributions and interests of diverse membership, and act to eliminate all forms of bias. Such an organizational state, referred to here as a culturally empowered environment, maximizes the likelihood of success for a diverse range of individuals and enhances the overall performance of the organization.

There are ten key areas connected to diversity empowerment in virtually every organization. These include mission and philosophy, institutional leadership, policies and procedures, climate and environment, staffing and retention, coaching and mentoring, human resource development, performance management, compensation and benefits, and program evaluation. Keep in mind that it is not necessary for an organization to address all ten areas at once. In fact, few institutions have the resources to do so. Your job as a consultant is to help the client determine which areas will provide the greatest return on investment given the goals of the organization and its strengths and weaknesses in each area.

1. Organizational Mission and Philosophy

Virtually all organizations articulate their philosophy and beliefs through a formal vision or mission statement. These statements are usually developed by leadership as a means of communicating the organization's purpose and reason for existence, as well as its core values. An emphasis in this area is absolutely necessary if the mission statement does not overtly specify a commitment to diversity. Ensuring that the organizational philosophy articulates such a commitment is of paramount importance because it tells organizational members, customers, and stakeholders that diversity is important to leadership and is a consideration in how the organization manages the various aspects of its business.

2. Institutional Leadership

One of the most common statements made regarding the facilitation of successful diversity interventions is the absolute need for leadership support. Indeed, few change initiatives of any type can be effective without the consistent support of top management. Therefore, ensuring that leadership provides visible, vocal, and continuous support for the organization's diversity program is vital. Leadership support can manifest itself in a number of ways, including leadership participation on diversity committees and design teams, verbal and written articulation of the rationale behind the initiative, consistent participation in diversity events, and taking proactive steps to increase the diversity of the leadership group.

3. Policies and Procedures

In order to understand the significance of policies and procedures as a diversity intervention point, we must clarify the difference between first-order and second-order change. First-order change is grounded in the individual. It is often referred to as "change without change" because it focuses on individual learning and development without a concomitant emphasis on the organization. Second-order change is referred to as "change with change" because it is geared toward changing the way the organization operates. The focus is on institutional policies and procedures and on how the work is done. Two points are significant here. First, to implement a successful diversity initiative, both first-order and second-order change are required. Second, the best way to facilitate second-order change is through the modification of organizational policies and procedures. Therefore, policies and procedures must be a consideration in every diversity intervention. Key focus areas will include policies on recruitment and selection, internal promotion, employee conduct, compensation and benefits, human resource development, and employee recognition and reward.

4. Climate and Environment

The fourth area of consideration is organizational climate. As mentioned earlier, a culturally empowered environment maximizes the likelihood of success for a diverse range of people and enhances individual and organizational performance. To determine whether this is an area in need of intervention, it is helpful to clarify employee perceptions regarding the current environment. Many organizations facilitate some type of employee satisfaction survey, which can give you an idea of the organization's strengths and weaknesses in areas such as quality of work life, organizational communication, work relationships, trust, teamwork, perceived level of support, leadership effectiveness, and employee satisfaction and morale. In addition, by examining the demographic breakdown of the survey, you can identify differences in perceptions between various cultural, ethnic, gender, and age groups. This will help the client gain a better sense of what needs to happen in order to improve the organization's diversity climate.

5. Staffing and Retention

In the study facilitated by SHRM and *Fortune* (2001), 75 percent of the responding organizations indicated that diversity recruitment was an area of focus in their diversity initiative. More than any other activity, organizations implement recruiting efforts specifically aimed at increasing employee diversity. The primary goal in this area is to create a human resources staffing process that increases the quality and diversity of candidate pools and ensures that the selection methods and criteria used to make hiring decisions are valid. In addition, there should be programmatic activities (such as a career development program) that motivate employees, particularly underrepresented group members, to remain with the organization.

6. Coaching and Mentoring

One of the most effective employee retention activities is systematic coaching and mentoring. Coaching is a conversation or a series of conversations between a leader and an employee designed to enhance the development of the employee and to improve overall job performance. Mentoring is also a series of conversations between a mentor and a protégé that is designed to enhance the protégé's overall development. However, unlike coaching, it is not specifically geared toward performance enhancement (although effective mentoring will often lead to this), but to facilitate the development of professional skills and networks on the part of the protégé. Mentoring also differs from coaching in that the interaction is not always between a supervisor and an employee. In fact, it frequently takes place between people with no reporting relationship and sometimes between people in separate organizations. The focus here is to provide opportunities for a diverse range of employees to receive both coaching and mentoring on a consistent basis.

7. Human Resource Development

In the SHRM/*Fortune* study (2001), two-thirds of the responding organizations indicated that diversity training and education was an area of emphasis in their diversity initiative. The first-order change discussed earlier can be facilitated through diversity-based human resource development efforts. The key is to identify the competencies individuals need to communicate, resolve conflict, and solve problems in culturally diverse settings. Such competencies can include self-awareness, diversity knowledge, multicultural communication skills, listening skills, conflict resolution skills, and team problem-solving skills. Other focus areas, especially for organizational leadership, can include the development of coaching, mentoring, and diversity recruitment skills.

8. Performance Management

Another common focus area for organizations that implement successful diversity programs is the evaluation of management's contribution to creating culturally empowered environments. Most organizations that are able to facilitate genuine institutional change make a significant effort in this area. Like policies and procedures, performance management is a good way to incorporate second-order change into the diversity process. The focus here is to evaluate each manager's contribution to the creation of culturally inclusive environments that have a positive impact on individual and organizational performance. This can be done by examining the extent to which managers have successfully accomplished diversity goals and by the use of a variety of measures and metrics (see Program Evaluation).

9. Compensation and Benefits

Although it is not as popular as some of the other opportunity areas, an emphasis on salary and benefits may be necessary for some organizations because of the significant impact compensation has on both recruitment and retention. Here, the goal is to make sure that the organization's compensation package is competitive and to ensure equality across racial and gender differences for equivalent jobs. Doing this can provide a significant competitive advantage because at least part of most decisions to accept a job offer or to remain with a particular organization is based on the compensation package. In order to attract a high-quality, culturally diverse pool of candidates, organizations must be confident that their salary and benefits package will be seen in a positive light.

10. Program Evaluation

Finally, every diversity initiative should include an evaluation component. In fact, no diversity activity should be implemented until it is clear how it will be evaluated. The primary concern is to identify specific measures and metrics to assess the overall effectiveness of the diversity initiative. Although an extensive review of diversity measures is beyond the scope of this article, some common metrics include cost per diversity hire, diversity hire percentage, candidate pool diversity percentage, staff diversity percentage, quality of diverse candidates and diversity hit rate, turnover rate, and stability rate (for more information on diversity measures and metrics, see Hubbard, 2001; Keller, 1996).

What Are the Benefits of Enhancing These Opportunity Areas?

Put another way, what do you have to gain by taking advantage of the chosen opportunity areas? It does not make sense to proceed with any type of diversity initiative if you have not clearly defined the benefits you hope to gain and the value it will provide for the organization. Generally speaking, the benefits accrued from diversity programs can be divided into three categories: individual and organizational performance, enhanced customer service, and improved bottom line.

1. Individual and Organizational Performance

Successful diversity initiatives should have a positive impact on individual and organizational performance. Individual employee skills and abilities, as well as overall organizational output, should measurably increase as a result of your efforts. Potential benefits include improved quality of the workforce, increased ability to attract and retain the best human resources, improved group performance, and an overall increase in the quality and productivity of work (for example, see Jackson & Ruderman, 1995; Ruderman, Hughes-James, & Jackson, 1996).

2. Enhanced Customer Service

Another potential benefit of performance-based diversity initiatives is the ability to tap into diverse markets and effectively serve a culturally diverse clientele. Benefits can include a greater ability to connect with and satisfy an increasingly diverse customer base and improved employee attitudes and morale (for example, see Schreiber & Lenson, 2001).

3. Improved Bottom Line

In any type of organizational change initiative, top leadership is generally interested in the impact on the organization's bottom line. Effective diversity programs can have a positive bottom line impact. Benefits can include increased organizational value and profitability, increased revenues, reduced cost-per-hire, reduced "bad" turnover, and reduction in racial/sexual harassment and accompanying legal costs (for example, see Hayles & Russell, 1997; SHRM & *Fortune*, 2001).

What Are Your Goals and How Do They Connect with Organizational Objectives?

Once you have identified your primary opportunity areas and clarified the benefits of enhancing those areas, it is time to specify goals. A goal is a statement of a desired end state. It specifies where you want to be at a given point in the diversity initiative and provides you with a means to evaluate progress. Effective diversity goals should be written using the SMART goal method. Specifically, each goal should have the following characteristics:

1. *Specific*—The goal is concise and stated in performance terms.

2. *Measurable*—It will be easy to determine whether the goal has been met.

3. *Achievable*—The goal is set high, but is also realistic and attainable.

4. *Relevant*—The goal is tied to organizational performance needs.

5. *Time-Bound*—The goal has an identifiable time frame for completion.

A diversity consultant can be of great assistance in this area because a common mistake on the part of organizations is to identify goals that fail to fully meet the SMART criteria. You can assist clients by using the following model to write a diversity SMART goal: "By the end of. . . , we will. . . , as demonstrated by. . . ." This ensures that the goal is time-bound, is measurable, is concise, and is stated in performance terms. Examples of well-written diversity SMART goals include the following:

- By the end of the first quarter of 2005, we will identify specific measures and metrics that will be used to assess managerial diversity performance, as demonstrated by the inclusion of those metrics in the company's formal performance appraisal system.

- By June 30, 2005, we will implement a formal diversity recruitment policy that facilitates the active participation of all managers, as demonstrated by increasing candidate pool diversity to 25 percent.

- By December 1, 2005, we will complete the multicultural communication skills training for managers, as demonstrated by successful completion, by at least 90 percent of the managers, of the Multicultural Communication Skills Proficiency Assessment.

In addition to creating SMART goals, it is important to clarify how these goals will connect with the organization's overall objectives. It is not enough to identify goals and processes that deliver a specified benefit. That benefit should be in line with larger organizational goals such as revenue generation, expense reduction, or the development of new markets.

How Will the Goals Be Achieved?

Your next step is to specify how each SMART goal will be achieved. This includes the key actions needed for successful completion, the identification of the key players needed for carrying out these actions, and a completion date for each activity. These action plans do not have to be overly detailed or particularly long. In fact, they work best when they are brief and include just the information required to clarify the requisite activities. The action plans should include a specification of the key roles and activities of the consultant and how this person will add value to the process. Although specific consultant actions can vary greatly from one organization to the next, some common, value-added activities include:

- Assessment of current organizational status and functioning;

- Communication of identified strengths and weaknesses to top leadership;

- Development of recommendations regarding specific areas of diversity program focus;

- Assisting with the creation of the diversity plan;

- Assisting with the development of diversity SMART goals;

- Assisting with the communication of the diversity goals and plans to organizational members;

- Assisting with the creation of diversity-friendly policies and procedures;

- Assisting with the development of diversity-friendly recruitment, selection, and retention processes;

- Development, implementation, and evaluation of diversity training and education activities;

- Development, implementation, and evaluation of diversity-friendly organization development programs such as career development and mentoring systems;

- Identification of diversity measures and metrics for use in program evaluation and management assessment; and

- Facilitation of diversity program evaluation activities.

How Will We Measure Success?

Finally, you will need to clarify how the diversity initiative will be evaluated. This is particularly important these days, since the value of some diversity activities has been called into question. The good news is that, once you have effectively addressed the first four questions, the final question is relatively easy. That's because well-constructed SMART goals have a built-in evaluation component. It's easy to tell whether the goal has been achieved. For example, if your goal is to increase the diversity of candidate pools by 10 percent, at the designated point in time you simply measure to see whether candidate pool diversity has increased by 10 percent or not.

In addition to the SMART goals, you may want to incorporate some of the measures and metrics described under Program Evaluation to assess the program's overall effectiveness. For example, if one of your primary focus areas is diversity recruitment, you can use staff diversity percentage and diversity hire percentage to assess long-term success. Examining staff diversity percentage (number of diverse employees divided by the total number of employees) tells you how effective you are at increasing diversity at various organizational levels. A review of the organization's diversity hire percentage (number of diverse hires divided by the total number of hires) tells you how effective you are at hiring diverse candidates from your candidate pools. The key is to use an evaluation strategy that matches the goals you have for your overall diversity initiative.

Conclusion

In today's world of global and multi-cultural organizations, few would argue with the need to both increase and take full advantage of diversity within organizations. The Diversity Consulting Model presented in this article can assist consultants in helping their clients to successfully implement performance-based diversity initiatives.

References

Carnevale, A.P., & Stone, S.C. (1995). *The American mosaic: An in-depth report on the future of diversity at work.* Alexandria, VA: American Society for Training and Development.

Carr-Ruffino, N. (1999). *Diversity success strategies.* New York: Elsevier.

Hayles, R., & Russell, A.M. (1997). *The diversity directive: Why some initiatives fail and what to do about it.* Alexandria, VA: American Society for Training and Development.

Hubbard, E.E. (2001). *Measuring diversity results: Volume one.* Petaluma, CA: Global Insights Publishing.

Jackson, S.E., & Ruderman, M.N. (1995). *Diversity in work teams: Research paradigms for a changing workplace.* Washington, DC: American Psychological Association.

Keller, J.M. (1996). *Evaluating diversity training: 17 ready-to-use-tools.* San Francisco, CA: Pfeiffer.

Ruderman, M.N., Hughes-James, M.W., & Jackson, S.E. (1996). *Selected research on work team diversity.* Washington, DC: American Psychological Association and the Center for Creative Leadership.

Schreiber, A.L., & Lenson, B. (2001). *Multicultural marketing.* Chicago, IL: NTC/Contemporary Publishing Group.

Society for Human Resource Management and *Fortune* Magazine (2002). *Survey on the changing face of diversity.* Alexandria, VA: Society for Human Resource Management.

Society for Human Resource Management and *Fortune* Magazine (2001). *Study of workplace diversity initiatives.* Alexandria, VA: Society for Human Resource Management.

Tyrone A. Holmes, Ed.D., *is the president of T.A.H. Performance Consultants, Inc., a full-service human resource development consulting firm specializing in the enhancement of individual and organizational performance. As a dynamic speaker, trainer, consultant, and coach, Dr. Holmes has helped countless individuals enhance their ability to communicate, resolve conflict, and solve problems in culturally diverse settings. He has created and copyrighted numerous training systems and speaks on a variety of communication, diversity, and consulting topics.*

The Write Stuff

Richard T. Whelan

Summary

In the constantly changing world of business needs and practices, the role of an educational/training consultant is both growing and changing. At times, there seem to be more consultants looking for clients than companies looking for consultants.

Because of this situation, it becomes necessary for successful consultants to be able to offer companies competent service with a distinctive style. This style may well be in the form of not just the spoken word, but the written word as well.

This article demonstrates one form a "written word" can take that will prove most beneficial to both the contracted company and to the consultant.

The Written Word as a Competitive Advantage

There is an old Chinese proverb that states, "A good picture is worth a thousand words." A national news broadcaster once said, "The right word can replace a thousand pictures."

In today's business world, training consultants primarily educate individuals through carefully selected visuals (videotape productions, slide shows, overhead projections, computer graphics, role plays, demonstrations, etc.) and words (presentations, audiotapes, recordings, readings, notes, books, journals, magazine articles, workshop manuals, etc.). These two formats assist consultants in achieving their goals to educate the workshop participants in learning new ideas, concepts, trends, work methods, and personal interactions and to provide resources to which the workshop participants may refer at a later time for refreshment or reinforcement.

However, because of the reduced availability of both time and money in many companies and organizations, it has become necessary for consultants, in an effort to remain competitive, to provide appropriate resources for organizations that will increase the likelihood that clients will view them as valuable assets. A proven way for this to occur is for Consultant "A" to create a more valuable, effective, creative, useful, and cost-saving educational method than Consultant "B."

Consultant B may leave a business card at the completion of a contracted assignment in hopes of receiving calls for more business. Consultant A, however, leaves something very different—written material that is provided to each workshop participant to reinforce what has been taught and learned and that may later be provided to other individuals in the contracted company to learn what has been designed and taught by the consultant.

This written material provided by the consultant serves several purposes:

- It allows the developed work of the consultant to be used continually by the company without the consultant having to be present at the company. The consultant may be earning additional income by providing services for other contracts, thus increasing the consultant's business arena.

- The consultant may be called back to the company if there is a need to update or modify the developed material.

- The consultant will also receive primary consideration in designing, developing, and delivering material for new workshop concepts for the company.

- This company will also enthusiastically refer the consultant to other companies. When this occurs, you, the consultant, can use the same basic material designed for the first company with the second company. You only have to meet with the appropriate personnel of the second company to obtain the information you need to make necessary changes in your written material so the finished product appears to have been designed specifically for the new contracted company. This allows you to work less, earn more, and still create the distinctive and valuable material for which you have received your excellent professional reputation.

Transitioning from Verbal to Written

Several questions may arise at this point:

- I know I can present verbally, but can I present in writing?

- In an actual presentation, I am there to answer any questions. How can that be done if I am not there?

- How can I write presentations that are both enjoyable for me to create and useful and inviting for the participants to use?

To begin answering these questions, think about how you develop and design your verbal presentations. You, more than likely, follow this type of process:

- Speak to knowledgeable personnel in the company or organization to learn about the business, its history, number and type of employees, the problems to be solved, and how the organization has addressed the issue in the past.

- Research how other companies or organizations have addressed similar issues.

- Speak to colleagues about their experiences.

- Research the problem or issue.

- Seek aids to be used in your presentation (videos, posters, tricks and techniques, guest speakers, assignments, etc.).

- Write notes on what to present and how to present, over a period of time, not in one sitting.

- Practice the presentation in front of a mirror or videotape it to watch as if you were the participating audience.

- Make final changes (and create back-up material in case it is needed) and give the workshop to the contracted company.

The same basic process is followed to create written material. The only significant difference is that the participants are reading what you write rather than listening to what you say.

A Process and Checklist for Writing

In deciding whether what you have written is what you wanted to write and what you want the readers to read, there are certain questions best asked at three times during your writing process:

1. Before you write;

2. While you are writing; and

3. After you have finished a particular stage of writing.

These necessary and important questions are

A. What is my goal in writing this/these stories?

B. What do I want each (this) story to say or present?

C. Am I consistent in keeping my goal in each story, so that either the whole book may be read and enjoyed or just one or two particular stories may be read and have my desired impact on the reader?

D. Who is my audience? Who do I want my audience to be (now and in the future)? If the audience is made up of people of different age ranges, educational backgrounds, geographic locations, religious backgrounds/practices, and/or experiences, have I included a particular style/knack that can be used to reach all of them?

E. Does the reader need to have experienced the same type of event to enjoy or understand the story (especially the way it was told), or can just reading it help the reader to actually picture what has occurred and identify with what has been described?

F. Using twenty-five words or less, what would I want the reader(s) to say if asked, "What is the lesson/story about?" (One hopes that an answer other than, "Oh, it's about three pages" would be given.)

G. How do my answers before I write each piece compare to the answers to the same questions after the piece is written?

H. How much reality do I want to have included in the lessons and/or stories?

I. May I include some created detail to add a little spice to raise the enjoyment and educational level without taking away from the believability of the story's usefulness?

After writing each story/lesson/portion, ask and check:

• What did I want to say? Did I say it?

• How did I want to say it? Did I say it that way?

• What kind of reactions do I want the reader to experience?

• If I am able to detach myself from the role of the writer, and become the reader, what is my reaction? (*Note:* This is usually best done a day or two after writing the piece or after two or three additional pieces have been written.)

- What do/did I want the reader(s) to learn?

- Are the reactions/learnings/effects from each story the same for all the stories? Do I want them to be the same for each story?

This may sound like a lot of work to include in something designed to be educational and entertaining. But after a very short time, you will discover you are automatically asking yourself these questions without having to look at them or spend time memorizing them. The questions listed will become part of your natural writing style, adding to—not interfering with—how and what you are writing. They will make it as much fun, and worthwhile, for you to present the stories and lessons as it will be for the readers to receive them. A famous movie actor once said he wanted the following statement written on his gravestone: "Dying is easy. Comedy is hard." You may have found in your experience that you would like to replace the word "comedy" with the word "writing." For you, this does not need to be the case. If you think of writing as a form of storytelling, you may find that it can be informative, educational, interesting, useful, and fun for all—and perhaps most important—easy, successful, and enjoyable for you!

There is also one additional value to this process. You may be able to sell your written material to other companies and organizations for use by their training professionals. Just be sure of at least two issues:

1. No specific names of companies, individuals, products, or locations identify your work with a specific company.

2. Your company name, address, and phone number appear on everything you write so you may easily be found and contacted for future business.

Conclusion

In your experience as a consultant, you may often have felt your value was with the contracted company only while you were physically present. Whether or not that is the case, leaving the company your knowledge, presentation, and material in a written form keeps you always present and available for additional consultation.

Richard T. Whelan *is a human resource consultant, published author, freelance writer, and a certified mental health counselor. He designs, develops, and delivers human resource and technical workshops for businesses, organizations, and agencies in the public and private sectors, both nationally and internationally. He is also the founder and director of Chesney Row Consortium and the Westminster Foundation.*

The Systemization of Facilitation

M.K. Key

Summary

The history and growth of facilitation is chronicled in the Pfeiffer *Annuals* from the early 1970s to present. The current challenge in training new facilitators has been to organize the swell of possible activities into a framework for helpful intervention. This article presents both a flow chart and a worksheet to help novice facilitators become comfortable with a process for facilitation.

Training new facilitators is quite a task, for what is seemingly an art must be reduced to something of a science. The complexity of the field is too difficult for the early learner to grasp—with task and group process, a plethora of tools, required use of intuition, balancing observation and intervention, and knowing correct timing and depth of work.

The Pfeiffer *Annuals* have led the field, full of experiential activities for training and facilitation. Lois Hart (1991) was kind enough to give us lesson plans with concrete modules on specific facilitator skills. That same year, Fran Rees (1991) presented us an overview of the structural aspects of meetings—the ground floor of facilitation. ASTD (1994) contributed an observation form for group task and maintenance activities. Trevor Bentley (1994) developed a spectrum of intervention, ranging from "doing nothing" to "highly directive" activity; the present author (Key, 2000) further refined the range of behaviors. And again that same year, W. Brendan Reddy (1994) expanded Edgar Schein's (1988) ideas about process consultation to explore the types and depth of interventions: from content to overt group issues, then covert issues, then individual values/beliefs/assumptions, and, finally, the unconscious. Reddy also described a paired flow of task and maintenance activities for the facilitator, time-ordered from contracting to closure. Roger Schwarz (1994) turned the downward flow of steps into a circle of diagnosis and intervention that repeated its six phases over and over. Weaver and Farrell (1997) expanded the facilitator role to encompass leaders and organized quick fixes for common problems. Bens (1999) put facilitator activities into a pocket-size guide. During all of this, manuals containing thousands of exercises to warm up, close down, energize, manage conflict, team build, and train teams proliferated.

What's a new facilitator to do? We still need an orderly approach to teach the steps of facilitation so that the student can tackle the first few meeting experiences without floundering and gain confidence with experience, without bombing out. This article is an attempt to integrate the facilitation process for them and to provide aids for elementary group work.

Integrating the Flow of the Facilitation Process

The flow of the facilitation process is illustrated in Figure 1, which will serve as the organizing structure for this section. Broadly, it is broken down into two main phases: Assessment and Intervention.

To assist new facilitators and provide some structure for the facilitation process, Exhibit 1 is provided. It is meant to be a double-sided form to take into a meeting to remind the facilitator of his or her options. The first side is dedicated to Assessment activities.

The Assessment Phase: Contract with Group

The first step in Figure 1 is to approach a group with a definition of your role as their facilitator—as a consultant to the team leader and the team, there to provide information to the team to enable people to make choices. This is sometimes referred to as "entry." Schwarz's (1994) distinction between basic facilitation (short-term, to help members solve a substantive problem) and developmental facilitation (over a period of time, to help members solve a problem while learning to improve their group process) is useful here. Education—often about team roles, meeting process, tools, and some introductory work on group process/relationships, e.g., warm-ups, openers, ground rules—is another entry task.

The Assessment Phase: Observe

Observation and attentive listening are the prime activities of the facilitator. Assessment has already begun at the moment when the facilitator was enlisted. Facilitators should ask questions about the purpose of the group and to obtain information on members, their history together, their roles and experience, and administrative details. Once in the meeting, sitting at the table, the first order of activity is looking, listening, and sensing. Interpreting nonverbal behavior and drawing on intuition are additional ways of acquiring data. The new facilitator can usually be helpful here by asking open questions

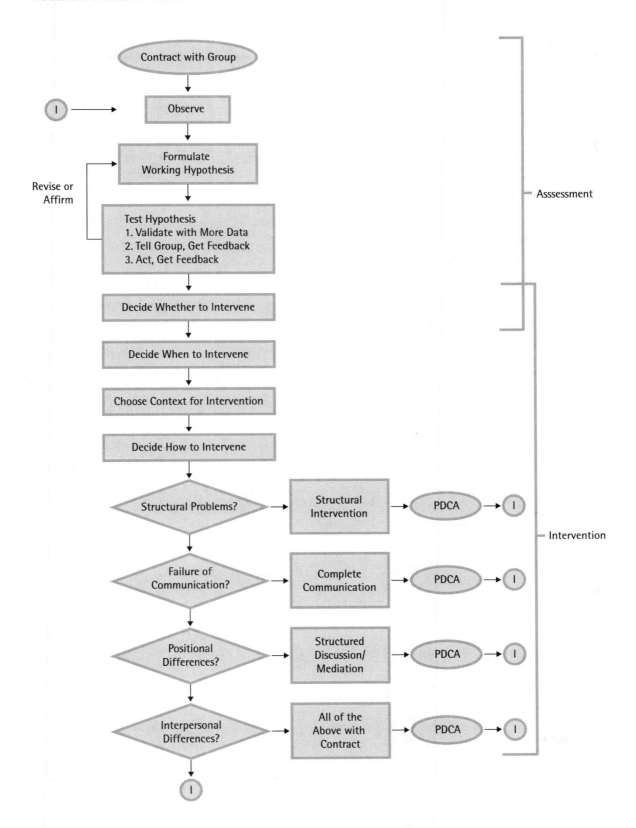

Figure 1. The Flow of the Facilitation Process

Exhibit 1.   Team Meeting Observation Form

Processes to Observe

- Participation/Commmitment
- Energy Level/Interest
- Communication
  - ○ Nonverbals
  - ○ Trust/Openness/Hidden Agendas
  - ○ Understanding
- Productivity
- Conflict Management
- Leadership/Decision Making
- Problem Solving
- Collaboration
- Team Building

Structural Observation

- Aim/Objective
- Agenda
- Membership
- Roles
- Time Management
- Contract
- Group Norms
- Tools (Generating, Deciding)
- Evaluation

Task or Content

Context

- Effective Culture
- Support from Without
- General Atmosphere
- Information
- Training

Notes

Sociogram:

Method of Assessment

- Pre-Meeting Assessment
- Observation
- Inquiry
- Questionnaire
- Dialogue—Process Check
- Intuition

Exhibit 1.   Team Meeting Observation Form. *continued*

Spectrum of Intervention

Do Nothing
Silence
Support
Question to Clarify
Descriptive Feedback
Evaluative Feedback
Questions to Move
Reframe
Teach
Share Your Idea
Make Suggestions
Guide
Direct

Supportive

Directive

Type of Intervention

Group Process

- Non-Intevention
- Nonverbal
- Communication
- Questions
- Feedback
- In-Process Intevention
- Conflict Management/Mediation
- Team Building
- Debriefing
- Training
- Dealing with Emotion
- Third-Party Intevention

Group Structure

- Procedural Suggestion
- Tool Suggestion
- Ground Rules
- Contracting/Group Agreement
- Agenda/Meeting Structure Change
- JIT/training

(what and how) for more information or to clarify the process. Facilitators may also provide their own feedback (mirror, reflect, paraphrase) to the group about what they observe; this can be done throughout a meeting, but at the very least, should be done at meeting's end. They may also be successful at taking notes (with the knowledge and permission of the group); part of this note taking might include drawing a sociogram of interpersonal interaction (ELI, 2002, p. 64). To create a sociogram for a team, draw and name a dot for each person in the group and the facilitator. Arrange the dots roughly the same as people are seated in the room. Each time someone speaks, draw a line from that person's dot. The direction of the line indicates to whom the person is speaking. The relative length of the line indicates for how long the person spoke. Punctuation describes the nature of the utterance.

Further elicitation of information can occur through structured questionnaires. Or the facilitator may conduct a process check—a "time out"—to ask the group members how they feel about the team's dynamics.

Exhibit 1 contains sample processes to observe, beginning with participation. Observation of group process is not the only area of assessment. The structural aspects of the meeting (aim, agenda, membership, roles, time management, contract, group norms, tools, and evaluation process), the task itself, and the organizational context (effective culture, support from external sources, general climate, information, and training) are other areas requiring attention.

The Assessment Phase: Formulate a Working Hypothesis

Facilitator observation feeds theories about whether the group process under study is within healthy limits—i.e., does it contribute to productivity and to good working relationships? The facilitator's interpretation of what he or she observes becomes a working hypothesis about behavior. Everyone carries around ideas about what constitutes healthy levels of a group's behavior—simply ask them about their best and worst team experiences, and the attributes of each will surface.

The Assessment Phase: Test Hypothesis

The facilitator needs sufficient data over time to spot a pattern and need not react to single events unless those events meet "damage control" criteria (see below). Facilitators may get more data by sharing their theory and observations and then asking for feedback from the group. Or they may intervene based on a hunch and get more data based on the reaction of the group. This is where assessment and intervention begin to overlap.

The Intervention Phase: Decide Whether and When to Intervene

The facilitator has choice about whether to intervene, when, where, and how. Some of the triggers (damage control criteria) for intervention are threats to safety and self-esteem, violation of an agreement, significant loss of productivity, need for information, and actual calls for help. Also bearing on the decision is whether the facilitator has the skills, whether the team is ready for it, and whether the team is becoming overly dependent on the facilitator. Generally, a good practice for facilitators is to hold back until a trend is observed and give the team an opportunity to self-correct.

The Intervention Phase: Choose Context for Intervention

The facilitator may intervene in-group or off-line-with individuals, a subgroup, or the entire group. A good practice here is to intervene with the whole group, describing observations in process language rather than characterizing team members (and their actions) as "good" or "bad." This way the group learns and takes responsibility for its own decisions. The off-line or out-of-group intervention should be reserved for issues holding potential for embarrassment or issues that are not the concern of the entire group.

The Intervention Phase: Decide How to Intervene

The facilitator has choices about the type of intervention. Definitions for the Spectrum of Intervention (Exhibit 1) can be found in Bentley (1994) and Key (2000). A good rule of thumb is to intervene at the lowest level possible to still be effective and yet be minimally intrusive. The novice facilitator can be coached to frame interventions as questions, always putting it back on the group to decide whether to use the suggestions.

Structural Problems?

The types of intervention are further subdivided into group structure and group process interventions—both can vary along the Spectrum. "Structural" refers to the mechanical aspects of the meeting, such as task, agenda, tools, ground rules, and training. The cleanest intervention here is to ask (1) what is the team trying to accomplish? and (2) what method or tool would be best used to accomplish that? The facilitator will find himself or herself mainly training and making procedural suggestions in this area. After making an intervention, its effectiveness should be checked using the Plan-Do-Check-Act (PDCA) model, also called the Deming Cycle (ELI, 2002). The facilitator then returns to observation and continues working down the flowchart again.

Failure of Communication?

Here the facilitator is urged to help the group complete its communication. To ensure listening, a helpful technique is to ask listeners to play back what the last speaker said before making their own point. This is a format for feedback that can be cycled until all agree they have been heard.

Positional Differences?

Here the facilitator has already assured that complete communication has taken place, and still people disagree. These differences constitute a type of conflict that requires a more advanced form of intervention—mediation. Mediation incorporates the completion of communication with structured discussion, where all parties go around and say what they believe and why. The facilitator listens to the interests, rationale, and data behind positions and then helps the group formulate an objective to optimize all parties' interests. The group then brainstorms ways to meet that objective, selects a path of action, and forms an agreement. This mediation process is described in more detail in Key (1996). Again the work is examined by PDCA thinking.

Interpersonal Differences?

These are the toughest problems for the early facilitator. Every tool of good communication comes into play, and the aim is to end up with a contract—an agreement about how people treat each other (ground rules), definition of what is off-limits, and maybe a behavior change request. The form of the contract may be guided by the facilitator, but the content should come from the group.

Bringing the Work to Closure

After numerous loops through the flow chart in Figure 1, the new facilitator should gain confidence in his or her ability to be helpful. The best measure of this is to ask the group, "In what ways have I been helpful, and how can I improve in my work with you?" This should occur at the end of a meeting and at the end of the group's tenure.

This model can bring some structure to our amorphous, artful field.

References

ASTD. (1994). *How to facilitate.* Alexandria, VA: ASTD.

Bentley, T. (1994). *Facilitation: Providing opportunities for learning.* London: McGraw-Hill.

Bens, I. (1999). *Facilitation at a glance: A pocket guide of tools and techniques for effective meeting facilitation.* Milwaukee, WI: AQP/Goal/QPC.

Hart, L.B. (1991). *Faultless facilitation: An instructor's manual for facilitation training.* Amherst, MA: HRD Press.

Executive Learning, Inc. (2002) *Handbook for improvement: A reference guide for tools and concepts.* Nashville, TN: Executive Learning, Inc.

Key, M.K. (1996) Across the great divide: A method for mediating differences. *The HR Handbook,* (pp. 397-401). Amherst, Mass: HRD Press.

Key, M.K. (2000). Continuum: Exploring the range of facilitator interventions. *The 2000 annual: Volume 2, consulting.* San Francisco, CA: Pfeiffer.

Reddy, W.B. (1994). *Intervention skills.* San Francisco, CA: Pfeiffer.

Rees, F. (1991). *How to lead work teams.* San Francisco, CA: Pfeiffer.

Schein, E.H. (1988). *Process consultation: Its role in organization development* (Vol. 1, 2nd ed.) Reading, MA: Addison-Wesley.

Scholtes, P. (1988). *The team handbook.* Madison, WI: Joiner Associates.

Schwarz, R.M. (1994). *The skilled facilitator: Practical wisdom for developing effective groups.* San Francisco, CA: Jossey-Bass.

Weaver, R.G., & Farrell, J.D. (1997). *Managers as facilitators: A practical guide to getting work done in a changing workplace.* San Francisco, CA: Berrett-Koehler.

M.K. Key, Ph.D., *is a clinical-community psychologist and the founder and principal of Key Associates in Nashville, Tennessee. She is a nationally recognized speaker on leadership, releasing the creative spirit, mediation of conflict, and team development. She has authored over forty publications on such topics as change management, continuous quality improvement, strategic business issues, and leadership during turbulent times. Her most recent releases are* Corporate Celebration: Play, Purpose and Profit at Work, *with Terrence E. Deal (1998), and* Managing Change in Healthcare: Innovative Solutions for People-Based Organizations *(1999). She has also served as adjunct professor of organization and human development at Vanderbilt University.*

Leadership Coaching:
Avoiding the Traps
Jan M. Schmuckler and Thomas J. Ucko

Summary

Leadership coaching is now being viewed as an effective tool for the workplace, and the number of coaches and HRD practitioners providing coaching services to organizations is on the rise. The number of training programs for coaches is also increasing. However, few of the programs look at coach self-awareness or teach individuals about the traps of coaching. This article examines some of the traps encountered during the most critical "contracting" phase of coaching and offers HRD practitioners an opportunity to look at some of the traps they might fall into. In addition, the article presents strategies for preventing and remedying the identified traps.

Is there any doubt that coaching has arrived in the workplace? A quick Google search reveals over one million entries on business coaching. Place "coaching" in the Amazon search window. Click. Over 2,000 titles emerge (granted, not all of these will be business or organization related). More than sixty training institutes are pumping out coaches: psychotherapists seeking to avoid the complexities of managed care, human resource development (HRD) practitioners wanting to expand their scope, and just plain folks out for new and exciting work are jumping on the coaching bandwagon.

There is both good news and not-so-good news in this renewed interest in and use of coaching. Certainly many managers and leaders are improving their performance and enhancing their careers through coaching. Others are being assisted to reshape company cultures, fine-tune their business strategies, and develop their teams. But there are dangers in the rapid growth of coaching. Many coaches or HRD practitioners providing coaching are insufficiently trained. (*Note:* To simplify, from here forward we will refer to all those providing coaching—whether HRD practitioners, designated coaches, or others—as "coaches.") They have simply decided to declare themselves coaches without benefit of acquiring sufficient skills. Others who have been trained in coaching techniques or who may otherwise have developed excellent one-on-one skills, such as therapists, often lack the organizational background to place their clients' issues in the proper context.

But the overriding concern we have about so many new or even well-trained coaches is their lack of self-awareness. Training programs that may do an excellent job of imparting knowledge and skills do not necessarily place much—if any—emphasis on developing awareness. Coaches who lack high levels of self-awareness are especially vulnerable to what we call the traps of coaching. Yet even the most self-aware coaches are not immune to the traps. In this article, we will identify the specific traps into which coaches are likely to fall during contracting—the critical phase of coaching that sets the stage for the coaching project and to a great extent determines the coaching project's success.

We will start by reviewing a basic coaching model and then explore the four traps we—along with a number of colleagues who assisted us—have identified as potentially most troublesome. For each trap, we discuss the trap itself and the strategy to avoid the trap.

Leadership Coaching Model

Our model of leadership coaching consists of six phases that are derived from our own experience and from organizational consulting frameworks such as Peter Block's (2000) model in *Flawless Consulting*. The phases are contracting; assessment; feedback; planning; ongoing coaching; and evaluation/completion (see Figure 1).

The first phase, contracting, is often considered the most critical step in the coaching assignment. It's the phase where all the factors of the coaching project will be discussed and decided on. During the contracting meeting, it is important to cover what the client wants and expects from the coaching process. It is equally important to tell the client what you, the coach, can offer and what you need from the client for the project to be successful.

After the contract is agreed to, the coach conducts the assessment phase. Survey instruments or interviews are used to examine the client's skills and behaviors.

After the assessment data has been collected and analyzed, the feedback phase begins. In this phase, coaches present the findings of the assessment phase to the client with a clear picture of the client's current behaviors and/or skills.

In the planning phase, clients prepare a development plan based on the feedback they received. The plan identifies the goals they want to work on, how they will work with the coach, and resources needed to achieve these goals.

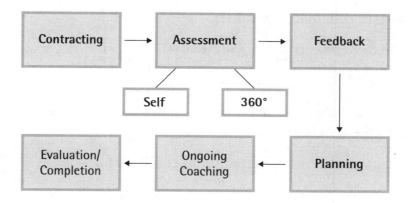

Figure 1. The Leadership Coaching Model

Ongoing coaching is next. During this phase, the client and the coach meet on a regular basis, in person or by phone, to work on the goals that the client has agreed to and that are part of the client's development plan.

The last phase in our coaching model is evaluation/completion. Here the coach is preparing the client for closure or coach and client are jointly determining whether or not to continue coaching and renew the contract.

Each of the phases in the coaching model has particular traps or pitfalls that the coach can easily fall into. When we are not aware of the traps or forget to stay alert, we can ensnare ourselves and limit our success as coaches.

Here, we examine four of the traps of the contracting phase, because this phase is most critical to project success.

1. Belief That We Can Coach Anyone Successfully

The Trap

A mistaken belief that we can coach anyone successfully can get us into trouble and result in the client not being well served.

Coaches sometimes think that they can work with any client who comes their way without evaluating the situation or the person for fit and readiness. Coaches can be caught up in the excitement of wanting to help or solve a problem. They may think, "This trap won't happen to me, because . . . " (e.g., "I am experienced"). In some cases, coaches may urgently need income or wish to please their organizational bosses and be blind to the obvious problems that are presented in the preliminary meeting.

A number of factors can interfere with our ability to be successful with a particular client. These include:

- Significant differences in values;

- Negative judgments about the client's behavior;

- Lack of sufficient coach availability;

- Insufficient personal "chemistry" (which may lead to the client not trusting the coach enough to be adequately open);

- Different philosophy/orientation to change; and

- Different coaching focus (for example, whole person versus business issues only).

As an example, Sarah, an external HRD consultant, was having a slow year. When a client company, a large financial institution, called regarding a coaching project, she fairly jumped at the chance. The individual in question, a sales manager, had been accused of harsh treatment by several of his reports. When Sarah met Ted, the coaching candidate, it soon became clear that he felt no need for coaching, but was going along with it to satisfy his boss's requirement. In addition, Sarah was low-key, soft-spoken, and slow-paced; she thought carefully before speaking. Ted, on the other hand, was loud, fast-paced, and spontaneous. To make matters worse, Ted's manager ruled out 360-degree feedback or any interviewing or surveying of Ted's reports on the grounds that "he wanted to keep this quiet." Not surprisingly, the project was unsuccessful, with none of the coaching objectives being reached. In retrospect, Sarah realized that the combination of her eagerness to get the work and her over-confidence in her ability to coach anyone had done her in.

The Strategy

It is important for coaches to understand their own styles, the type of clients with whom they work best, and the situational elements that can undermine the project. As in the example above, when the coach and client's styles are vastly different, and when some basic conditions of a successful outcome are not met, we know that the fit is not good. Similarly, the coach must examine other aspects of fit, as described in "The Trap" section above—negative judgments, availability, chemistry, philosophy, and focus.

It is as important to know when to stop a coaching project as it is to know whether to start in the first place. Sometimes, the lack of fit is not apparent until well into the coaching cycle. Either way, at the front end or once the project is underway, when the coach perceives a problem with fit, the coach must raise the issue with the client and offer to make an appropriate referral. None of us can be successful with every client who comes our way. The important thing is to determine whether you can work well with the person and, if not, to take the necessary steps to transfer the client to another coach. If in doubt about fit, it may be worthwhile to discuss the issue, in confidence, with a trusted advisor.

2. Failing to Ask for What You Need

The Trap

Sometimes, as coaches we spend so much time concentrating on what the client's needs are that we forget to ask for what we need. In a coaching project at a semi-conductor company, for example, the client, Jim, was at odds with his boss, who seemed to favor other members of his team. The coach spent a good deal of time listening to the client and trying to sort out what Jim needed. However, the coach did not hold Jim accountable for his homework assignments and for the new behaviors Jim was to try out with his manager. By not asking for specific commitments to completing homework assignments and to working on coaching goals outside the coaching session, the coach was not successful in engaging the client in taking the coaching process seriously. As a result, the project failed to meet its intended outcomes.

The Strategy

To have a successful coaching engagement, it is important for coaches to negotiate for their own needs and wants as well as to focus on the client's wants and needs. There are certain conditions that enhance a coaching assignment, and it's up to the coach to get those conditions met by the client. A good strategy for coaches is to develop a list of their wants and needs prior to a contracting meeting so that they can be certain of asking for everything they need. These may include, for example, administrative assistance in scheduling interviews, prompt return of phone calls, periodic feedback from the client or the client's manager, and completion of homework assignments.

3. Failing to Contract with All the Right People

The Trap

Even experienced coaches can fall into the trap of thinking that their initial work is complete when they have contracted with the individual client. This ignores their key relationship with their client's manager and the role of internal human resources or organization development practitioners. Failing to include the client's manager can have several undesirable consequences. For example, the client's development may be out of alignment with the organization's strategic directions or with the manager's expectations for his or her report. Not including the manager in contracting also reduces the possibility that you can advise the manager on how best to assist in your client's development.

If you don't include the internal human resources or organization development practitioner in your contracting, you have not only failed to make a valuable ally in your work, but you have likely alienated your referral source—and perhaps limited your opportunities for further assignments. You may also experience lack of cooperation and, in extreme cases, even sabotage. (As externals, we have experienced sabotage more than once from internal consultants who believe they should have received the assignment or who resent the greater stature of external coaches.)

The Strategy

The obvious cure is to consider who else needs to be in the loop in any particular coaching project. Certainly the client's manager and internal HR, HRD, or OD practitioners are likely candidates. In some organizations, even the manager's manager may need to be included. You may want to informally coach the client's manager to gain maximum leverage in your assignment. Often, the boss is part of the problem and contributes to less-than-stellar client performance by failing to communicate expectations clearly or by softening feedback when the client is off course. We like to contract with the manager (at whatever level) by saying that we'd like to offer our recommendations on how he or she can best manage the client. This gives us the opening—or "permission"—to give the manager feedback as needed. Additionally, HRD practitioners can be a valuable resource for skills training opportunities and for seeing clients on a regular or daily basis to reinforce the coaching goals or to give feedback when the client is on or off target.

4. Not Contracting to Raise Difficult Issues

The Trap

Like all of us, our clients have blind spots. They have self-perceptions that don't match how others see them. A significant part of our job as coaches is to shed light on these blind spots and help our clients see themselves as others see them. Yet we may hold back from giving straightforward and direct feedback. We may "pull our punches" and soften our feedback or avoid it entirely, fearing the client may become angry, dislike us, or send us away.

The Strategy

The trick here is to raise the issue at the very beginning of the project during the contracting phase. One way is to alert the client that difficult issues always come up in a coaching project, that these issues must be put on the table for the project to be successful, and that you want to make sure that you are both okay with raising difficult issues with one another. Another way is to tell the client that you will be providing feedback—both from the assessment and as needed during the project—and that some of it may be difficult to hear. Then ask, "How would you like to receive difficult feedback?" In our experience, most clients, when asked this question, will act surprised and say something like, "Why, just give it to me straight." If the client takes exception to receiving difficult feedback, this is cause for discussion. Perhaps the client is not ready for coaching. Whichever method you adopt, you will have gained permission in advance to raise difficult issues and give straight feedback. This will make the actual conversation, when it comes, immeasurably easier.

Conclusion

As we have illustrated, there are many traps that await us in the coaching process, especially in the contracting phase. No matter how much experience we have, we must recognize that we may not be able to coach everyone successfully. Unless we are continually vigilant, we may fail to ask for what we need, to contract with all the right people, or to raise difficult issues. In this article, we have offered strategies that our colleagues and we have found to be effective in avoiding these traps. By honing both our self-awareness and our awareness of the traps that await us, we can enhance our effectiveness in this critical contracting phase and increase the likelihood of achieving the desired coaching outcomes.

Reference

Block, P. (2000). *Flawless consulting: A guide to getting your expertise used* (2nd ed.). San Francisco, CA: Pfeiffer.

Jan M. Schmuckler, *organizational psychologist and leadership coach, works with executives and managers to achieve outstanding business results. Her more than twenty-five years' experience with leading companies in high technology, biotechnology, and financial sectors around the world brings unique perspectives for competing more effectively. Currently, Dr. Schmuckler is director of the Coaching Certification Program at John F. Kennedy University, as well as heading her own consulting firm. Her Ph.D. in organizational psychology is from the Wright Institute.*

Thomas J. Ucko *is a leadership coach and organizational consultant who assists leaders and leadership teams to achieve their business and career goals. His clients range from global enterprises to startups. Mr. Ucko teaches in the Coaching Certificate Program at John F. Kennedy University and is the author of* Selecting and Working with Consultants: A Guide for Clients. *He holds an MBA from Fordham University and an M.A. in counseling psychology from Columbia University.*

Corporate Values and Bottom-Line Performance:
The Value of Values
Steve Terrell

Summary

Companies that define, integrate, and consistently demonstrate a strong set of core values within their organizational practices, processes, decisions, and actions experience greater long-term success than companies that do not pursue this course or that do so partially or inconsistently. The recent epidemic of high-profile, corporate ethical failures and scandals provides clear evidence that failure to pay adequate attention to values comes with a high price. At the same time, an increasing number of leading companies have recognized the impact of culture and values on their ability to be competitive and, by paying close attention to their values, are reaping the many rewards of their efforts.

This article provides insight into how and why companies address corporate values, reviews research on the impact of corporate values on organizational performance, and explains the business case for defining and implementing corporate values. It also describes practices related to the development and implementation of corporate values and introduces the reader to a practical approach to supporting implementation of corporate values.

Corporate ethics, values, and culture are in the news virtually every day. And it's usually bad news: the stories of greed, theft, deception, fraud, and lack of integrity give us ample evidence that, in some quarters, things are going terribly wrong. Fortunately, it's not like that everywhere. In many organizations, positive corporate values are put front and center and integrated into all aspects of the business. Every employee is expected to "live the values," demonstration of the corporate values is rewarded, and a strong values-based culture is seen as a critical contributor to competitive advantage. In fact, many leading organizations point to their culture and values as being key drivers of their ability to perform, grow, and succeed.

However, the reality is that most organizations struggle with successfully instilling values throughout their organizations. They wrestle with tough questions such as. . .

- "Do we really 'walk the talk'?"

- "Are our leaders acting as effective role models?"

- "How do we get everyone consistently demonstrating the values in their day-to-day work lives?"

Effectively instilling values throughout an organization is a significant challenge. But the organizations that successfully build a culture in which positive values are shared and "lived" by people at all levels will almost certainly experience greater long-term success than those that do not.

The Current Reality

First, There's Bad News: "Houston, We Have a Problem."

It's almost impossible to avoid hearing about the epidemic of ethics failure. Merely reading the newspaper or watching national news reports brings the problem with corporate values home. Headlines, lead stories, and magazines chronicle the sad state of affairs on a regular basis, as companies and leaders once admired for their innovative and successful strategies are revealed to be engaged in unethical and illegal practices. At one time, *Forbes* published a "Corporate Scandal Sheet" that listed an ever-growing number of companies and their ethical dilemmas, including such organizations as Adelphia Communications, AOL Time Warner, Arthur Andersen, Bristol-Myers Squibb, CMS Energy, Duke Energy, Dynegy, El Paso, Enron, Global Crossing, Halliburton, Homestore.com, K-Mart, Merck, Mirant, Nicor Energy, Peregrine Systems, Qwest Communications International, Reliant Energy, Tyco, WorldCom, and Xerox (Patsuris, 2002).

In one of the most infamous cases, Enron was accused of boosting profits, hiding over one billion dollars of debt, bribery, and manipulation of the California energy market. Kenneth Lay, who was once regarded as a great business leader and a hero on Wall Street, became yet another symbol of corporate greed and hypocrisy. In a January 24, 2002 article, BBC News Online reported, "In the space of a few months, Kenneth L. Lay has turned from being a Wall Street hero into public enemy number one. He is the man who turned an unspectacular natural gas pipeline company into a financial powerhouse, winning himself a place in the Texas Business Hall of Fame and several surveys of the world's top management. Ironically, Mr. Lay also lectured on government-business relations" (Hale, 2002). And in her book, *Value Shift*, Harvard Business School professor Dr. Lynn Sharp Paine states, "By January 2002, when the New York Stock Exchange suspended trading in Enron shares, they were valued at $.60. Copies of the Enron code of ethics, some advertised jokingly as 'never been read,' were trading on eBay for as much as $10 to $20 each" (pp. 34–35). If it wasn't so tragic for so many people, it would be funny. Enron's top executives enriched their personal fortunes at shareholders' and employees' expense while thousands of Enron employees lost both their jobs and their entire retirement savings. Clearly, these leaders just gave lip service to Enron's corporate values of communication, respect, integrity, and excellence, rather than actively living them on a day-to-day basis.

In another high-profile values and ethics disaster, Tyco's ex-CEO, Dennis Kozlowski, was indicted for tax evasion in May 2002. Shortly before his indictment, Kozlowski held a lavish, $2 million birthday party for his wife on the island of Sardinia and charged half the expense to the company. Video of the party was broadcast around the world for weeks and became emblematic of Tyco's many questionable practices and excesses. It also created a stark contrast to the company's stated values of integrity, teamwork, communication, and accountability.

Another case involved MCI/WorldCom, which ran into trouble when it was discovered to have overstated its cash flow and to have given former CEO Bernie Ebbers $400 million in off-the-books loans. Following bankruptcy, the company responded to its ethical issues by hiring a chief ethics officer and implementing a range of new efforts aimed at bolstering its image and ethics capabilities:

- Ethics training for 55,000 U.S.-based employees and contractors;

- Code of Ethics and Business Conduct enhanced and distributed to all employees;

- "Zero-tolerance policy" on suspected violations of the ethics code;

- Confidential ethics hotline;

- Ethics pledge signed by top 100 executives; and

- New set of ten "guiding principles" (Hindo, 2003).

It remains to be seen whether MCI's program will succeed.

The problem is one of not "walking the talk," of saying one thing but doing another. As Ralph Waldo Emerson said, "What you do speaks so loudly that I cannot hear what you say." All the values statements, pledges, training programs, and codes of ethics in the world won't make any difference unless those values are translated into action and consistently reinforced throughout the organization at all levels.

. . . But There's Also Good News!

Interestingly, while these and other scandals and ethical failures have been coming to light, an increasing number of companies have recognized the impact of culture and values on their ability to be competitive. Several factors in the business environment have contributed to this awareness and have led executives to pay more attention than ever to the so-called "soft" side of management:

1. *Ethical issues*—As just discussed, the seemingly never-ending tide of news about companies experiencing ethical and values meltdowns has demonstrated the risks of not being proactive in articulating and effectively implementing ethics and values and holding people accountable for practicing those ethics and values on a day-to-day basis.

2. *Changing workplace/workforce*—Many factors in the workplace contribute to an increased emphasis on values and ethics, including workers seeking greater meaning from their jobs, wanting to "make a difference" or "have an impact" no matter what they do; workers' desire for greater work/life balance; the ongoing development of a networked (and even wireless) workplace; and generational differences (Zemke, Raines, & Filipczak, 2000).

3. *Increased awareness of "emotional intelligence" factors*—The popularity and increased visibility/awareness of the impact of "emotional competencies" on leaders' effectiveness and organizational performance has given rise to an emphasis on developing leaders who demonstrate emotional competencies that align with and support corporate values (Goleman, 1998).

4. *Compelling research on organizational performance*—Over the past two decades, there has been a steady stream of research into the factors that cause organizations to succeed. One of the most common, recurring findings is that there is a strong, clear connection between organizational values and organizational performance.

"Survey Says!"

More and more companies are focusing on values. *The Journal of Business Ethics* (Murphy, 1995) reports that more than 80 percent of the Forbes 500 companies that had adopted values statements, codes of conduct, or corporate credos created or revised these docu-

Table 1. AMA Survey Results

Information about corporate values discussed in:	Employee handbooks	71 percent
	Company brochures	67 percent
	Staff meetings	65 percent
	Annual meeting	55 percent
Corporate values linked to performance evaluations and compensation:	64 percent	
Stated values: (top 5)	Customer satisfaction	77 percent
	Ethics/integrity	76 percent
	Accountability	61 percent
	Respect for others	59 percent
	Open communication	51 percent
To what extent is each value practiced "Most/all of the time"?	Customer satisfaction	76 percent
	Ethics/integrity	72 percent
	Accountability	61 percent
	Respect for others	60 percent
	Open communication	44 percent

Copyright © 2002, American Management Association. Used with permission.

ments in the 1990s. And the 2000 National Business Ethics Survey, Volume I (Joseph, 2000), reports that ethics guidelines and training is widespread:

- 79 percent of U.S. employees surveyed in 1999/2000 indicated their companies had written ethics guidelines.

- 55 percent said their company offered ethics training, up from 33 percent in 1994.

More recently, in a 2002 survey conducted by the American Management Association (AMA) and completed by 175 AMA executive members and AMA council members, 86 percent of the respondents indicated that their organizations had corporate values, written or stated. Other selected highlights from the AMA survey are shown in Table 1.

The "good news" is that the vast majority of survey respondents reported that their companies have corporate values, written or stated. However, this is good news only in relative terms when you look at the extent to which each value is practiced (or not practiced):

- Customer satisfaction is practiced, on average, most or all of the time, by about three-fourths (76 percent) of the respondents' companies. One can only wonder how customers at the other companies fare.

- Ethics/integrity is practiced, on average, most or all of the time by 72 percent of the respondents' companies. What about the other 28 percent?

- Accountability is practiced, on average, most or all of the time by 61 percent of respondents' companies. Almost 40 percent of these companies do not practice accountability!

- Respect for others is practiced most or all of the time by only 60 percent. The other 40 percent fall behind in practicing respect for others.

- Only 44 percent of respondents indicated that their companies practice open communication most/all of the time, meaning that 56 percent of the respondents' believe their companies don't do a very good or consistent job of practicing open communication. Can you demonstrate respect for others if you don't practice open communication?

Results of a similar online survey conducted by Aspire Consulting in November 2003, completed by fifteen HR professionals attending a professional conference, vary somewhat from the AMA survey results (Terrell, 2003). (See Table 2.)

There are two broad "takeaways" from the results of these two surveys:

1. Regardless of the difference in focus or degree of integration into the organization, a large number of organizations have espoused/written/stated values and are actively engaged in some kind of activity to promote those values.

2. A significant percentage of those organizations are not practicing their espoused values on a consistent, day-to-day basis.

Living Corporate Values: An Example

The survey results discussed above illustrate one of the main challenges that organizations face in relation to corporate values: it's one thing to define corporate values, and it's something entirely different for an entire organization to "live" the values in everyday work life. To fully align an organization around shared, core values requires

Table 2.　Aspire Consulting Survey Results

Corporate values written or stated	73 percent	
Information about corporate values discussed in:	Websites	67 percent
	Employee handbooks	53 percent
	Recruiting literature	53 percent
	Staff meetings	53 percent
Stated values: (top 5)	Ethics/Integrity	73 percent
	Community service	53 percent
	Customer focus	53 percent
	Respect for others	53 percent
	Diversity	47 percent
To what extent is each value practiced "Most/all of the time"?	Ethics/Integrity	82 percent
	Community service	58 percent
	Customer focus	70 percent
	Respect for others	50 percent
	Diversity	50 percent

To what degree are corporate values integrated into your organizations:

	Completely Integrated	Somewhat Integrated
Recruiting and Selection Process	21 percent	43 percent
Orientation/On-Boarding Process	31 percent	38 percent
Training and Development Programs	23 percent	38 percent
Performance Management Process	43 percent	43 percent
Recognition Programs	23 percent	54 percent
Compensation and Rewards	15 percent	62 percent
Succession Planning/Talent Mgt.	23 percent	46 percent
Decision-Making Processes/Practices	21 percent	57 percent

much more than merely defining and communicating the values to "the troops," posting them on plaques, or putting them on wallet cards. It requires executive sponsorship, integration of the values into all aspects of the organization's operation and business and human resource practices, and a relentless focus on the impact of the values on decisions and actions.

Those companies that integrate their values throughout the entire organization—its systems, practices, decisions, and culture—find that there's a powerful payoff, even though some still encounter problems or challenges from time to time. Bank of America is an example of an organization that makes a concerted effort to instill values throughout their culture. Bank of America has had a long history of focus on values, which were first codified in a predecessor bank, NationsBank. The author co-led the task force at NationsBank that defined and wrote up the values and then developed the tools and resources to disseminate the values throughout the organization. The initial set of tools included a set of instructional materials and case studies that were used to train personnel managers both on the values and on how to help the managers they supported apply the values in day-to-day work life and business decisions. From there, the values were integrated into leadership development programs, and a comprehensive suite of recognition programs was designed to reinforce and reward consistent demonstration of the values. The values are now integrated into the bank's performance management system, talent management, and other vital systems and human capital management processes.

Today, the bank is facing several values-related challenges. Allegations of involvement in improper stock market trading practices, mutual funds management, and possible improprieties related to the sale of bonds and other business it structured for a client all demonstrate the impact of just one questionable decision or action that ideally would be prevented by values-based decision making. These situations have drawn the scrutiny of federal regulators, created questions for shareholders, and produced concern for customers and bank associates. Executive management is now faced with the difficult task of maintaining a steady hand on the wheel while cooperating with investigators to uncover the truth about what happened, all the while taking action to reassure its constituents that any wrongdoers have been dealt with and the bank is treating them honestly, fairly, and with integrity. In fact, for its constituents, the key indicator of the bank's integrity may be just how ethics and values violations and violators are dealt with and whether bad behavior is tolerated if it is uncovered in the future.

Bank of America faces the same challenge that any large organization faces in terms of creating alignment around its values. Even though the bank's values are communicated and integrated throughout the organization, and despite robust, corporate-wide programs designed to reinforce the values and reward values-based behavior, bank associates are evaluated and rewarded for meeting aggressive growth and performance goals. They must learn how to balance bank expectations that they "deliver results" while at the same time "living the values." Without constant organizational and management attention, reinforcement, and strong accountability, it is very difficult to ensure a high degree of alignment around core values in any organization.

Why Corporate Values Are So Important

Corporate values are important because values and culture drive organizational performance. While it is not currently possible to demonstrate a direct cause-and-effect relationship between values and organizational financial performance, the value chain is clear. Values and culture drive employee satisfaction, loyalty, and productivity, which in turn drive customer satisfaction and loyalty, which drive organizational financial performance (see Figure 1). There are clearly many factors that influence organizational financial performance, and values and culture are just a couple among those many. But managers are paying more and more attention to the effects of culture and values on their organizations' ability to fulfill their vision, execute their strategy, and achieve their objectives.

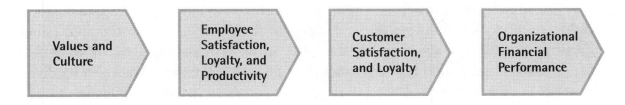

Figure 1. The Value Chain

Over twenty years ago, Tom Peters began talking about values in what he called the "excellent" organization. In his now classic book, *In Search of Excellence*, Peters wrote, "Every excellent company we studied is clear on what it stands for and takes the process of value shaping seriously. In fact, we wonder whether it is possible to be an excellent company without clarity on values and without having the right sorts of values" (Peters & Waterman, 1982, p. 280).

Now, many of the organizations he categorized as "excellent" no longer exist or have fallen out of favor. Clearly, having strong values is no panacea or "silver bullet" that guarantees success. Any number of factors can intervene to influence organizational performance:

- Products (lifecycle, new products, competitor products);

- Effectiveness of sales and marketing campaigns and personnel;

- Economic conditions (expansion, retraction);

- Change in organizational leadership, leadership effectiveness;

- Ethical issues; and

- New competitors.

So are corporate values just another leftover fad from the 1980s or a revisited "flavor of the month" to merely endure, keeping your head down until the urge to do something passes? Not really.

The Value of Values

Values haven't faded away like many fads. Instead, interest in values has continually grown since the 1980s, with more research studies on values in the past five years than in the previous twenty years. But what does it mean to embrace the value of values? To answer that, let's first consider the impact of not embracing the value of values.

The cost of having and espousing corporate values, but not actively, consistently, and visibly supporting, reinforcing, rewarding, and integrating them into day-to-day work life at all levels is extremely high. To illustrate, when you tell someone (friend, spouse, co-worker) that you value something, ask for his or her commitment to value the same thing, and you then violate the value, a trust is broken. And, as we all know, trust is easy to break and very hard to win back. So what happens when you espouse values as an organization and you tell employees you expect them to adhere to the values, but you don't really actively live those values on a day-to-day basis? Some of the consequences of this lack of alignment between espoused values and demonstrated behavior/actions include:

- Employee cynicism about the values;

- Employee disbelief and distrust of management;

- Loss of management credibility;

- Poor employee morale;

- Suboptimal employee productivity;

- Un-engaged employees;

- Increased undesirable turnover;

- Limited capacity for change;

- Reduced organizational resiliency;

- Negative company impression on customers; and

- Lower organizational/financial performance.

In the same vein, what happens when you do live the values you espouse? Not surprisingly, the value that organizations realize from embedding corporate values into day-to-day work life at all levels by actively, consistently, and visibly supporting, reinforcing, and rewarding their demonstration is very high. Some of the consequences from a strong degree of alignment between espoused values and demonstrated behavior/actions include:

- Employee support for the values;

- Employee belief in and trust of management;

- Management credibility;

- Solid employee morale;

- Increased employee satisfaction and loyalty;

- Increased employee productivity;

- Reduced undesirable turnover;

- Increased capacity for change;

- Enhanced organizational resiliency;

- Positive impression on customers; and

- Higher organizational/financial performance.

Clearly, organizations that embrace the value of values will reap the rewards!

Research on Corporate Values

Research conducted during the past twelve years has demonstrated that there is a strong, clear connection between organizational values and organizational performance. For example:

- Positive employee morale increases shareholder returns. The companies included in *Fortune* magazine's 2002 edition of the "100 Best Companies to Work For" are "not just great to work for, they're also fabulous to invest in. Frank Russell Co. put together an index and discovered that, had you bought the public companies when the 1998 list came out, and reinvested in the new list each year, you would have earned 10.6 percent annually. That wallops the S&P 500's 5.7 percent annual return over the same period" (Watson, 2002).

- Values for trust and camaraderie increase shareholder value (Levering & Moskowitz, 2000).

- Organization change efforts fail when culture is ignored (Cameron & Quinn, 1999).

- Values-based leadership increases job satisfaction and bottom-line performance (Wilson Learning, 1999).

- Profits are higher when personal and organizational values are aligned. Of *Fortune*'s Top 100 Companies to Work For, forty-five earned annual returns to shareholders of 27.5 percent versus 17.3 percent for a comparison group, and earned 23.4 percent versus 14.8 percent over ten years (Grant, 1998).

- Companies with an enduring core ideology outperform the stock market; superior market performance is possible without making profit a primary value. In a six-year research project, eighteen "visionary" companies, compared to the performance of eighteen peer organizations over a sixty-four-year period, achieved fifteen times greater stock value growth than the general stock market. Profit is only one of several driving factors that companies achieving this "extraordinary long-term performance" focus on—they also focus on their core values and sense of purpose beyond just making money (Collins & Porras, 1994).

- Firms that consider the interests of employees, customers, and stockholders greatly outperform those that do not (Kotter & Heskett, 1992).

The bottom line is impressively clear. Organizations that:

- Clearly define and articulate their values;

- Communicate their values in a compelling, easily understood manner;

- Proactively instill those values throughout the organization; and

- Consistently and repetitively reward and reinforce people for living by those values on the job.

Achieve:

- Higher levels of employee satisfaction, loyalty, and productivity;

- Higher levels of customer satisfaction and loyalty;

- Increased organizational resiliency and capacity for change; and

- "Extraordinary" long-term financial performance and success.

Best Practices

Okay, let's say we believe in the "value of values." We think the argument is correct, and there is a business case for defining and integrating values throughout an organization's systems, processes, practices, decisions, and actions. Just exactly how do you do that? What do you actually do to instill the values into your organizational DNA, to infuse them into the organization's bloodstream?

Organizations that embrace the value of values, that build a strong core ideology into their culture, and that experience outstanding success as a result do five things very, very well. They actively, visibly, and consistently:

1. Articulate,

2. Communicate,

3. Demonstrate,

4. Integrate, and

5. Celebrate

the corporate values in day-to-day work life at all levels. Some examples of the specific actions that organizations take are noted in Table 3.

There are many ways organizations can effectively and successfully implement best practices such as these. Most importantly, successful implementation of these best practices requires a clear and strong commitment from senior executive leadership. Unless senior executives demonstrate public and private support for the values, any effort to introduce and instill values into an organization will fail or, at best, sub-optimize. But as important as senior executive sponsorship is, it's not enough by itself; in other words, it's necessary but not sufficient. In addition to sponsorship, organizations need to provide people with the "how to"—the resources and tools that make it possible to translate values into action.

Very often, people know all about the values; they can tell you what the values are and even express commitment to fulfilling them. But they fall short in a behavioral understanding of what the values mean on a day-to-day basis, on the job, where decisions are made and customers are served. People need practical tools to help bridge the knowing-doing gap. They know what they are expected to do, but they can't figure out how to do it. The best advice we can give is to follow the actions from Table 3.

Table 3.   Actions That Embrace the Value of Values

Articulate	Define your organization's values in clear, simple language.
	Engage employees at all levels in the process to generate buy-in.
Communicate	Plan and execute a communication campaign designed to develop awareness and understanding of the values and their implications for all employees.
	Make expectations clear.
	Leaders share their personal perspectives on the values with employees.
Demonstrate	Senior leaders walk the talk.
	Look for and take every opportunity to reinforce your words with actions that are aligned with the values.
	Invite others to provide you with candid feedback on your personal demonstration of the values in your day-to-day work life.
	Hold people accountable for living the values, and enforce appropriate consequences for failure to do so.
Integrate	Build the values into key organizational systems and processes, including recruiting/selection, performance management, reward and recognition, management/leadership development, talent management.
	Provide practical tools and resources to managers that help them instill the values in their teams.
	Implement a long-term campaign designed to develop buy-in, commitment, and behavioral change in multiple ways.
Celebrate	Use recognition as a tool to help instill and reinforce demonstration of the values.
	Publicly acknowledge employees who have demonstrated a high degree of commitment to the values.

Conclusion

Companies that define and consistently demonstrate a strong set of core values experience greater long-term success than companies that do not define and consistently demonstrate a strong set of core values. Those companies that embrace the value of values by building a strong core ideology into their culture also build and enhance their competitive advantage, since it is impossible to copy or steal! Effectively instilling values throughout an organization is a significant challenge. But the organizations that successfully build a culture in which positive values are shared and lived by people at all levels will almost certainly experience greater long-term success than those that do not.

References

American Management Association. (2002). *AMA 2002 corporate values survey* [Online]. Available: www.amanet.org/research/pdfs/2002_corp_value.pdf.

Cameron, K.S., & Quinn, R.E. (1999). *Diagnosing and changing organizational culture: Based on the competing values framework.* New York: Addison-Wesley.

Collins, J., & Porras, J. (1994). *Built to last: Successful habits of visionary companies.* New York: HarperCollins.

Goleman, D. (1998). *Working with emotional intelligence.* New York: Bantam Books.

Grant, L. (1998). The 100 best companies to work for: Happy workers, high returns. *Fortune* [Online]. Available: www.fortune.com/fortune/articles/0,15114,379146,00.html.

Hale, B. (2002, January 24). Kenneth Lay: A fallen hero. *BBC NEWS* [Online]. Available: http://news.bbc.co.uk/1/hi/business/1779445.stm.

Hindo, B. (2003, November 3). Teaching MCI right from wrong. *Business Week.*

Is your company up to speed? (2003, June). *Fast Company* [Online]. Available: www.fastcompany.com/magazine/71/uptospeed.html.

Joseph, J. (2000). *2000 national business ethics survey, Volume I.* Ethics Resource Center [Online]. Available: www.ethics.org/2000survey.html.

Kotter, J., & Heskett, J. (1992). *Corporate culture and performance.* New York: The Free Press.

Levering, R., & Moskowitz, M. (2000). The 100 best companies to work for: With labor in short supply, these companies are pulling out all the stops for employees. *Fortune* [Online]. Available: www.fortune.com/fortune/articles/0,15114,368658,00.html.

Murphy, P.E. (1995). Corporate ethics statements: Current status and future prospects. *Journal of Business Ethics, 14,* 727-740.

Paine, L.S. (2003). *Value shift: Why companies must merge social and financial imperatives to achieve superior performance.* New York: McGraw-Hill.

Patsuris, P. (2002, August 26). The corporate scandal sheet. *Forbes.com* [Online]. Available: www.forbes.com/2002/07/25/accountingtracker_print.html.

Peters, T., & Waterman R. (1982). *In search of excellence: Lessons from America's best-run companies.* New York: HarperCollins.

Terrell, S. (2003). Aspire Consulting, Inc. [Online]. Available: www.aspireconsulting.net/2003_Corp_Value.pdf.

Watson, N. (2002). The 100 best companies to work for: Happy companies make happy investments. *Fortune* [Online]. Available: www.fortune.com/fortune/investing/articles/0,15114,374129,00.html.

Wilson Learning. (1999). *The leader's role in improving employee satisfaction.* Eden Prairie, MN: Author.

Zemke, R., Raines, C., & Filipczak, B. (2000). *Generations at work: Managing the clash of veterans, boomers, xers, and nexters in your workplace.* New York: AMACOM.

Steve Terrell *is president and founder of Aspire Consulting, a management consulting firm that specializes in developing leadership capabilities needed for success. Prior to founding Aspire Consulting, he was executive director of consulting services for Executive Development Associates, director of the Leadership Development Practice for Dove Consulting, a senior manager in change navigation with Andersen Consulting, and senior vice president in leadership development at Bank of America.*

Contributors

Kristin J. Arnold, CMC, CPF, CSP
Quality Process Consultants, Inc.
11304 Megan Drive
Fairfax, VA 22030
(703) 278-0892
email: karnold@gpcteam.com

Robert Alan Black, Ph.D., CSP
Cre8ng People, Places, & Possibilities
P.O. Box 5805
Athens, GA 30604
(706) 353-3387
email: alan@cre8ng.com

W. Warner Burke, Ph.D.
Teachers College
Columbia University
525 West 120th Street, Box 24
New York, NY 10027
(212) 678-3831
fax: (212) 664-1554
email: wwb3@columbia.edu

Doug Campbell
PacifiCorp
825 NE Multnomah, Suite 1700
Portland, OR 97232
(503) 813-5032
email: Doug.Campbell@PacificCorp
.com

Phyliss Cooke, Ph.D.
1935 Harton Road
San Diego, CA 92123
(858) 569-5144
fax: (858) 569-7318
email: phyliss6@earthlink.net

Susan Crosson
Santa Fe Community College
3000 NW 83 Street
Gainesville, FL 32606
(352) 395-5137
fax: (352) 395-5286
email: susan.crosson@sfcc.edu

Charles L. Fields
P.O. Box 754
Tolland, CT 06084
(860) 875-8892
fax: (860) 871-1705
email: clfields@snet.net

Peter R. Garber
PPG Industries, Inc.
One PPG Place
Pittsburgh, PA 15272
(412) 434-2009
fax: (412) 434-3490
email: garber@ppg.com

Barbara Pate Glacel, Ph.D.
12103 Richland Lane
Oak Hill, VA 20171
  (703) 262-9120
  fax: (703) 264-5314
  email: BPGlacel@glacel.com
  URL: www.glacel.com

Donna L. Goldstein, Ed.D.
Managing Director
Development Associates
  International, Inc.
3389 Sheridan Street #309
Hollywood, FL 33021
  (954) 893-0123
  fax: (954)893-0170
  email: Devasscint@aol.com
  URL: www.DAInt.org

Gail Hahn, MA, CSP, CPRP, CLL
Fun*cilitators
11407 Orchard Green Court
Reston, VA 20190
  (866) 386-2896
  fax: (530) 326-2979
  email: Gail@funcilators.com
  URL: www.funcilators.com
  URL: http://866.fun.at.work

Tyrone A. Holmes, Ed.D., L.P.C.
30307 Sterling Drive
Novi, MI 48377
  (248) 669-5294
  fax: (248) 669-5295
  email: tyrone@doctorholmes.net

Cher Holton, Ph.D.
The Holton Consulting Group, Inc.
4704 Little Falls Drive, Suite 300
Raleigh, NC 27609
  (919) 783-7088
  (800) 336-3940
  fax: (919) 781-2218
  email: cher@holtonconsulting.com

John Howes
PacifiCorp
825 NE Multnomah, Suite 1700
Portland, OR 97232
  (503) 813-6236
  email: John.Howes@PacificCorp.com

Brenda Hubbard
Florida Institute of Certified Public
  Accountants
325 West College Avenue
Tallahassee, FL 32301
  (850) 224-2727, ext. 419
  fax: (850) 681-2433
  email: hubbardb@ficpa.org

M.K. Key, Ph.D.
Key Associates
1857 Laurel Ridge Drive, Suite 100
Nashville, TN 37215
  (615) 665-1622
  fax: (615) 665-8902
  email: keyassociates@mindspring.com

Deborah Spring Laurel
Laurel and Associates, Ltd.
917 Vilas Avenue
Madison, WI 53715
  (608) 255-2010
  fax: (608) 260-2616
  email: dlaurel@ameritech.net

Rajnish Kumar Misra, Ph.D.
Institute of Business Administration
  & Training
KIIT Campus 1
Bhubaneswar, Orissa 751024
India
  91-674-2741389
  fax: 91-674-271747
  email: rajnish@ibat.ac.in

Luis R. Morales
2001 Northeast 211 Street
North Miami Beach, FL 33179
  (305) 933-1576

Ira J. Morrow, Ph.D.
Department of Management
The Lubin School of Business
Pace University
1 Pace Plaza
New York, NY 10038
  (212) 346-1846
  email: imorrow@pace.edu

Mohandas K. Nair
A2 Kamdar Building
607 Gokhale Road (S)
Dadar, Mumbai - 400 028
India
  (91-22) 2422 6307; 2432 1914
  email: mknair@vsnl.net
  email: nair_mohandas@hotmail.com

Phalgu Niranjana, Ph.D.
Institute of Business Administrations
  & Training
B-School of KIIT, Deemed University,
  KIIT Campus 1
Bhubaneswar, Orissa 751024
India
  91-674-274 1998/274 1389
  fax: 91-674-274 1465
  email: phalgu_niranjana@yahoo.com

Biswajeet Pattanayak, Ph.D.
Institute of Business Administrations
  & Training
KIIT Campus 1, Patia
Bhubaneswar, Orissa 751024
India
  91-674-2742103/274 1998/274 1389
  fax: 91-674 1465
  email: bpattanyak@yahoo.com

Connie Phillips
City of Anaheim, Human Resources
200 S. Anaheim Boulevard, Suite 332
Anaheim, CA 92805
  (714) 765-5256
  fax: (714) 765-5211
  email: cphillips1@anaheim.net

A. Venkat Raman
Faculty of Management Studies
University of Delhi - South Campus
Benito Juarez Road
New Delhi - 110 021
India
  +91-11- 2687 5875
  fax: +91-11- 2611 3353
  email: venkatfms@yahoo.co.in

Carrie Reese
PacifiCorp
825 NE Multnomah, Suite 1700
Portland, OR 97232
  (503) 813-7123
  email: Carrie.Reese@PacificCorp.com

Jeffrey Russell
Russell Consulting, Inc.
1134 Winston Drive
Madison, WI 53711-3161
  (608) 274-4482
  fax: (608) 274-1927
  email: RCI@RussellConsultingInc.com

Linda Russell
Russell Consulting, Inc.
1134 Winston Drive
Madison, WI 53711-3161
  (608) 274-4482
  fax: (608) 274-1927
  email: RCI@RussellConsultingInc.com

Parth Sarathi
Additional General Manager
Bharat Heavy Electricals Ltd.
Plot No., 25, Sector-16-A
NOIDA-201 301 (U.P)
India
  91-120-2515417
  fax: 91-120-2515431
  email: ps@hrd.bhel.co.in
  email: saranth@bol.net.in

Jan M. Schmuckler, Ph.D.
Jan M. Schmuckler Ph.D. Consultation
3921 Burckhalter Avenue
Oakland, CA 94605
  (510) 562-0626
  email: jan@janconsults.com
  URL: www.janconsults.com

Robert Shaver
Program Director
University of Wisconsin-Madison
School of Business
601 University Avenue
Madison, WI 53715-1035
  (608) 441-7334
  fax: (608) 441-7325
  email: bshaver@bus.wisc.edu

Saundra Stroope
c/o PacifiCorp
1407 West North Temple, Suite 230
Salt Lake City, UT 84116
  (801) 220-4062
  email: Saundra.Stroop@pacificorp.com

Steve Terrell
President
Aspire Consulting, Inc.
1312 Chelbrook Road
Chesapeake, VA 23322
  (757) 546-7347
  fax: (757) 546-8679
  email: steve@aspireconsulting.net

Teresa Torres-Coronas, Ph.D.
Universitat Rovira i Virgili
Av. Universitat, s/n 43204 Reus
  (Tarragona)
Spain
  email: mttc@fcee.urv.es

Thomas J. Ucko
602 Chapman Drive
Corte Madera, CA 94925
  (415) 924-7010
  email: tom@ucko.com
  URL: www.ucko.com

Lorraine L. Ukens
Team-ing With Success
4302 Starview Court
Glen Arm, MD 21057-9745
  (410) 592-6050
  fax: (410) 592-5502
  email: ukens@team-ing.com

Arthur B. VanGundy, Ph.D.
VanGundy & Associates
428 Laws Drive
Norman, OK 73072-3851
  (405) 447-1946
  email: avangundy@aol.com

Richard T. Whelan, M.A., C.C.L.
520 Collings Avenue, Suite B823
Collingswood, NJ 08107
  (856) 858-9496

Contents of the Companion Volume, *The 2005 Pfeiffer Annual: Training*

Editor's Choice

Inventories, Questionnaires, and Surveys

Articles and Discussion Resources

**Topic is "cutting edge."

How to Use the CD-ROM

System Requirements

PC with Microsoft Windows 98SE or later
Mac with Apple OS version 8.6 or later

Using the CD with Windows

To view the items located on the CD, follow these steps:

1. Insert the CD into your computer's CD-ROM drive.

2. A window appears with the following options:

    Contents: Allows you to view the files included on the CD-ROM.

    Software: Allows you to install useful software from the CD-ROM.

    Links: Displays a hyperlinked page of websites.

    Author: Displays a page with information about the Author(s).

    Contact Us: Displays a page with information on contacting the publisher or author.

    Help: Displays a page with information on using the CD.

    Exit: Closes the interface window.

If you do not have autorun enabled, or if the autorun window does not appear, follow these steps to access the CD:

1. Click Start -> Run.

2. In the dialog box that appears, type d:<\\>start.exe, where d is the letter of your CD-ROM drive. This brings up the autorun window described in the preceding set of steps.

3. Choose the desired option from the menu. (See Step 2 in the preceding list for a description of these options.)

In Case of Trouble

If you experience difficulty using the CD-ROM, please follow these steps:

1. Make sure your hardware and systems configurations conform to the systems requirements noted under "System Requirements" above.

2. Review the installation procedure for your type of hardware and operating system.

It is possible to reinstall the software if necessary.

To speak with someone in Product Technical Support, call 800-762-2974 or 317-572-3994 M–F 8:30 a.m.–5:00 p.m. EST. You can also get support and contact Product Technical Support through our website at www.wiley.com/techsupport.

Before calling or writing, please have the following information available:

- Type of computer and operating system
- Any error messages displayed
- Complete description of the problem.

It is best if you are sitting at your computer when making the call.

Pfeiffer Publications Guide

This guide is designed to familiarize you with the various types of Pfeiffer publications. The formats section describes the various types of products that we publish; the methodologies section describes the many different ways that content might be provided within a product. We also provide a list of the topic areas in which we publish.

FORMATS

In addition to its extensive book-publishing program, Pfeiffer offers content in an array of formats, from fieldbooks for the practitioner to complete, ready-to-use training packages that support group learning.

FIELDBOOK Designed to provide information and guidance to practitioners in the midst of action. Most fieldbooks are companions to another, sometimes earlier, work, from which its ideas are derived; the fieldbook makes practical what was theoretical in the original text. Fieldbooks can certainly be read from cover to cover. More likely, though, you'll find yourself bouncing around following a particular theme, or dipping in as the mood, and the situation, dictate.

HANDBOOK A contributed volume of work on a single topic, comprising an eclectic mix of ideas, case studies, and best practices sourced by practitioners and experts in the field.

An editor or team of editors usually is appointed to seek out contributors and to evaluate content for relevance to the topic. Think of a handbook not as a ready-to-eat meal, but as a cookbook of ingredients that enables you to create the most fitting experience for the occasion.

RESOURCE Materials designed to support group learning. They come in many forms: a complete, ready-to-use exercise (such as a game); a comprehensive resource on one topic (such as conflict management) containing a variety of methods and approaches; or a collection of like-minded activities (such as icebreakers) on multiple subjects and situations.

TRAINING PACKAGE An entire, ready-to-use learning program that focuses on a particular topic or skill. All packages comprise a guide for the facilitator/trainer and a workbook for the participants. Some packages are supported with additional media—such as video—or learning aids, instruments, or other devices to help participants understand concepts or practice and develop skills.

- *Facilitator/trainer's guide* Contains an introduction to the program, advice on how to organize and facilitate the learning event, and step-by-step instructor notes. The guide also contains copies of presentation materials—handouts, presentations, and overhead designs, for example—used in the program.

- *Participant's workbook* Contains exercises and reading materials that support the learning goal and serves as a valuable reference and support guide for participants in the weeks and months that follow the learning event. Typically, each participant will require his or her own workbook.

ELECTRONIC CD-ROMs and web-based products transform static Pfeiffer content into dynamic, interactive experiences. Designed to take advantage of the searchability, automation, and ease-of-use that technology provides, our e-products bring convenience and immediate accessibility to your workspace.

METHODOLOGIES

CASE STUDY A presentation, in narrative form, of an actual event that has occurred inside an organization. Case studies are not prescriptive, nor are they used to prove a point; they are designed to develop critical analysis and decision-making skills. A case study has a specific time frame, specifies a sequence of events, is narrative in structure, and contains a plot structure—an issue (what should be/have been done?). Use case studies when the goal is to enable participants to apply previously learned theories to the circumstances in the case, decide what is pertinent, identify the real issues, decide what should have been done, and develop a plan of action.

ENERGIZER A short activity that develops readiness for the next session or learning event. Energizers are most commonly used after a break or lunch to stimulate or refocus the group. Many involve some form of physical activity, so they are a useful way to counter post-lunch lethargy. Other uses include transitioning from one topic to another, where "mental" distancing is important.

EXPERIENTIAL LEARNING ACTIVITY (ELA) A facilitator-led intervention that moves participants through the learning cycle from experience to application (also known as a Structured Experience). ELAs are carefully thought-out designs in which there is a definite learning purpose and intended outcome. Each step—everything that participants do during the activity—facilitates the accomplishment of the stated goal. Each ELA includes complete instructions for facilitating the intervention and a clear statement of goals, suggested group size and timing, materials required, an explanation of the process, and, where appropriate, possible variations to the activity. (For more detail on Experiential Learning Activities, see the Introduction to the *Reference Guide to Handbooks and Annuals*, 1999 edition, Pfeiffer, San Francisco.)

GAME A group activity that has the purpose of fostering team spirit and togetherness in addition to the achievement of a pre-stated goal. Usually contrived—undertaking a desert expedition, for example—this type of learning method offers an engaging means for participants to demonstrate and practice business and interpersonal skills. Games are effective for team building and personal development mainly because the goal is subordinate to the process—the means through which participants reach decisions, collaborate, communicate, and generate trust and understanding. Games often engage teams in "friendly" competition.

ICEBREAKER A (usually) short activity designed to help participants overcome initial anxiety in a training session and/or to acquaint the participants with one another. An icebreaker can be a fun activity or can be tied to specific topics or training goals. While a useful tool in itself, the icebreaker comes into its own in situations where tension or resistance exists within a group.

INSTRUMENT A device used to assess, appraise, evaluate, describe, classify, and summarize various aspects of human behavior. The term used to describe an instrument depends primarily on its format and purpose. These terms include survey, questionnaire, inventory, diagnostic survey, and poll. Some uses of instruments include providing instrumental feedback to group members, studying here-and-now processes or functioning within a group, manipulating group composition, and evaluating outcomes of training and other interventions.

Instruments are popular in the training and HR field because, in general, more growth can occur if an individual is provided with a method for focusing specifically on his or her own behavior. Instruments also are used to obtain information that will serve as a basis for change and to assist in workforce planning efforts.

Paper-and-pencil tests still dominate the instrument landscape with a typical package comprising a facilitator's guide, which offers advice on administering the instrument and interpreting the collected data, and an initial set of instruments. Additional instruments are available separately. Pfeiffer, though, is investing heavily in e-instruments. Electronic instrumentation provides effortless distribution and, for larger groups particularly, offers advantages over paper-and-pencil tests in the time it takes to analyze data and provide feedback.

LECTURETTE A short talk that provides an explanation of a principle, model, or process that is pertinent to the participants' current learning needs. A lecturette is intended to establish a common language bond between the trainer and the participants by providing a mutual frame of reference. Use a lecturette as an introduction to a group activity or event, as an interjection during an event, or as a handout.

MODEL A graphic depiction of a system or process and the relationship among its elements. Models provide a frame of reference and something more tangible, and more easily remembered, than a verbal explanation. They also give participants something to "go on," enabling them to track their own progress as they experience the dynamics, processes, and relationships being depicted in the model.

ROLE PLAY A technique in which people assume a role in a situation/scenario: a customer service rep in an angry-customer exchange, for example. The way in which the role is approached is then discussed and feedback is offered. The role play is often repeated using a different approach and/or incorporating changes made based on feedback received. In other words, role playing is a spontaneous interaction involving realistic behavior under artificial (and safe) conditions.

SIMULATION A methodology for understanding the interrelationships among components of a system or process. Simulations differ from games in that they test or use a model that depicts or mirrors some aspect of reality in form, if not necessarily in content. Learning occurs by studying the effects of change on one or more factors of the model. Simulations are commonly used to test hypotheses about what happens in a system—often referred to as "what if?" analysis—or to examine best-case/worst-case scenarios.

THEORY A presentation of an idea from a conjectural perspective. Theories are useful because they encourage us to examine behavior and phenomena through a different lens.

TOPICS

The twin goals of providing effective and practical solutions for workforce training and organization development and meeting the educational needs of training and human resource professionals shape Pfeiffer's publishing program. Core topics include the following:

Leadership & Management

Communication & Presentation

Coaching & Mentoring

Training & Development

e-Learning

Teams & Collaboration

OD & Strategic Planning

Human Resources

Consulting